GABRIEL FAURÉ

Complete Songs

Volume 1: 1861–1882

medium voice / voix moyennes / mittlere Stimme

34 songs for voice and piano
34 mélodies pour chant et piano
34 Lieder für Singstimme und Klavier

Critical edition by / Édition critique de / Kritische Ausgabe von
Roy Howat & Emily Kilpatrick

Urtext

ALLE RECHTE VORBEHALTEN · ALL RIGHTS RESERVED
EDITION PETERS
PUBLISHED BY FABER MUSIC
LEIPZIG · LONDON · NEW YORK

Cover Painting:

Boulevard des Italiens, c. 1880. Oil on canvas. Gustave Caillebotte (1848–1894)

© 2014 by Peters Edition Ltd, London

Alle Rechte vorbehalten · All rights reserved
Vervielfältigungen jeglicher Art sind gesetzlich verboten.
Any unauthorized reproduction is prohibited by law.

ISMN 979-0-014-11761-0

CONTENTS

General Preface VI
Preface to Volume 1 VII

Préface générale XII
Préface au 1ᵉʳ volume XIII

Allgemeines Vorwort XVIII
Vorwort zu Band 1 XX

Index of Songs / Table des mélodies / Liederverzeichnis XXVI

Poetic texts / Textes poétiques des mélodies / Liedtexte XXVIII

Select Bibliography / Bibliographie sélective / Auswahlbibliographie XLII

Songs / Mélodies / Lieder 1

Table of known chronology / Tableau chronologique / Chronologie 128

Critical Commentary 130

Appendix / Appendice / Anhang 152

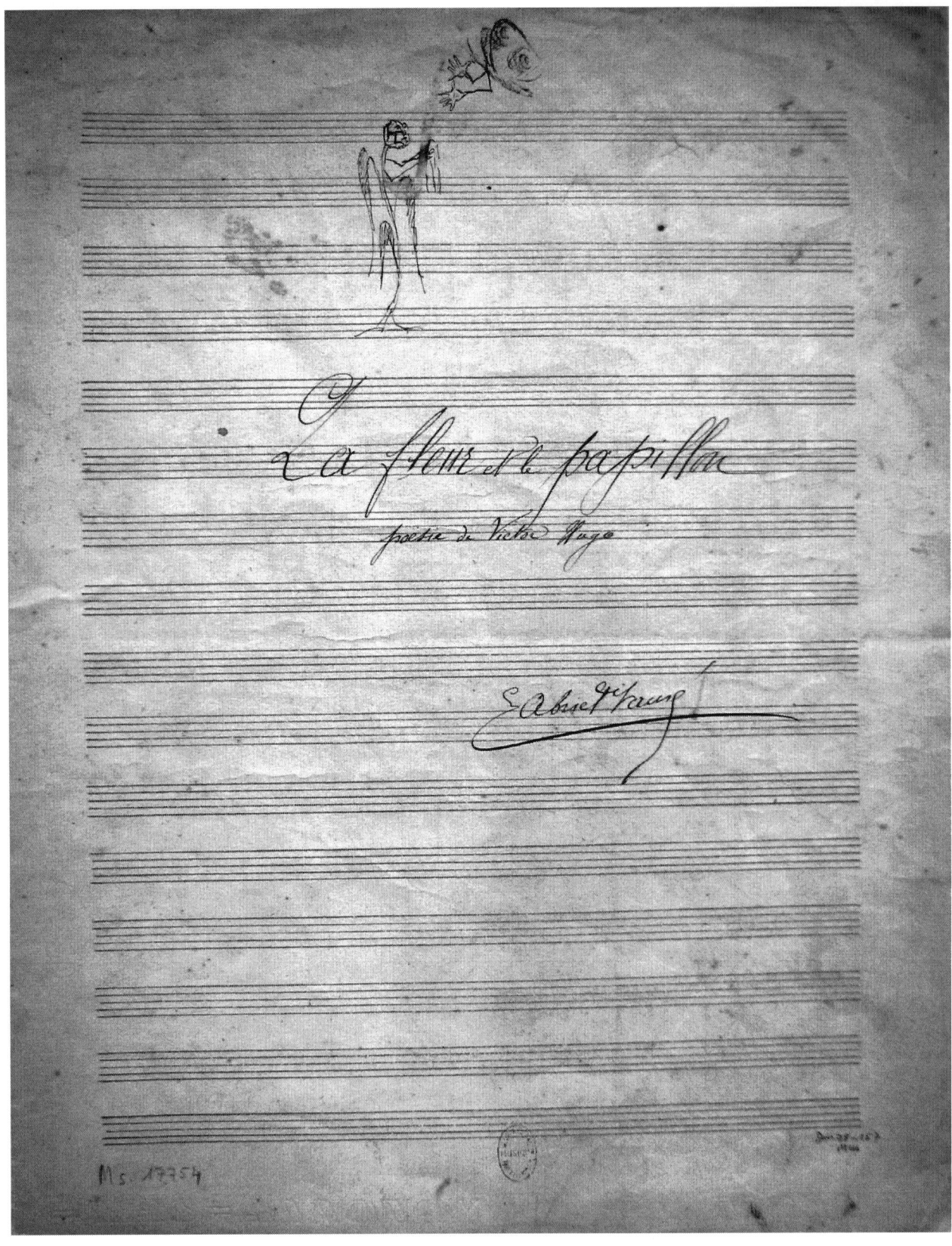

Le Papillon et la fleur: autograph title page,
showing a variant title and a drawing attributed to Camille Saint-Saëns.

Le Papillon et la fleur: page de titre autographe,
montrant une variante du titre et un dessin attribué à Camille Saint-Saëns.

Le Papillon et la fleur: Titelseite Autograph,
mit einer Variante des Titels und einer Camille Saint-Saëns zugeschriebenen Zeichnung.

Reproduced by kind permission of the Bibliothèque nationale de France.

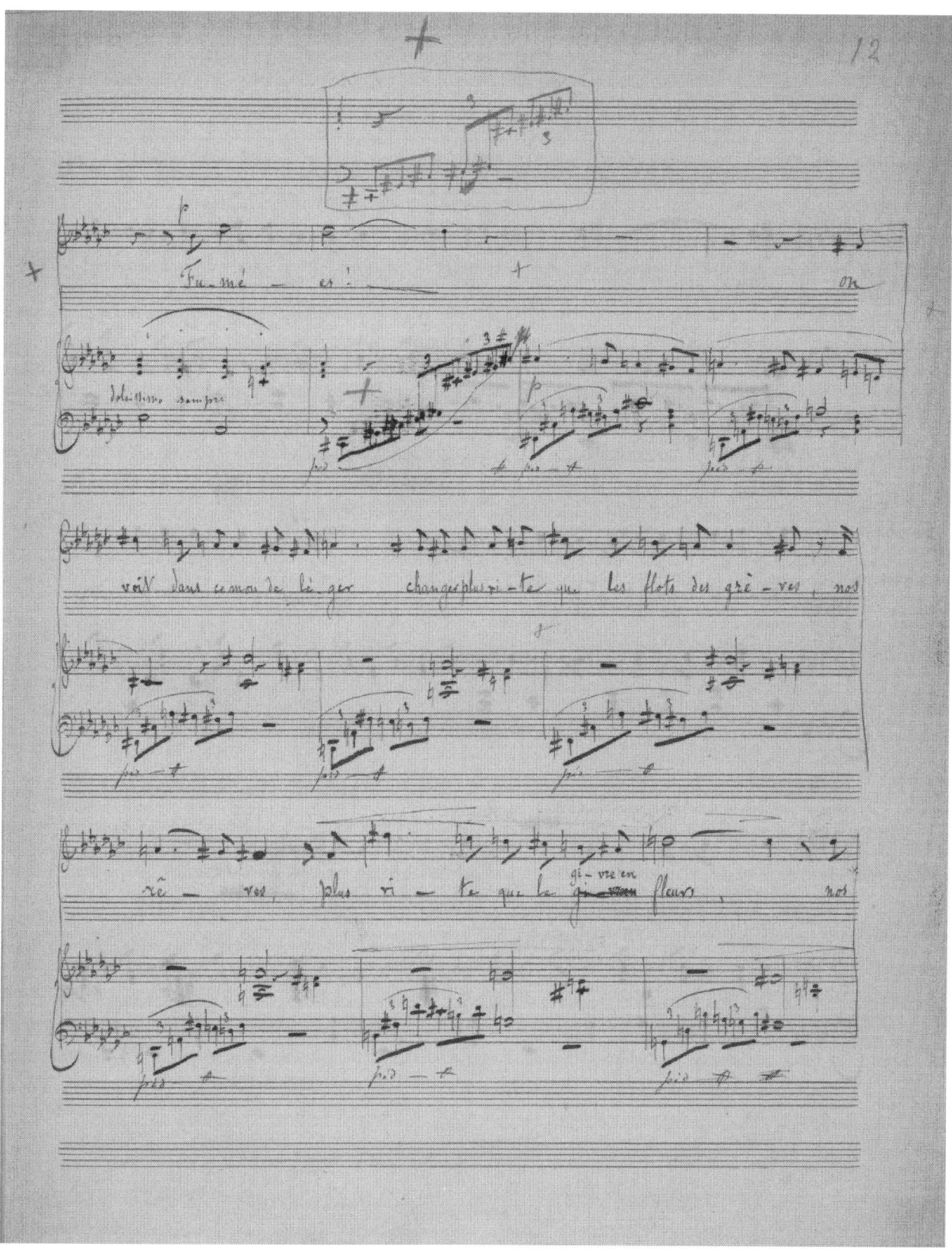

"Adieu" (*Poème d'un jour*). Autograph manuscript of bars 11–20,
showing various revisions and enharmonic spelling of the central episode.

« Adieu » (*Poème d'un jour*). Manuscrit autographe des mes. 11-20,
montrant diverses révisions et la notation enharmonique de l'épisode central.

„Adieu" (*Poème d'un jour*). Autograph der Takte 11–20,
mit diversen Korrekturen und enharmonischer Notation des Mittelteils.

Reproduced by permission of the Harry Ransom Center, The University of Texas at Austin.

General Preface

It is truly in his songs that Fauré reveals the flower of his genius.
— Maurice Ravel[1]

No composer made a more substantial and varied contribution to the French song repertoire than Gabriel Fauré. *Mélodies* span his career, from the delightful *Le Papillon et la fleur* of 1861 to the masterly cycle *L'Horizon chimérique*, composed sixty years and more than a hundred songs later. The importance of this contribution has long been compromised by its erratic publication history: dispersed across different publishers and collections, many of the songs have been marred by serious misprints and conflicting readings across different printed versions. This first complete critical edition presents a text both authoritative and flexible, bringing together the familiar compendium of sixty songs (as established by the publisher Hamelle in 1908) with other songs and cycles issued separately, including three songs unpublished during Fauré's lifetime as well as four songs for more than one voice. The associated volume of Fauré's collected *Vocalises* (EP 11385) includes his wordless *Vocalise-Étude* first published in 1907, alongside forty-four others published for the first time.

With its focus both practical and scholarly, the present edition aims to encourage creative, confident and well-informed performance. Founded on study of hundreds of manuscript and printed sources, it has been tested internationally in masterclasses, workshops, seminars, concerts and recordings, with the participation of professional singers, students, teachers, coaches and specialists. In this it takes a lead from the composer, who prepared his own editions on the basis of performing experience. The edition also assimilates interpretative insights from musicians who worked with Fauré, as well as from his documented performing preferences.

Sources and editorial approach

Fauré's principal song publishers were Choudens (1869–1879), Hamelle (1880–1904), Heugel (1905–1910) and Durand (1915–1921); various of his songs were also issued at different times by Hartmann, Durand & Schœnewerk, Fromont, and the London firm Metzler (plus some secondary American editions derived from French originals). Most of his songs were published singly before being brought together in collections, the first of these in 1879 (Choudens), the second in 1897 (Hamelle), and the third in 1908 (Hamelle).[2] These collections, like most of the single prints, were issued in high- and medium-voice keys; some songs were published separately in additional transpositions. Against this wealth of printed sources, manuscripts are more sparsely preserved. Of those now traced, many – particularly for the earlier songs – are early drafts, presentation copies or intermediate versions.

Editorial treatment of such varied sources demands care. Manuscripts, for all the valuable corrections, verifications and variants they offer, have to be treated with caution, particularly when they were not directly in the source chain leading to publication. Meanwhile, even from the plethora of printed sources it is often impossible to adhere to one source as representing a "final" or definitive composer's text, for every source mixes essential information with problems and corruptions (again, most notably in the earlier songs). In order to present a text as faithful as possible to Fauré's corrections over many years, the present edition has had to combine the best of various sources within bounds of logical source priority and musical sense, always respecting coherence across single songs, groupings, cycles and collections, and taking into account all that is known about Fauré's composing, revising and performing habits, along with any circumstantial evidence. *Ossia* versions are given wherever more than one reading is clearly viable. These include some early readings that clarify aspects of compositional intent, elements that were sometimes masked by later revisions aimed at "fireproofing" the music against inept performance. The **Critical Commentary** provides full explanations.

Keys

There is no evidence whatever that Fauré was opposed to transposition of his songs, in principle or practice.[3] Several of his songs exist in more than one autograph key (including some post-publication transpositions), others first appeared in a key (or keys) different from surviving manuscripts, while for songs whose manuscripts are lost it is sometimes impossible to identify an original key from the printed sources, let alone any authorially preferred one. (Even in the established Hamelle collections, "Original key" labels are not always reliable.)[4] As a lifelong practical musician, accompanist and skilled choirmaster, Fauré was used to working with a large range of voices. Surviving concert programmes show that he regularly performed his songs with different voice-types, often in circumstances that clearly involved transpositions (including a few important premieres). Like any composer, for a few songs Fauré did have intrinsic preferences of tessitura or key colour; any such evidence is quoted here and taken into editorial account.

In those respects the present edition honours Fauré's own pragmatic approach, in making his songs accessible to as many singers as possible within appropriate bounds of taste and scholarship. The high- and medium-voice keys of the three long-established collections are mostly maintained, except when a source offers a more compelling option or suggests this was Fauré's preference, and occasionally to offer a more realistic distinction between high and medium voices. Practicality at the keyboard is also a consideration. In a very few cases the present edition adopts a new transposed key, prompted by musical sense and tessitura along with consideration of sources. For those few songs published in only one key or unpublished in Fauré's lifetime, a second key has been determined editorially. In a few select cases, where sources present additional useful keys, a third key is available online through www.fabermusic.com/editionpetersresources. For each song the present edition lists original known key (or keys); where no manuscript is traced or original printed keys differ, the latter are shown in parentheses, using bold print for keys indicated as original in the Hamelle collections.

Performance

Witness accounts of Fauré's playing and interpretative preferences all indicate his assumption of forward motion, with a strong aversion to any gratuitous slowing, rubato or sentimental affectation.[5] His sense of tempo relates to the natural pace of the spoken poem; his close colleague, the distinguished mezzo-soprano Claire Croiza, emphasised the importance he attached to the poem and its articulation in song. Croiza further recalled:

Fauré was a metronome incarnate ... Above all, slowing him down distorts him ... For Fauré more than anyone else the expression has to be found within a framework of keeping in time ... I once heard *Après un rêve* sung by a singer who [almost] literally ground to a halt. Dining with Fauré that evening, I asked him, "What tempo do you really want in *Après un rêve, maître?*" And he said, "*Sans ralentir, sans ralentir.*"[6]

While emphasising the intensity of tragic moments (*Chanson du pêcheur* or *Prison*), Croiza repeatedly warns against treating Fauré's more melancholy songs in a dolorous manner, the essence of refinement and understatement in this idiom lying in not exaggerating or caricaturing what the composer has already balanced finely.[7] Among Fauré's early songs in particular, an overtly melancholy poem like *Tristesse* can entail a degree of parody or self-mockery,[8] to which Fauré responds with a light touch that relates to numerous accounts, via his family and colleagues, of his lively sense of humour and inherent gaiety right through to his final years.[9]

Editorial presentation

Ossia readings are transposed as necessary from their source keys. Any debatable musical readings are footnoted. Editorial ties and slurs (and slur completions) are printed in broken lines; other editorial additions are placed in square brackets. Cautionary accidentals in parentheses appear thus in sources. Parentheses are also added around non-essential breath marks that appear only in some sources, and around useful dynamics and other indications that come from secondary sources, as detailed in the **Critical Commentary**.

London, 2014   *Roy Howat & Emily Kilpatrick*

---

[1] Maurice Ravel, 'Les Mélodies de Gabriel Fauré', *La Revue musicale* 3 (October 1922), in Arbie Orenstein (ed.), *Maurice Ravel: Lettres, écrits, entretiens* (Paris: Flammarion, 1990), p. 325.

[2] The 1908 publication of the Third Collection coincided with Hamelle's reissue of the First and Second Collections (he bought out the First Collection from Choudens in 1887 and issued a high-voice edition of it in 1890), and involved some redistribution of contents; see **Critical Commentary**.

[3] For detailed discussion of this and other editorial issues vital to the present edition, see the present editors' articles "Editorial Challenges in the Early Songs of Gabriel Fauré" and "Gabriel Fauré's Middle-Period Songs".

[4] These are indicated only in the Hamelle Second and Third Collections, from op. 18 onwards. Nor was pitch then standard through Europe – across borders it could vary by a semitone or more – although over Fauré's professional life it was regulated in France (by parliamentary decree of 1859) at $a' = 435$ Hz, slightly lower than today's norms of 440 or slightly above.

[5] Several of these witness accounts, from his family and musical colleagues, are quoted in Roy Howat, *The Art of French Piano Music* (London and New Haven: Yale UP, 2009), p. 247 and generally through Chapters 17, 18 and 21.

[6] Quoted in Abraham (ed.), *Un Art de l'interprétation*, pp. 199 and 212, and partly in Bannerman (ed.), *The Singer as Interpreter*, p. 82; the latter adds a specific reference that prompts the present edition's "(*sans ralentir*)" at bar 46. Fauré's violinist colleague Hélène Jourdan-Morhange corroborates this trait, adding an anecdote about a (nameless) singer given to pausing and languishing over phrase-ends: accompanied by Fauré once at an afternoon concert, "she was horrified to find herself being propelled by the piano along an undulation-free road... the motorway of the future!" (Jourdan-Morhange, *Mes amis musiciens*, pp. 22–23).

[7] See Bannerman (ed.), *The Singer as Interpreter*, pp. 84–88, and Abraham, *Un Art de l'interprétation*, pp. 31, 40 and 212.

[8] Vladimir Jankélévitch (*Gabriel Fauré et ses mélodies*, p. 49) similarly observes, "Again we shouldn't regard any of this tragically. Fauré was immune to the wave of neuraesthenia which, with Duparc and Chausson, starts to descend on France ... and the melancholy of *Tristesse* isn't too serious."

[9] The composer's daughter-in-law remembered him thus: "Fauré était un méridional, très gai et enclin à la plaisanterie [Fauré was a southerner, very merry by nature and inclined to jocularity]" ("Brève rencontre avec Blanche Fauré-Fremiet", *Journal de Vichy*, 28 June 1958). Hélène Jourdan-Morhange referred to him as having never lost something of the "street urchin [*l'esprit gavroche*]" (*Mes amis musiciens*, p. 24). Some memoirs that Fauré penned in his late seventies recount, with undisguised glee, adolescent pranks he and his classmates used to perpetrate on their teachers at the École Niedermeyer ("Souvenirs", *La Revue musicale* 4/11, special Fauré number, 1 November 1922, pp. 3–9).

Preface to Volume 1

This volume presents all Fauré's songs up to op. 27 of 1882, comprising the twenty of the original "First Collection" (including *Barcarolle*), three songs unpublished during Fauré's life (the present nos. 2, 5 and 7), and the first four opus groups from the traditional "Second Collection", including Fauré's first song cycle, *Poème d'un jour*. The history of these collections and groupings is explained in the **Critical Commentary**.

A primary task here is to ascertain as reliable an ordering as possible, given that most of Fauré's songs prior to the op. 18 set were published in haphazard order, up to a dozen years after their composition. Nor is their ordering within the traditional First Collection chronological (except for the first two songs), and there is no musical logic to the later appending of the opus numbers 1–8 across that volume.[1] More than half of these songs can be dated only within two to five years (see the **Table of known chronology** on pages 128–129). As described below, *Poème d'un jour* also appears to predate the op. 18 songs, despite its higher printed opus number.

The present volume proposes a sequence for the first twenty-three songs which, with just one exception, establishes consistent poet-based groupings within known bounds of chronology. This also reveals a remarkably coherent stylistic development through Fauré's early songs. The only resulting exception to chronological order is Fauré's last Victor Hugo song, *L'Absent*, which must postdate at least *Lydia*, *Hymne* and *Seule!* Since even then its exact chronological place cannot be determined, in this one case the present edition prioritizes poet grouping over strict chronology.

The songs

Le Papillon et la fleur reveals the 16-year-old Fauré already displaying the easy melodic grace and rhythmic liveliness that characterizes much of his output. "My first song", as Fauré recalled, it was "written in the school refectory [of the École Niedermeyer], amid the aromas of cooking... and Saint-Saëns was my first interpreter".[2] Its surviving manuscript features a title-page cartoon probably drawn by Saint-Saëns (see facsimile on p. IV), newly employed as the school's – and Fauré's – piano professor (the two composers were to remain lifelong friends). *Puisque j'ai mis ma lèvre* (1862) similarly dates from Fauré's École Niedermeyer years; while its mandolin-like accompaniment anticipates later songs like *Clair de lune* and *Mandoline*, its most audible and remarkable link is to the second of Liszt's piano *Consolations* (a resemblance that perhaps explains why Fauré left the song unpublished). Two more Hugo *romances*, *Mai* and *S'il est un charmant gazon*, date from between 1862 and early 1864. The latter was published only in 1875, as *Rêve d'amour!*, a title imposed by the publisher Choudens, to Fauré's dismay.[3] An early presentation manuscript shows this song with a livelier tempo heading, a more aerated piano texture and a more compact ending, all suggesting a lithe, witty treatment of the poem. This version is sufficiently distinct from the long-published one to be printed here in its entirety as a viable alternative.[4]

These early Hugo settings feature in a letter of early 1864 from Hugo's factotum Paul Meurice to the poet himself:

> A young pupil of Niedermeyer's, a M. Gabriel Fauré, has set some of your poetry to music; he is prepared to pay you for the rights, but I know that several pieces are reserved, and I am sending you the titles of those he has taken in order that you can tell me whether they are excluded: *La Fleur et le papillon* [sic], *Puisque mai tout en fleurs*, *S'il est un charmant gazon*, *Puisqu'ici-bas toute âme*, *L'aube naît*, *Puisque j'ai mis ma lèvre*.[5]

Around 1865 (the year in which he took up a position as organist at the church of Saint-Sauveur in Rennes), Fauré tried his hand at a very different Hugo poem, *Tristesse d'Olympio*. Surviving only in what appears to be a scribal copy, this setting takes an excerpt from a longer dramatic poem, with a declamatory opening and restless strophic *Allegro* in the manner of a Schubertian *scena*. *Dans les ruines d'une abbaye* probably followed soon after; in 1869 it would be issued along with *Le Papillon et la fleur*, as the composer's first published songs.

The only traced source of *L'Aurore* (c. 1868–1870) is again a non-autograph copy, with a few retouches in Fauré's hand. Its texture is in the same vein as *Lydia* (composed around the same time) and the later *Green* (from op. 58), while its middle section shares a striking progression with two famous later songs, *Après un rêve* of 1877 and *Prison* of 1894. Why Fauré left this attractive song unpublished is uncertain, though it might relate – as with *Tristesse d'Olympio* – to its having set only a small portion of Hugo's much longer poem.

Fauré's final solo setting of Hugo reflects a more sombre context: dated "3 avril 1871", *L'Absent* was composed during the upheaval of the Paris Commune. With its poem taken from Hugo's collection *Les Châtiments*, written in furious reaction to Napoléon III's 1851 coup, the song might be read as a deadly apt rejoinder, marking the violent end of the resultant Second Empire. By this time Fauré had made his first excursion into the poetry of Leconte de Lisle, with *Lydia* (which famously opens in Lydian mode). As Jean-Michel Nectoux has observed,[6] this is most probably the "petite mélodie" that Fauré promised, in a letter of June 1870, to send Julien Koszul along with his "romance" *S'il est un charmant gazon*. Fauré's explicit stylistic distinction there marks a watershed between the lighter *romances* of the 1860s and the more concentrated, adventurous *mélodies* that follow.[7]

Fauré's three settings of Charles Baudelaire show a new dramatic intensity and structural boldness which, taken together, mark one of the biggest stylistic leaps of his career. His chosen poems could be read as embodying a thoroughly Baudelairean trilogy of love (*Hymne*), reason (*La Rançon*) and mortality (*Chant d'automne*), the last of these answering the "salut d'immortalité" in *Hymne*. Although *Hymne* was published in 1871 and the other two only in 1879, their close musical links suggest they all date from 1870–1871, indicating a possible collusion with Fauré's friends Duparc and Chabrier, whose first Baudelaire settings similarly date from 1870; Fauré's dedication of *La Rançon* to Duparc also stands out here as the only song he ever dedicated to another major composer.[8] Traditionally dispersed across the established First Collection, these three songs respond to Baudelaire's rich and complex poetry with a sophistication that has often been underestimated. Their sequential presentation here clarifies their remarkable relationship and coherence, notably through their shared structural and stylistic elements (the rising chromatic lines that permeate the first and third of them, and the texturally related transitions to the major mode in the second and third).[9]

These dramatic heights are followed by the very different verse of Théophile Gautier, again in four contrasted texts: *Les Matelots* (revisiting the simpler strophic form of the earlier *romances*); the darkly brooding *Seule!*; the plangent *Chanson du pêcheur (Lamento)*; and *Tristesse*, an unashamedly maudlin text redolent of the *café-concert* ("même mon petit chien" in the final strophe must count as doggerel in the full sense), as reflected in Fauré's gently ironic waltz rhythm. *Chanson du pêcheur* is dedicated to the great mezzo-soprano Pauline Viardot, Chopin protégée, composer and salon hostess, to whom Fauré was introduced by Saint-Saëns in the early 1870s. He soon became a regular member of her musical circle – in 1877 he would be briefly engaged to her daughter Marianne – and his next songs, *Aubade* and *Barcarolle*, set words by Viardot intimates Louis Pomey and Marc Monnier.

In the mid-1870s a venture into the poetry of Sully Prudhomme (*Ici-bas* and *Au bord de l'eau*) brought to Fauré's song-writing an added sense of sinuous dialogue between voice and piano. *Ici-bas* dates from no later than 1874, *Au bord de l'eau* probably from summer 1875, which Fauré spent at the home of his musically supportive friends Camille and Marie Clerc: an early fragment of the song rubs shoulders on a manuscript page with his First Violin Sonata, mostly composed that summer.

The late 1870s saw Fauré select two Tuscan poems in free translations by his singer friend Romain Bussine. *Après un rêve* (1877) has become Fauré's most famous song, while *Sérénade toscane* suggests a true tenor serenade. The present edition renders both songs fully singable for the first time in the original Tuscan (an option offered by the original editions, but with such defective syllabification as to have left at least *Sérénade toscane* unsingable in that form).

Sylvie, to a text by Paul de Choudens (an aspiring but mediocre poet, the son of Fauré's publisher), bears witness to a compromise Fauré undertook to hasten a first collective publication of twenty of his songs.[10] The volume in question duly appeared from Choudens *père* in December 1879 – ironically just a month after Fauré signed his first contract with Julien Hamelle, for works including the three songs of op. 18. By then he may already have sold the triptych *Poème d'un jour* to the publisher Durand & Schœnewerk; its manuscript shows the deleted annotation "op. 17".[11] Although the manuscript presents the songs in high-voice keys (D♭ major, F♯ minor and G♭ major), Durand & Schœnewerk first published the cycle in medium-voice transposition, in keys Fauré noted for that purpose on the manuscript. When a high-voice version eventually appeared in 1894, the last two songs were re-transposed into F minor and major, presumably by oversight. The present high-voice edition restores their original keys. As with *Sylvie*, his Tuscan songs and Pomey's *Aubade*, Fauré probably obtained these poems directly from their author; no published source is known for Charles Grandmougin's texts.

Opus 18 sets a pattern Fauré was to maintain for some decades, of mixing poets within his own defined opus groups. With *Nell* he made a happy return to Leconte de Lisle,[12] the song's lyrical flow contrasting with the much darker *Le Voyageur* and *Automne*.[13] These latter two are the first of Fauré's twelve settings of Armand Silvestre, another poet he knew personally (in 1881 the two planned an *opéra-comique*, *Lizarda*, though nothing came of it).[14] Nine Silvestre songs (from the years 1878–1884) are spread across the opus groups 18, 23, 27 and 39, in addition to the op. 35 *Madrigal* for SATB; again Fauré almost certainly sourced most of his texts from the poet himself. If rarely profound, Silvestre's poetry displays an attractive diversity of form, character and subject that appealed to the fluid and creative *mélodiste* Fauré had by now become. Tellingly, these first nine Silvestre settings were all designated by the poet as *Vers pour être chantés* [Lines to be sung].[15]

Composed between 1879 and 1881, the op. 23 songs again include two Silvestre settings, the tender *Le Secret* – which Maurice Ravel regarded as "one of Fauré's most beautiful songs"[16] – and the exuberant *Notre amour*, one of his lightest and most agile. *Les Berceaux*, marking Fauré's last return to the poetry of Sully Prudhomme, follows *Ici-bas* and *Au bord de l'eau* in exploring active dialogue between voice and piano: at the song's climax the piano is effectively invited to drown the voice's last syllable like a breaking wave. Another pair of Silvestre settings, from 1882, comprises op. 27. *Chanson d'amour* turns one of Silvestre's less remarkable poems into a playground of musical and poetic *enjambment*, while in the playfully ironic *La Fée aux chansons* Fauré may have ruefully recognized some of his own experience in vocal coaching.

Notes on the edition and performance

Keys

Most of the songs are presented here in the keys established by the Choudens–Hamelle collections. For *Mai*, *Au bord de l'eau*, "Toujours" and "Adieu" (*Poème d'un jour*) and *La Fée aux chansons*, however, the present high-voice edition restores tonalities from manuscript sources. The case of *Poème d'un jour* is discussed above; for *La Fée aux chansons* Fauré's original E major seems better suited to both voice and piano than the established high-voice key of F. *Chant d'automne* and *Le Voyageur* are analogously restored to their original high-voice keys (respectively C♯ and A minor rather than the C and G minor of the established collections), in which they lie more idiomatically, including some key-specific piano fingering in *Chant d'automne*.[17] *Dans les ruines d'une abbaye*, *Ici-bas* and *Au bord de l'eau* have all traditionally been printed in high- and medium-voice keys a semitone apart. For the first of these the present edition adopts G major for medium-voice transposition in preference to the established A♭; for *Au bord de l'eau* the D minor of Fauré's early draft is adopted as the high-voice key in preference to the long-published C♯ minor (retaining C minor, the key of all three complete manuscripts, as the medium-voice key). For *Ici-bas*, with its intrinsically high tessitura, the original manuscript's F♯ minor tonality, printed since 1890 as medium-voice key, is taken here as the high-voice key in place of the traditional G minor, and E minor adopted as the medium-voice key (the piano part also lies better in this sharp-based tonality). For *Sérénade toscane* the present edition takes its medium-voice key of A minor (rather than the traditional B♭) from a separate edition of 1901, bringing the song more within mezzo and baritone range. The manuscript keys of *L'Aurore* and *Tristesse d'Olympio* are adopted here for respectively the high-voice and medium-voice editions, with transposed keys chosen editorially; *Puisque j'ai mis ma lèvre* is given in its two manuscript keys.

Tempo, metre and rhythm

Besides the comments in the **General Preface** above, knowledge of Fauré's habits and performing preferences can illuminate some notational and editorial quirks peculiar to his early songs. His use of *Allegretto* is typically very near *Allegro*, but with more lightness of texture and character. His frequent use of *Andante* – often qualified by *quasi allegretto* or even *quasi adagio* – can be read as signifying moderate, flowing tempi in the present-day sense, embodying the literal sense of *andante* as "moving" and of *adagio* as "at ease" – and indeed of *quasi adagio* as "almost at ease". This notably affects *Lydia*, *Chant d'automne*, "Rencontre" and *Nell*, as well as *Seule !* and *L'Absent*. For these last two, the present edition restores the 𝄵 of their manuscripts and first editions (in place of the 𝄴 printed in subsequent editions), underlining their intrinsic half-bar tread and sense of forward motion. The texture and flow in *Lydia* and *Chanson d'amour* (for which no manuscripts remain) prompt corresponding editorial suggestions of [𝄵], supported in the case of *Lydia* by its textural affinity with *L'Aurore*, whose quavers flow very similarly to the crotchets in *Lydia*.

Fauré's tempo headings often make best sense when read against melodic lines and underlying harmonic rhythms, rather than against busier accompanying figurations. In *Aubade*, for example, the double element in the tempo heading suggests a fairly lively start from the piano to help the singer sustain the extended vocal phrases. This applies even more in *Chant d'automne*, whose opening *Andante* tempo is crucially defined in retrospect by the later metric equivalence into the coda.

Fauré's perennial tinkering with tempo headings has left several songs with variant indications across high- and medium- or low-voice editions. While most of these suggest variant descriptions of the same musical concept (like *Allegretto* versus *Allegro non troppo* in *Le Papillon et la fleur* and *Dans les ruines d'une abbaye*), *Ici-bas* is more complex: headed *Andantino* in all early sources and the later high-voice collection, since 1879 it has appeared in the medium-voice collection under the heading *Adagio*, with concomitant thickening of the piano part. Priority is given here to the *Andantino* version as intrinsic to Fauré's original conception and to the poem (wistful rather than tragic); the alternative reading is shown in footnotes. The only song from the original First Collection to have been given a metronome marking was *Barcarolle* (when it was later moved to Hamelle's Second Collection, as noted in the **Critical Commentary**). For a few songs the original metronome markings appear unsustainably slow: in particular, ♩ = 66 in *Nell* suggests an error for 96, while those in *Chanson d'amour* and *Notre amour* belie the songs' playful, even breathless character.[18] In such cases editorial suggestions are appended in square brackets alongside the source markings.

Fauré's intrinsic sense of forward motion shows itself in a penchant for sometimes restoring tempo (after a brief *ritard.*) just before a cadence or main beat rather than on it, as with his manuscript placing of *a tempo* indications in *Mai* (bars 26 and 59) and *L'Aurore*. In the former case this involves moving straight through a comma in the text – doubtless in part to forestall singers taking a leisurely breath there. *Au bord de l'eau* and *Chanson d'amour* show a related gesture, a slur marked (in just some sources) across text punctuation. While Fauré endorses this in *Au bord de l'eau* by specifying a breath a few notes later (bars 15 and 31, via a pleasing moment of piano bass imitation), Claire Croiza quotes him as later disavowing it in favour of taking a breath at the text punctuation.[19] Such varying treatment, over a long and busy compositional life, reflects an inherent flexibility of conception discussed more below.

Fauré's music is suffused with rhythmic play, notably in the form of hemiolas (sounding $\frac{3}{4}$ or $\frac{3}{2}$ patterns across a $\frac{6}{8}$ or $\frac{3}{4}$ background), a device that permeates his piano Barcarolles in particular and has roots in the folk idioms of his native southern France. This penchant springs out of the very first vocal entry in *Le Papillon et la fleur*, setting off most of the poem's syllabification in effective $\frac{3}{4}$ rhythm against the piano's $\frac{6}{8}$, a trait equally observable in parts of *Au bord de l'eau* and the opening lines of *Notre amour*.[20] Performers have to be alert to such rhythmic play, bearing in mind that placing weak syllables on apparent strong beats is not *per se* a fault in French sung prosody, given the language's inherent plasticity of stress and rhythmic patterns.

Musical sources

The twenty songs of the original First Collection – the present nos. 1, 3–4, 6 and 8–23 – have come to us through various early editions with a sometimes bewildering array of variants, resulting from their multiple publishers, engravings, keys and amended reprints over Fauré's lifetime. Each successive source tends to mix new revisions with corruptions or reversals of earlier revisions, to the extent that no single source can be taken as a coherently definitive version. Autograph manuscripts are traced for just fourteen of the present volume's songs: the only one of these manuscripts specifically drawn up for publication was *Poème d'un jour*, though a few others may have figured in the source chain leading to publication. Some predate publication by up to a decade and show a song in an earlier state, or suggest just one of several compositional conceptions: three clean autographs of *Au bord de l'eau*, for example, all from around 1875–1876, show varying realizations of texture and nuances throughout. Although essentially superseded by the published versions, these manuscripts help resolve misprints or clarify details of voicing and layout; they also show many revealing variants, sometimes from when a song was freshest in the composer's mind. The most important of these figure among the present edition's *ossia* readings, and provide one complete alternative version (of *S'il est un charmant gazon*).

To some degree all this reveals an intrinsic fluidity of conception in Fauré's early songs, an important characteristic that the present edition accepts, indeed embraces. While the most coherent reading of each song is presented here as the main musical text, viable variants are shown on *ossia* staves or in footnotes. Essential corrections are taken into the musical text from whatever source supplies them; some less essential but useful indications from secondary sources are incorporated in parentheses.

Taking all the above into consideration, the most reliable source for the songs published during Fauré's life theoretically ought to be the revised 1908 printings of the first two Hamelle Collections, which underwent no further changes during Fauré's life. Unfortunately that ideal is repeatedly thwarted by variants of tempo, syllabification, dynamics and articulation across their high- and medium-voice versions. This particularly affects the First Collection, whose 1890 first edition for high voice took its musical text mainly from separate prints farther back in the source chain, losing many of the careful revisions Fauré had incorporated in the volume's (mostly medium-voice) original publication of 1879. Instead the 1890 high-voice edition shows a different array of revisions, probably entered at the last minute and ranging from makeshift to indispensable. These discrepancies, never remedied, oblige us now to choose between the high- and medium-voice volumes as a priority source for each song, according to which version suggests the more thorough preparation or revision. Whichever is given precedence still needs supplementing from other sources to arrive at a text that respects Fauré's careful work of revision over several decades, while remaining coherent within itself.

Fauré's earlier songs also show numerous variants of syllabification across sources, as he sought in successive editions to refine the fluidity and practicality of his text-setting. While many of his amendments address potentially awkward or unidiomatic accentuations, others suggest a reaction to performers failing to grasp the rhythmic or emphatic flexibility of an original reading. The present edition shows the more interesting of these variants as *ossias*; notable examples come near the end of *La Rançon* (providing a better *enjambment* at the expense of a prolonged weak syllable) and at bars 28–30 in *Seule!* (providing more emphatic focus than the later, safer readings). Alert performance can obviate many of the inherent hazards.

Text

Fauré often modified the text of poems he set, substituting words, amending word order or excising lines and verses to mould the poem to his musical designs. His retouches usually have a musically astute purpose, making the words as smoothly melodic and singable as possible. The present edition respects these amendments, which are shown in brackets alongside the original texts on pp. XXVIII–XLI.

More complex are Fauré's modifications of the poems' punctuation and capitalization: across the many manuscript and printed sources, many details of punctuation are omitted, innumerable others appear differently, and occasionally new punctuation symbols appear. Patterns of capitalization can be equally variable, sometimes respecting the poetic originals and sometimes appearing in quite different arrangements. When such discrepancies across sources of a single song appear to result from compositional or engraving oversight, the present edition tacitly follows whichever musical sources maintain the poem's own punctuation and capitalization. Where musical sources show no punctuation or unviable alternatives, that of the printed poem is editorially restored, as noted in the **Critical Commentary**.

Often, however, musical sources show plausible or interpretatively useful amendments to a poem's punctuation or formatting, in ways that suggest deliberate compositional initiatives. These include simplifying densely punctuated passages, exchanging exclamation marks, commas, semicolons or full stops, introducing semicolons or full stops to define the end of stanzas or musical paragraphs, using exclamation marks as an indicator of dynamic intensity, and introducing commas to indicate a breath or a non-elision (*Mai* and *L'Absent* in particular show many such adjustments). Just as it respects Fauré's word modifications, the present edition attempts to discern and respect deliberate and systematic amendments to punctuation and capitalization, provided no syntactic or musical problems result.[21] These variants, generally unlisted in the **Critical Commentary**, can easily be identified by comparing the musical text with the poems in their original forms (as quoted on pages XXVIII–XLI). Poetic source punctuation and capitalization are restored to a greater degree in the songs Fauré left unpublished, whose manuscripts show less methodical treatment.

Acknowledgments

The editors' grateful thanks are extended to all those who kindly made sources available for study or helped in practical ways, including librarians and private collectors worldwide (with particular thanks to the music staff of the Bibliothèque nationale de France) and numerous individuals, notably Helen Abbott, Thierry and Pierrette Bodin, Mimi Segal Daitz, Denis Herlin, Peter Jost, Edmond Lemaître (and Éditions Durand), Roger Nichols, Robert Orledge and Herbert Schneider, and to Angela Newport, Valeria Schiavone and Diego Ropele for assistance with the Tuscan texts. Performing and teaching colleagues and students have provided supportive enthusiasm, expertise and invaluable musical feedback through workshops and concerts; the editors thank in particular Mary Dibbern, Amber Evans, Guy Flechter, François Le Roux, Robert Macfarlane, Rosalind Martin, Kurt Ollmann, Christopher Underwood and Darlene Wiley. The editorial project's base at the Royal Academy of Music, London, has been supported by a Project Grant from the Arts and Humanities Research Council (UK); special thanks there go to Nicole Tibbels for an immeasurable degree of enthusiastic cooperation and insights in practical and linguistic matters, to Richard Stokes for kindly authorising reproduction of his English translations of song texts, and to the Academy's postgraduate singing students, along with David Gorton, Neil Heyde and Timothy Jones.

London, 2014   *Roy Howat & Emily Kilpatrick*

---

[1] The numbers were superimposed on the existing sequence of the First Collection by Hamelle in 1896, as part of Fauré's candidature for the Institut de France. For convenience of reference, the present edition shows them in parentheses (as also with op. 21: see note 11 below). Regarding more detailed discussion of this and other editorial issues in Fauré's early songs, see **Select Bibliography**.

[2] Letter of 14 July 1922, in Fauré-Fremiet (ed.), *Gabriel Fauré: Lettres intimes*, p. 282.

[3] Letter to Julien Koszul of June 1870, in Nectoux (ed.), *Gabriel Fauré: His Life through his Letters*, p. 25.

[4] Surviving source evidence suggests that Fauré may have retained only rough drafts of some early songs after giving away carefully-marked presentation manuscripts (notably of *Mai* and *S'il est un charmant gazon*), the latter thus being no longer accessible when the opportunity for publication arose years later.

[5] In Nectoux (ed.), *Gabriel Fauré: His Life through his Letters*, p. 18 (letter undated); Hugo accorded his permission in a reply dated 29 May 1864. *Puisqu'ici-bas* was published in 1879 as a vocal duet (see *Complete Songs*, vol. 2); if *L'Aube naît* was set, it is now untraced.

[6] In Nectoux (ed.), *Gabriel Fauré: His Life through his Letters*, pp. 24–25.

[7] In 1911 Fauré was to opine that he had never succeeded in setting Victor Hugo (and only rarely Leconte de Lisle) to his satisfaction: "their poetry is too full, too rich, too self-sufficient for the music to adapt to it successfully" ("Sous la Musique que faut-il mettre?", *Musica* 101, February 1911, p. 38). This might be read as Fauré (like many an older composer) being overly self-deprecating about his early works, given the natural charm and lightness of touch that pervade these songs.

[8] Baudelaire had previously been set to music only by his *chansonnier* friends. Fauré, Duparc and Chabrier were also co-founders, in 1871, of the Société nationale de musique, whose express purpose was to promote new French music. *Chant d'automne* is first documented only in 1878 (in a letter from Fauré to Marie Clerc: "I have dedicated *Chant d'automne* to Mme M. Camille Clerc – is that all right?"; in Nectoux (ed.), *Gabriel Fauré: His Life through his Letters*, p. 82), but Fauré's wording, evidently prompted by imminent publication, suggests a song familiar to her rather than something new.

[9] For more detail see the present editors' "Wagnérisme de Fauré : *Pénélope* (1913) et les mélodies", in Marie-Cécile Leblanc and Danièle Pistone (ed.), *Wagner, 1913–2013, Ruptures et Continuité*, Paris, Presses de la Sorbonne-Nouvelle, in press for 2015.

[10] "I have performed a labour of Hercules, *viz.* setting to music some lines by Choudens (Paul)! Yes, dear Madame, Lucette [the name presumably a joke] will be walking through life with an escort of four flats and twelve semiquavers per bar ... Now that I have put myself right with Choudens I hope that publication of the volume of songs will proceed smoothly." (Letter of October 1878 to Marie Clerc; translation slightly amended from Nectoux (ed.), *Gabriel Fauré: His Life through his Letters*, pp. 81–82.)

[11] No trace remains of the contract in the archives of Éditions Durand; it was probably signed in 1879. The opus number 21 was first attached to the cycle in 1897, the number 17 having been appropriated by Hamelle in 1880 for his publication (in 1881) of Fauré's *Romances sans paroles* for piano, which had been composed many years earlier.

[12] Leconte de Lisle's *Nell* derives from Robert Burns's *Handsome Nell*, an ode to his teenage sweetheart Nellie Kilpatrick.

[13] An apparent attempt by Hamelle to sentimentalize these titles was, this time, successfully resisted by Fauré: "I much prefer the title *Le Voyageur* because it is the one the poet gave his poem. As for the other song, I have thought it over and the title *Juin* does not seem to suit it as well as the title *Nell*. June, with the delights of its blossom and sunshine, is invoked purely for the purposes of comparison with the fervour of the love that Nell has inspired in the poet's heart. It is Nell who is the subject, not June. Why don't we put – to *Nell* – ?" (letter to Hamelle, 24 June 1880; translation slightly amended from Nectoux (ed.), *Gabriel Fauré: His Life through his Letters*, p. 96).

[14] Nectoux, *Gabriel Fauré: A Musical Life*, p. 137.

[15] The settings are drawn from two collections, *Le Pays de roses* and *Les Ailes d'or*, which both include sections thus titled.

[16] Ravel, "Les Mélodies de Gabriel Fauré", *La Revue musicale* 3 (October 1922), in Arbie Orenstein (ed.), *A Ravel Reader: Correspondence, Articles, Interviews*, New York, 1990, p. 385.

[17] The change to C minor for the First Collection may result from a publisher's preference for an "easier" key signature.

[18] The opening vocal entry of *Notre amour* makes this point from the outset: too moderate a tempo leaves a weak syllable overexposed on the top note. No manuscript sources verify these metronome indications, added more than fifteen years after the songs' first publication (see **Critical Commentary**). Analogous misprints in Fauré's output include the first of his *Pièces brèves* for piano, whose first edition misprinted his 69 indication as 96.

[19] Abraham (ed.), *Un Art de l'interprétation*, p. 138; Bannerman (ed.), *The Singer as Interpreter*, p. 83.

[20] The 1879 publication of the First Collection amended the opening voice entry of *Le Papillon et la fleur*, at bar 10, to start on the beat with an unambiguous $\frac{6}{8}$ pattern (see **Critical Commentary**); the main aim of this was probably to ensure a secure vocal entry, rather than any rethinking of syllabification, given that $\frac{2}{4}$–$\frac{6}{8}$ cross-rhythms then continue unchanged through most of the song (including bar 11). Fauré's decision to restore the original reading of bar 10 in all subsequent editions was certainly a deliberate one, for it entailed amending the plates of the First Collection.

[21] For a detailed discussion of this issue see Kilpatrick, "Moot point: Editing poetry and punctuation in Fauré's early songs".

Préface générale

C'est vraiment dans ses mélodies que Fauré nous livre la fleur de son génie.
— Maurice Ravel[1]

Nul compositeur n'a fait de contribution plus substantielle et plus variée au répertoire de la mélodie française que Gabriel Fauré. La mélodie couvre toute sa carrière, du charmant *Papillon et la fleur* de 1861 au magistral cycle *L'Horizon chimérique*, composé soixante ans et plus de cent mélodies plus tard. L'importance de cette contribution a longtemps été compromise par l'histoire erratique de la publication des mélodies : dispersées dans différents recueils et chez divers éditeurs, bon nombre d'entre elles ont eu à pâtir de graves fautes d'impression et de leçons contradictoires dans les différentes versions imprimées. Cette première édition critique complète présente un texte qui fait autorité mais reste flexible, rassemblant la collection connue de soixante mélodies (telle qu'établie en 1908 par les éditions Hamelle), d'autres mélodies et cycles publiés séparément, dont trois mélodies restées inédites du vivant de Fauré, ainsi que trois mélodies à deux voix et un quatuor vocal. Le volume associé des *Vocalises* complètes de Fauré (EP 11385) comprend sa *Vocalise-Étude* sans paroles publiée pour la première fois en 1907, ainsi que quarante-quatre autres vocalises restées inédites jusque-là.

Avec son caractère à la fois pratique et scientifique, la présente édition vise à encourager les interprétations créatives, assurées et bien informées. Fondée sur l'étude de centaines de manuscrits et sources imprimées, elle a été éprouvée au plan international dans des master-classes, ateliers, séminaires, concerts et enregistrements, avec la participation de chanteurs professionnels, étudiants, professeurs, répétiteurs et spécialistes. En cela elle s'inspire du compositeur, qui préparait ses propres éditions sur la base de l'expérience interprétative. L'édition intègre aussi les idées d'interprètes qui ont travaillé avec Fauré, ainsi que ses propres préférences attestées dans ce domaine.

Sources et principes d'édition

Les principaux éditeurs des mélodies de Fauré étaient Choudens (1869-1879), Hamelle (1880-1904), Heugel (1905-1910) et Durand (1915-1921) ; diverses mélodies de lui furent également publiées à différents moments par Hartmann, Durand & Schœnewerk, Fromont, et la firme londonienne Metzler (outre certaines éditions américaines secondaires tirées d'originaux français). La plupart de ses mélodies furent imprimées séparément avant d'être réunies en recueils : le premier d'entre eux parut en 1879 (Choudens), le deuxième en 1897 (Hamelle), et le troisième en 1908 (Hamelle)[2]. Ces recueils, comme la plupart des éditions séparées, parurent dans des tonalités destinées aux voix élevées et aux voix moyennes ; et certaines mélodies furent publiées séparément dans des transpositions supplémentaires. À l'opposé de cette abondance de sources imprimées, les manuscrits conservés sont moins nombreux. Parmi ceux qui ont maintenant été retrouvés, beaucoup – en particulier pour les premières mélodies – sont des ébauches, des manuscrits de présentation ou des versions intermédiaires.

Des sources aussi variées demandent à être traitées avec attention par l'éditeur. Les manuscrits, malgré les précieuses corrections, vérifications et variantes qu'ils offrent, réclament une certaine prudence, surtout lorsqu'ils n'étaient pas directement dans la chaîne de sources conduisant à la publication. Dans le même temps, même parmi la pléthore de sources imprimées, il est souvent impossible de s'en tenir à une source unique qui représenterait le texte « final » ou définitif du compositeur, car chacune des sources mêle des informations essentielles à des problèmes et des corruptions (là encore, le plus apparents dans les premières mélodies). Pour présenter un texte aussi fidèle que possible aux corrections faites par Fauré au fil des ans, la présente édition a dû recourir aux meilleures parmi les sources variées tout en restant dans les limites de la priorité logique des sources et du bon sens musical, en respectant toujours la cohérence au sein des mélodies uniques, groupes, cycles et recueils, et en prenant en compte tout ce qu'on sait des habitudes de Fauré en matière de composition, révision et interprétation, ainsi que toute indication circonstancielle. Des *ossia* sont donnés partout où plusieurs leçons sont manifestement viables. Il s'agit entre autres de quelques leçons anciennes qui clarifient certains aspects des intentions du compositeur – éléments qui furent parfois masqués par des révisions ultérieures visant à « protéger » la musique des interprétations ineptes. Le **commentaire critique** donne à ce sujet des explications complètes.

Tonalités

Absolument rien ne dit que Fauré s'opposait à la transposition de ses mélodies, en principe ou en pratique[3]. Plusieurs de ses mélodies existent dans différentes tonalités autographes (dont des transpositions faites après publication), d'autres ont d'abord paru dans une ou plusieurs tonalités qui diffèrent des manuscrits qui subsistent, tandis que pour les mélodies dont le manuscrit est perdu il est parfois impossible d'identifier à partir des sources imprimées la tonalité originale, et à plus forte la tonalité préférée de l'auteur. (Même dans les recueils d'Hamelle, on ne peut se fier toujours aux indications « ton original »[4].) Fauré, qui fut toute sa vie un musicien pratique, un accompagnateur et un habile chef de chœur, avait l'habitude de travailler avec une large palette de voix. Les programmes de concert qui subsistent montrent qu'il interprétait régulièrement ses mélodies avec différents types de voix, souvent dans des circonstances qui supposaient manifestement une transposition, notamment plusieurs créations importantes. Comme tout compositeur, Fauré avait ses propres préférences de tessiture ou de couleur tonale pour quelques mélodies ; toute indication de ce genre est citée ici et prise en compte.

À cet égard, la présente édition respecte la démarche pragmatique de Fauré lui-même, en rendant ses mélodies accessibles à autant de chanteurs que possible dans les limites appropriées du goût et de la rigueur. Les tonalités pour voix élevées et voix moyennes des trois recueils traditionnels sont pour la plupart maintenues, sauf lorsqu'une source offre une option plus convaincante ou laisse à penser que c'était la préférence de Fauré, et parfois pour faire une distinction plus réaliste entre voix élevées et moyennes. L'aspect pratique au clavier est également pris en considération. Dans quelques rares cas, la présente édition adopte une nouvelle tonalité transposée, pour des raisons de logique musicale et de tessiture, en tenant compte des sources. Pour les quelques mélodies publiées dans une seule tonalité du vivant de Fauré, une deuxième tonalité a été déterminée par l'éditeur. Dans certains cas, lorsque les sources présentent d'utiles tonalités supplémentaires, une troisième tonalité est disponible en ligne à www.fabermusic.com/editionpetersresources. Pour chaque mélodie, la présente édition indique la ou les tonalités originales connues ; lorsque le manuscrit est perdu ou que la tonalité originale imprimée diffère, cette dernière est indiquée entre parenthèses, en gras pour les tonalités données comme originales dans les recueils Hamelle.

INTERPRÉTATION

Les témoignages sur le jeu et les préférences interprétatives de Fauré indiquent tous qu'il tenait à ce que la musique avance, avec une forte aversion pour tout ralentissement, rubato ou affectation sentimentale gratuits[5]. Son sens du tempo était lié au rythme naturel du poème parlé, et sa collègue Claire Croiza, mezzo-soprano distinguée, soulignait l'importance qu'il attachait au poème et à son articulation dans la mélodie. Croiza rapporte en outre :

> Fauré était un vivant métronome. [...] Par-dessus tout, c'est en le ralentissant qu'on le déforme. [...] Pour Fauré plus que pour quiconque il faut trouver l'expression dans le cadre de la mesure. [...] J'ai entendu une fois chanter *Après un rêve* par un chanteur qui mourait littéralement. Le soir même, dînant avec Fauré, je lui dis : « Enfin, Maître, dans quel mouvement voulez-vous *Après un rêve* ? » Et lui : « Sans ralentir, sans ralentir ! »[6]

Tout en soulignant l'intensité des moments tragiques (*Chanson du pêcheur* ou *Prison*), Croiza met en garde à plusieurs reprises contre une interprétation douloureuse des mélodies plus mélancoliques de Fauré, l'essence du raffinement et de la retenue de ce langage étant de ne pas exagérer ni caricaturer ce que le compositeur a déjà subtilement équilibré[7]. Parmi les premières mélodies de Fauré, en particulier, un poème ouvertement mélancolique comme *Tristesse* peut receler un certain degré de parodie ou d'autodérision[8], à quoi Fauré répond avec une touche légère qui rappelle de nombreux témoignages de ses amis et collègues sur son humour vivace et sa gaieté innée jusque dans ses dernières années[9].

PRÉSENTATION

Les *ossia* sont transposés, suivant les besoins, à partir de leur tonalité source. Toute leçon musicale sujette à discussion fait l'objet d'une note de bas de page. Les liaisons ajoutées (ou complétées) par l'éditeur sont en pointillés ; les autres ajouts de l'éditeur sont entre crochets. Les altérations de précaution entre parenthèses apparaissent telles quelles dans les sources. Des parenthèses sont également ajoutées autour des respirations non essentielles qui apparaissent uniquement dans certaines sources, et autour de nuances et d'autres indications utiles provenant de sources secondaires, comme le détaille le **commentaire critique**.

Londres, 2014
Roy Howat et Emily Kilpatrick
(Traduction : Dennis Collins)

---

[1] Maurice Ravel, « Les mélodies de Gabriel Fauré », *La Revue musicale* 3, octobre 1922, dans Arbie Orenstein (éd.), *Maurice Ravel : Lettres, écrits, entretiens*, Paris, Flammarion, 1990, p. 325.

[2] La publication du troisième recueil en 1908 coïncidait avec la réédition par Hamelle des deuxième et troisième recueils (il racheta le premier recueil à Choudens en 1887 et en publia une édition pour voix élevée en 1890), avec quelques modifications dans la répartition du contenu ; voir **commentaire critique**.

[3] Pour une discussion détaillée de cette question éditoriale et d'autres, essentielles pour la présente édition, voir nos articles « Editorial Challenges in the Early Songs of Gabriel Fauré » et « Gabriel Fauré's Middle-Period Songs ».

[4] Celles-ci ne figurent que dans les deuxième et troisième recueils Hamelle, à partir de l'op. 18. Le diapason n'était alors pas standardisé en Europe – il pouvait varier d'un demi-ton de l'autre côté de la frontière –, même si, pendant la carrière de Fauré, il était fixé en France (par décret parlementaire de 1859) à la^3 = 435 Hz, un peu plus bas que la norme actuelle, de 440 Hz ou un peu plus.

[5] Plusieurs de ces témoignages, provenant de sa famille et de ses collègues musiciens, sont cités dans Roy Howat, *The Art of French Piano Music*, Londres et New Haven, Yale UP, 2009, p. 247, et de façon générale dans les chapitres 17, 18 et 21.

[6] Cité dans Abraham (éd.), *Un art de l'interprétation*, p. 199 et 212, et en partie dans Bannerman (éd.), *The Singer as Interpreter*, p. 82 ; ce dernier ouvrage ajoute une référence spécifique qui explique le « (sans ralentir) » de la présente édition à la mesure 46. La collègue violoniste de Fauré, Hélène Jourdan-Morhange, confirme ce trait, livrant une anecdote sur une chanteuse (anonyme) qui avait l'habitude de marquer des pauses et de traîner sur les fins de phrase : accompagnée par Fauré un jour pour un concert dans l'après-midi, « elle fut horrifiée d'être entraînée par le piano dans une route sans vallonnements... l'autostrade future ! » (Jourdan-Morhange, *Mes amis musiciens*, p. 22-23).

[7] Voir Bannerman (éd.), *The Singer as Interpreter*, p. 84-88, et Abraham (éd.), *Un art de l'interprétation*, p. 31, 40 et 212.

[8] Vladimir Jankélévitch (*Gabriel Fauré et ses mélodies*, p. 49) note de même : « Toujours ne prenons rien au tragique. Fauré reste en dehors de la vague de neurasthénie qui, avec Duparc et Chausson, commence à s'abattre sur la France [...] et la mélancolie de *Tristesse* n'est pas trop sérieuse. »

[9] La belle-fille du compositeur se souvenait ainsi de lui : « Fauré était un méridional, très gai et enclin à la plaisanterie » (« Brève rencontre avec Blanche Fauré-Fremiet », *Journal de Vichy*, 28 juin 1958). Hélène Jourdan-Morhange disait qu'il n'avait jamais perdu son « esprit gavroche » (*Mes amis musiciens*, p. 24). Certains souvenirs que Fauré nota vers la fin de sa vie évoquent, avec une jubilation non déguisée, les farces d'adolescent que lui et ses condisciples faisaient subir à leurs professeurs à l'École Niedermeyer (« Souvenirs », *La Revue musicale* 4/11, numéro spécial Fauré, 1er novembre 1922, p. 3-9).

Préface au 1er volume

Ce volume réunit toutes les mélodies de Fauré jusqu'à l'op. 27 de 1882 et comprend les vingt du « premier recueil » (dans sa forme primitive, avec *Barcarolle*), trois mélodies inédites du vivant de Fauré (nos 2, 5 et 7 ici), et les quatre premiers opus du « deuxième recueil » traditionnel, avec le premier cycle de Fauré, *Poème d'un jour*. L'historique de ces recueils et de ces groupements est expliqué dans le commentaire critique.

La première tâche ici a été de déterminer un ordre aussi fiable que possible, étant donné que la plupart des mélodies de Fauré avant l'op. 18 furent publiées dans un ordre aléatoire, jusqu'à une douzaine d'années après leur composition. Leur ordre dans le premier recueil traditionnel n'est pas non plus chronologique (sauf pour les deux premières mélodies), et il n'y a pas de logique musicale à l'ajout ultérieur des numéros d'opus 1-8 tout au long de ce volume[1]. Plus de la moitié de ces mélodies ne peuvent être datées qu'approximativement, à l'intérieur d'une période de deux à cinq ans (voir le **tableau chronologique** pages 128-129). Comme nous l'expliquons ci-dessous, *Poème d'un jour* semble également précéder les mélodies op. 18, malgré son numéro d'opus supérieur.

Le présent volume propose pour les vingt-trois premières mélodies un ordre qui, à une seule exception près, définit des groupements cohérents sur la base des poètes dans le cadre des limites connues de la chronologie. Cet ordre révèle également une évolution stylistique d'une remarquable cohérence au long des premières mélodies de Fauré. La seule exception à l'ordre chronologique qui en résulte est la dernière mélodie de Fauré sur un poème de Victor Hugo, *L'Absent*, qui doit être postérieure au moins à *Lydia*, *Hymne* et *Seule!* Comme cette exacte place chronologique ne peut être déterminée, dans ce cas-ci nous donnons la priorité au groupement par poète.

LES MÉLODIES

Le Papillon et la fleur révèle déjà chez le jeune Fauré, âgé de seize ans, la grâce mélodique et la vivacité rythmique qui caractérisent tant de son œuvre. « C'est là, en effet, écrit Fauré, ma toute première mélodie, composée dans le réfectoire de l'École [Niedermeyer], parmi les parfums de cuisine... et mon premier interprète fut Saint-Saëns[2]. » Le manuscrit qui subsiste comporte en page de titre une caricature probablement dessinée par Saint-Saëns (voir fac-similé, p. IV), nouvellement engagé comme professeur de piano de l'école, et de Fauré (les deux compositeurs allaient rester amis pour la vie). *Puisque j'ai mis ma lèvre* (1862) date de même des années de Fauré à l'École Niedermeyer; si son accompagnement à la manière d'une mandoline préfigure des mélodies ultérieures come *Clair de lune* et *Mandoline*, c'est avec la deuxième des *Consolations* pour piano de Liszt que le lien est le plus audible et le plus remarquable (ressemblance qui explique peut-être que Fauré ait laissé la mélodie inédite). Deux autres romances d'après Hugo, *Mai* et *S'il est un charmant gazon*, datent d'entre 1862 et 1864. La seconde ne fut publiée qu'en 1875, sous le titre *Rêve d'amour!* imposé par l'éditeur, Choudens, au grand dam de Fauré[3]. Un manuscrit de présentation ancien révèle cette mélodie avec une indication de tempo plus animée, une écriture pianistique plus aérée et une fin plus compacte, qui reflètent un traitement leste, spirituel, du poème. Cette version est suffisamment distincte de la version publiée depuis longtemps pour être imprimée ici dans son entier en tant que variante viable[4].

Ces premières mélodies d'après Hugo sont citées dans une lettre du début de 1864 de son homme de confiance, Paul Meurice, au poète lui-même:

> Un jeune homme, élève de Niedermeyer, M. Gabriel Fauré, a fait de la musique sur des vers de vous; il est prêt à payer le droit de vos pauvres, mais je sais que plusieurs pièces sont réservées, et je vous envoie les titres de celles qu'il a prises pour que vous me disiez si elles sont exclues: *La Fleur et le papillon* [sic], *Puisque mai tout en fleurs*, *S'il est un charmant gazon*, *Puisqu'ici-bas toute âme*, *L'aube naît*, *Puisque j'ai mis ma lèvre*[5].

Vers 1865 (année où il assuma les fonctions d'organiste de l'église Saint-Sauveur de Rennes), Fauré s'essaya à un poème d'Hugo très différent, *Tristesse d'Olympio*. Cette mélodie, qui ne subsiste que dans ce qui semble être un manuscrit de copiste, est écrite sur un extrait d'un poème dramatique plus long, avec un début déclamatoire et un *Allegro* strophique agité à la manière d'une *scena* schubertienne. *Dans les ruines d'une abbaye* suivit probablement peu de temps après; en 1869, avec *Le Papillon et la fleur*, ce furent les premières mélodies publiées du compositeur.

La seule source connue de *L'Aurore* (v. 1868-1870) est de nouveau une copie non autographe, avec quelques retouches de la main de Fauré. L'écriture est dans la même veine que *Lydia* (composé vers le même moment) et *Green* (plus tardif, de l'op. 58), tandis que la section médiane partage une saisissante progression avec deux célèbres mélodies ultérieures, *Après un rêve* de 1877 et *Prison* de 1894. On ne sait pas pourquoi Fauré laissa cette séduisante mélodie inédite, encore que ce puisse être lié –comme pour *Tristesse d'Olympio*– au fait que la mélodie n'emploie qu'une petite partie du poème beaucoup plus long d'Hugo.

L'ultime mélodie de Fauré sur des vers d'Hugo reflète un contexte plus sombre: daté du « 3 avril 1871 », *L'Absent* fut composé pendant les soulèvements de la Commune de Paris. Avec son poème emprunté au recueil *Les Châtiments* d'Hugo, écrit en réaction furieuse au coup d'État de Napoléon III en 1851, la mélodie pourrait se lire comme une riposte parfaitement appropriée, marquant la fin violente du Second Empire. À cette époque Fauré avait déjà fait ses premières incursions dans la poésie de Leconte de Lisle, avec *Lydia* (qui débute, on le sait, en mode lydien). Comme le note Jean-Michel Nectoux[6], il s'agit très probablement de la « petite mélodie » que Fauré, dans une lettre de juin 1870, promettait d'envoyer à Julien Koszul avec sa « romance » *S'il est un charmant gazon*. La distinction stylistique explicite que fait Fauré trace une ligne de partage entre les romances plus légères des années 1860 et les mélodies plus concentrées, plus aventureuses, qui suivent[7].

Les trois poèmes de Charles Baudelaire mis en musique par Fauré révèlent une intensité dramatique et une audace structurelle nouvelles qui, ensemble, marquent l'un des plus grands bonds stylistiques de sa carrière. Les poèmes choisis pourraient se lire comme une trilogie profondément baudelairienne d'amour (*Hymne*), raison (*La Rançon*) et mortalité (*Chant d'automne*), ce dernier volet répondant au « salut d'immortalité » d'*Hymne*. Si *Hymne* fut publié en 1871 et les deux autres en 1879 seulement, leurs liens musicaux étroits laissent à penser que les trois mélodies datent toutes de 1870-1871, reflétant une éventuelle connivence avec deux amis de Fauré, Duparc et Chabrier, dont les premières mélodies d'après Baudelaire datent elles aussi de 1870; *La Rançon*, dédié à Duparc, se distingue aussi comme la seule mélodie que Fauré ait jamais dédiée à un autre compositeur majeur[8]. Traditionnellement réparties à travers le premier recueil, ces trois mélodies répondent à la poésie riche et complexe de Baudelaire avec un raffinement qu'on a souvent sous-estimé. Leur présentation groupée ici clarifie leur relation et leur cohérence remarquables, révélées notamment par leurs éléments structurels et stylistiques partagés (les lignes chromatiques ascendantes qui imprègnent la première et la troisième, et la parenté d'écriture dans les transitions vers le mode majeur des deuxième et troisième[9]).

Ces sommets dramatiques sont suivis de la poésie très différente de Théophile Gautier, de nouveau dans quatre textes contrastés: *Les Matelots* (qui revient à la forme strophique simple des romances plus anciennes); *Seule!*, mélodie sombre et pensive; la mélancolique *Chanson du pêcheur (Lamento)*; et *Tristesse*, texte ouvertement larmoyant qui rappelle le café-concert, comme le suggère le rythme de valse délicatement ironique de Fauré. La *Chanson du pêcheur* est dédiée à la grande mezzo-soprano Pauline Viardot, protégée de Chopin, compositrice et hôtesse de salon, à qui Fauré fut présenté par Saint-Saëns au début des années 1870. Il devint bientôt un habitué de son cercle musical –en 1877, il fut brièvement fiancé à sa fille Marianne–, et ses mélodies suivantes, *Aubade* et *Barcarolle*, sont écrites sur des poèmes de deux intimes des Viardot, Louis Pomey et Marc Monnier.

Au milieu des années 1870, une incursion dans la poésie de Sully Prudhomme (*Ici-bas* et *Au bord de l'eau*) ajouta une autre dimension aux mélodies de Fauré, avec un dialogue sinueux entre voix et piano. *Ici-bas* date de 1874 au plus tard, *Au bord de l'eau* probablement de l'été 1875, que Fauré passa chez ses amis et soutiens Camille et Marie Clerc : sur une feuille de papier à musique, une ébauche ancienne de la mélodie côtoie sa Première Sonate pour violon, composée pour l'essentiel cet été-là.

À la fin des années 1870, Fauré choisit deux poèmes toscans dans des traductions libres de son ami chanteur Romain Bussine. *Après un rêve* (1877) est devenu la mélodie la plus célèbre de Fauré, tandis que la *Sérénade toscane* évoque une véritable sérénade de ténor. La présente édition rend pour la première fois les deux mélodies entièrement chantables dans la version toscane originale (option offerte dans les éditions originales, mais avec une syllabification si défectueuse qu'au moins la *Sérénade toscane* était inchantable sous cette forme).

Sylvie, sur un texte de Paul de Choudens (médiocre aspirant poète, fils de l'éditeur de Fauré), témoigne d'un compromis accepté par Fauré pour hâter la première publication en recueil de vingt de ses mélodies[10]. Le volume en question parut comme prévu chez Choudens père en décembre 1879 – paradoxalement, un mois seulement après que Fauré eut signé son premier contrat avec Julien Hamelle, pour des œuvres comprenant les trois mélodies de l'op. 18. Il avait peut-être alors déjà vendu le triptyque *Poème d'un jour* à l'éditeur Durand & Schœnewerk, car le manuscrit comporte l'annotation biffée « op. 17 »[11]. Bien que le manuscrit de Fauré présente les mélodies dans des tonalités pour voix élevée, (ré♭ majeur, fa♯ mineur et sol♭ majeur), Durand & Schœnewerk publia d'abord le cycle en transpositions pour voix moyenne, dans des tonalités que Fauré nota à cette fin sur le manuscrit. Quand une version pour voix élevée parut ensuite en 1894, les deux dernières mélodies furent retransposées en *fa* mineur et majeur, sans doute par oubli. La présente édition pour voix élevée rétablit leur tonalité originale. Comme pour *Sylvie*, ses mélodies toscanes et *Aubade* de Pomey, Fauré obtint peut-être ces poèmes directement de leur auteur ; on ne connaît pas de source publiée de ces textes de Charles Grandmougin.

L'op. 18 instaure un modèle que Fauré allait suivre pendant plusieurs décennies, mêlant plusieurs poètes au sein d'opus qu'il définissait lui-même. Avec *Nell*, il fit un heureux retour à Leconte de Lisle[12], le débit lyrique de la mélodie contrastant avec *Le Voyageur* et *Automne*, beaucoup plus sombres[13]. Ces deux dernières mélodies sont les premières des douze œuvres que Fauré écrivit sur des vers d'Armand Silvestre, autre poète qu'il connaissait personnellement (en 1881, les deux hommes envisagèrent d'écrire un opéra-comique, *Lizarda*, mais le projet n'aboutit pas[14]). Neuf mélodies d'après Silvestre (des années 1878-1884) sont réparties sur les opus 18, 23, 27 et 39, outre le *Madrigal* op. 35 pour SATB ; là encore, Fauré obtient très probablement la plupart de ses textes du poète lui-même. Bien qu'elle soit rarement profonde, la poésie de Silvestre révèle une séduisante diversité de forme, de caractère et de sujet qui plaisait au mélodiste fluide et créatif que Fauré était alors devenu. Il est significatif que les neuf premiers de ces poèmes mis en musique aient tous été baptisés par le poète *Vers pour être chantés*[15].

Composées entre 1879 et 1881, les mélodies op. 23 comportent de nouveau deux poèmes de Silvestre, le tendre *Secret* – que Maurice Ravel considérait comme « l'un des plus beaux lieder de Fauré[16] » – et *Notre amour*, mélodie exubérante qui est l'une de ses plus légères et de ses plus agiles. *Les Berceaux*, qui marque le dernier retour de Fauré à la poésie de Sully Prudhomme, suit *Ici-bas* et *Au bord de l'eau* en explorant le dialogue actif entre voix et piano : au point culminant de la mélodie, le piano est effectivement invité à noyer la dernière syllabe de la voix telle une vague déferlante. Une autre paire de mélodies d'après Silvestre, de 1882, forme l'op. 27. *Chanson d'amour* transforme l'un des poèmes moins remarquables de Silvestre en un terrain de jeu pour l'enjambement musical et poétique, tandis que dans l'ironie enjouée de *La Fée aux chansons* Fauré pourrait avoir reconnu avec regret un peu de sa propre expérience de répétiteur.

Notes sur l'édition et l'interprétation

Tonalités

La plupart des mélodies sont présentées dans les tonalités établies par les recueils Choudens-Hamelle. Pour *Mai*, *Au bord de l'eau*, « Toujours » et « Adieu » (*Poème d'un jour*) et *La Fée aux chansons*, toutefois, la présente édition pour voix élevée rétablit la tonalité à partir de sources manuscrites. Le cas de *Poème d'un jour* est évoqué plus haut ; pour *La Fée aux chansons*, le *mi* majeur original de Fauré semble mieux convenir tant à la voix qu'au piano que la tonalité traditionnelle de *fa* pour voix élevée. *Chant d'automne* et *Le Voyageur* sont de même rétablis dans leur tonalité originale pour voix élevée (respectivement *ut*♯ mineur et *la* mineur plutôt que l'*ut* mineur et le *sol* mineur des recueils originaux), ce qui donne une disposition plus idiomatique, avec quelques doigtés spécifiques à la tonalité dans *Chant d'automne*[17]. *Dans les ruines d'une abbaye*, *Ici-bas* et *Au bord de l'eau* ont tous été traditionnellement imprimés dans les tonalités pour voix élevée et pour voix moyenne à distance de demi-ton. Pour la première de ces mélodies, la présente édition adopte *sol* majeur comme tonalité de la transposition pour voix moyenne de préférence au *la*♭ traditionnel ; pour *Au bord de l'eau*, le *ré* mineur de l'ébauche ancienne de Fauré est adopté comme tonalité de voix élevée de préférence à l'*ut*♯ mineur du recueil traditionnel (*ut* mineur, la tonalité des trois manuscrits complets, étant conservé comme tonalité de voix moyenne). Pour *Ici-bas*, avec sa tessiture intrinsèquement aiguë, la tonalité de *fa*♯ mineur du manuscrit original, publiée depuis 1890 comme tonalité de voix moyenne, est prise ici comme tonalité de voix élevée au lieu du *sol* mineur traditionnel, *mi* mineur étant adopté comme tonalité de voix moyenne (cette tonalité diésée convient mieux aussi à la partie de piano). Pour *Sérénade toscane*, la présente édition prend sa tonalité de *la* mineur pour voix moyenne (au lieu du *si*♭ traditionnel) d'une édition séparée de 1901, qui met davantage la mélodie dans l'ambitus de mezzo et de baryton. Les tonalités de *L'Aurore* et de *Tristesse d'Olympio* dans les manuscrits sont adoptées ici pour les éditions pour voix élevée et pour voix moyenne, respectivement, les tonalités transposées étant le choix de l'éditeur ; *Puisque j'ai mis ma lèvre* est donné dans les deux tonalités des manuscrits.

Tempo, mètre et rythme

Outre les commentaires de la **préface générale** ci-dessus, connaître les habitudes et les préférences de Fauré en matière d'interprétation peut expliquer certaines particularités de notation et d'édition propres à ses premières mélodies. *Allegretto* tel qu'il l'emploie est généralement très proche d'*allegro*, mais avec plus de légèreté dans l'écriture et le caractère. Son *andante* – souvent précisé par *quasi allegretto* voire *quasi adagio* – peut se comprendre comme un tempo modéré et coulant au sens actuel, représentant le sens littéral d'*andante* (« allant ») et d'*adagio* (« à l'aise ») – et du reste de *quasi adagio* (« presque à l'aise »). Ceci concerne notamment *Lydia*, *Chant d'automne*, « Rencontre » et *Nell*, ainsi que *Seule!* et *L'Absent*. Pour ces deux dernières mélodies, la présente édition rétablit le ¢ des manuscrits et des premières éditions (à la place du C imprimé dans les éditions ultérieures), soulignant leur allure intrinsèque à la demi-mesure et leur mouvement vers l'avant. L'écriture et le débit de *Lydia* et de *Chanson d'amour* (mélodie pour laquelle il ne subsiste pas de manuscrit) justifient le [¢] suggéré par l'éditeur, suggestion étayée, dans le cas de *Lydia*, par l'affinité sur le plan de l'écriture avec *L'Aurore*, dont les croches coulent de manière très semblable aux noires de *Lydia*.

Les indications de tempo de Fauré sont souvent le plus logiques lorsqu'on les lit par rapport aux lignes mélodiques et aux rythmes harmoniques sous-jacents, plutôt qu'en fonction des figurations d'accompagnement plus actives. Dans *Aubade*, par exemple, le double élément de l'indication de tempo suggère un départ relativement rapide du piano pour aider le chanteur à soutenir les longues phrases vocales. Cela s'applique plus encore à *Chant d'automne*, dont le tempo *Andante* initial est défini rétrospectivement de manière cruciale par l'équivalence métrique ultérieure dans la coda.

Les constantes révisions de Fauré aux indications de tempo ont laissé plusieurs mélodies avec des variantes entre les éditions pour voix élevée et voix moyenne ou grave. Si la plupart d'entre elles semblent correspondre à un même concept musical décrit de manière différente (ainsi *Allegretto* plutôt que *Allegro non troppo* dans *Le Papillon et la fleur* et *Dans les ruines d'une abbaye*), *Ici-bas* est plus complexe : marquée *Andantino* dans toutes les sources anciennes et dans le recueil ultérieur pour voix élevée, depuis 1879 la mélodie est apparue dans le recueil pour voix moyenne sous l'indication *Adagio*, avec un épaississement concomitant de la partie de piano. Priorité est donnée ici à la version *Andantino*, considérée comme inhérente à la conception originale de Fauré et au poème (plus mélancolique que tragique) ; la variante figure en note. La seule mélodie du premier recueil original à avoir reçu une indication métronomique est la *Barcarolle* (quand elle fut ensuite déplacée dans le deuxième recueil d'Hamelle, comme noté dans le **commentaire critique**). Pour quelques mélodies, les indications métronomiques originales paraissent d'une lenteur excessive : en particulier, ♩ = 66 dans *Nell* suggère une erreur pour 96, tandis que celles de *Chanson d'amour* et de *Notre amour* semblent contredire le caractère enjoué, voire haletant, des mélodies[18]. Dans de tels cas, les suggestions de l'éditeur sont ajoutées entre crochets à côté de l'indication de la source.

Le mouvement vers l'avant auquel Fauré était attaché se manifeste dans une tendance à parfois rétablir le tempo (après un bref *ritard.*) juste avant, plutôt que sur, une cadence ou un temps principal, comme c'est le cas avec les indications manuscrites *a tempo* placées dans *Mai* (mesures 26 et 59) et *L'Aurore*. Dans la première mélodie, Fauré demande ici au chanteur d'avancer malgré la virgule dans le texte – sans doute en partie pour éviter qu'il ne respire tranquillement. *Au bord de l'eau* et *Chanson d'amour* présentent des gestes analogues, une liaison notée (dans certaines sources seulement) par-dessus une ponctuation du texte. Si Fauré la confirme dans *Au bord de l'eau* en spécifiant une respiration quelques notes plus loin (mesures 15 et 31, en passant par un agréable moment d'imitation dans la ligne de basse), Claire Croiza dit cependant que Fauré désavoua par la suite la liaison en faveur d'une respiration à la ponctuation du texte[19]. Un tel traitement changeant, sur une période longue et active d'une carrière de compositeur, témoigne d'une flexibilité essentielle de conception évoquée plus en détail ci-dessous.

La musique de Fauré est pleine de jeux rythmiques, notamment sous forme d'hémioles (des formules qui sonnent à 3/4 ou à 3/2 dans un contexte à 6/8 ou à 3/4), procédé qui imprègne ses Barcarolles pour piano en particulier et prend ses racines dans les musiques traditionnelles de son Midi natal. Ce penchant jaillit de la toute première entrée vocale du *Papillon et la fleur*, qui déclenche la syllabification du poème dans un rythme effectif à 3/4 contre le 6/8 du piano, trait qu'on observe également dans certaines parties d'*Au bord de l'eau* et les premiers vers de *Notre amour*[20]. Les interprètes doivent être attentifs à ces jeux rythmiques, en se rappelant que placer les syllabes faibles sur d'apparents temps forts n'est pas une faute en soi dans la prosodie chantée française, étant donné la plasticité intrinsèque de l'accentuation et des formules rythmiques de la langue.

Sources musicales

Les vingt mélodies du premier recueil original – les présents nos 1, 3-4, 6 et 8-23 – nous sont parvenues à travers diverses éditions anciennes avec parfois un stupéfiant ensemble de variantes, résultant de leurs multiples éditeurs, gravures, tonalités et retirages corrigés du vivant de Fauré. Chaque source successive tend à mélanger de nouvelles révisions à des corruptions ou à des versions antérieures, à tel point qu'aucune source unique ne peut être prise comme version définitive cohérente. Des manuscrits autographes ont été retrouvés pour seulement quatorze mélodies du présent volume ; le seul d'entre eux spécifiquement destiné à la publication était *Poème d'un jour*, bien que quelques autres aient pu figurer dans la chaîne de sources conduisant à la publication. Certains précèdent la publication d'une dizaine années parfois, et dévoilent la mélodie dans un état antérieur, ou n'indiquent que l'une de plusieurs conceptions compositionnelles : trois copies au net d'*Au bord de l'eau*, par exemple, toutes d'environ 1875-1876, révèlent différentes textures et nuances tout du long. Bien que supplantés pour l'essentiel par les versions publiées, ces manuscrits aident à corriger les fautes d'impression ou à clarifier des détails de la polyphonie et de la disposition ; ils comportent aussi de nombreuses variantes révélatrices, datant parfois du moment où la mélodie était le plus fraîche dans l'esprit du compositeur. Les plus importantes d'entre elles figurent parmi les *ossia* de la présente édition, et l'un des manuscrits livre une variante complète (*S'il est un charmant gazon*).

Dans une certaine mesure, tout cela révèle une fluidité intrinsèque de conception dans les premières mélodies de Fauré, caractéristique importante que la présente édition accepte, y voyant même un atout. Tout en présentant la leçon la plus cohérente de chaque mélodie en tant que texte musical principal, elle donne aussi les variantes viables sous forme d'*ossia* ou en note. Les corrections essentielles sont intégrées au texte musical en provenance de la source qui les fournit ; quelques indications moins essentielles mais néanmoins utiles provenant de sources secondaires sont incorporées entre parenthèses.

Compte tenu de tout cela, la source la plus fiable pour les mélodies publiées du vivant de Fauré devrait théoriquement être les impressions révisées des deux premiers recueils Hamelle publiées en 1908, qui ne subirent pas d'autres changements du vivant de Fauré. Malheureusement, cet idéal est contredit à plusieurs reprises par des variantes de tempo, de syllabification, de nuances et d'articulation entre les versions pour voix élevée et pour voix moyenne. Elles affectent plus particulièrement l'ancien premier recueil, dont la première édition pour voix élevée (1890) tirait son texte musical essentiellement d'éditions séparées plus éloignées dans la chaîne des sources, perdant bon nombre des révisions soigneuses que Fauré avait incorporées dans la publication originale du volume (essentiellement pour voix moyenne) en 1879. L'édition pour voix élevée de 1890 montre un ensemble différent de révisions, probablement faites à la dernière minute, qui vont de l'improvisé à l'indispensable. Ces divergences, qui n'ont jamais été réglées, nous obligent désormais à choisir la source prioritaire pour chaque mélodie entre les volumes pour voix élevée et pour voix moyenne, suivant la version qui semble la préparation ou la révision la plus minutiese. La version choisie demande néanmoins à être complétée par d'autres sources pour aboutir à un texte qui respecte le travail soigneux de révision fait par Fauré sur plusieurs décennies, tout en restant cohérent en soi.

Les plus anciennes mélodies de Fauré révèlent également de nombreuses variantes de syllabification d'une source à l'autre, car il cherchait dans les éditions successives à raffiner la fluidité et le caractère pratique de sa mise en musique. Si bon nombre de ses corrections concernent des accentuations potentiellement maladroites ou non idiomatiques, d'autres semblent refléter une réaction à des interprétations qui ne parvenaient pas à saisir la flexibilité de rythme ou d'emphase d'une leçon originale. La présente édition donne les variantes les plus intéressantes sous forme d'*ossia* ; des exemples notables s'en trouvent vers la fin de *La Rançon* (donnant un meilleur enjambement aux dépens d'une syllabe faible prolongée) et aux mesures 28-30 de *Seule !* (donnant un caractère plus emphatique que les versions ultérieures, plus prudentes). Une interprétation alerte peut éviter bon nombre des risques intrinsèques.

Texte

Fauré modifiait souvent le texte des poèmes qu'il mettait en musique, substituant des mots, changeant l'ordre ou coupant des vers et des strophes pour façonner le poème conformément à ses desseins musicaux. Ses retouches recouvrent généralement une judicieuse intention musicale, visant à rendre les mots aussi fluides et chantables que possible. La présente édition respecte ces changements, qui sont donnés entre crochets à côté des textes originaux p. XXVIII–XLI.

Les modifications faites par Fauré à la ponctuation et à la capitalisation du poème sont plus complexes : d'un manuscrit et d'une source imprimée à l'autre, de nombreux détails de ponctuation sont omis, d'innombrables autres apparaissent différemment, et parfois de nouveaux signes de ponctuation s'ajoutent. La capitalisation peut elle aussi être variable, tantôt respectant le poème original, tantôt s'en écartant sensiblement. Lorsque de telles divergences entre les sources d'une mélodie unique semblent le résultat d'une simple omission du compositeur ou du graveur, la présente édition suit tacitement la source qui préserve la ponctuation et la capitalisation du poème. Lorsque les sources musicales ne comportent pas de ponctuation, ou lorsque ses variantes ne sont pas viables, nous rétablissons celle du poème imprimé, comme noté dans le **commentaire critique**.

Souvent, cependant, les sources musicales révèlent des changements plausibles ou utiles, pour l'interprète, dans la ponctuation ou le découpage d'un poème, qui semblent refléter une initiative délibérée du compositeur : simplification de passages densément ponctués, changement de points exclamation, virgules, points-virgules ou points pour définir la fin de strophes ou de sections musicales, utilisation de points d'exclamation pour souligner l'intensité dynamique, introduction de virgules pour indiquer une respiration ou la non-élision (on en voit en particulier de nombreux ajustements de ce genre dans *Mai* et *L'Absent*). De même qu'elle respecte les modifications faites par Fauré aux mots, la présente édition tente de discerner et de respecter les changements délibérés et systématiques de ponctuation et de capitalisation, à condition qu'il n'en résulte pas de problèmes syntaxiques ou musicaux[21]. On identifiera facilement ces variantes, qui ne sont généralement pas répertoriées dans le **commentaire critique,** en comparant le texte musical aux poèmes dans leur forme originale telle qu'elle est donnée pages XXVIII–XLI. La ponctuation et la capitalisation des sources poétiques sont rétablies dans une plus large mesure pour les mélodies que Fauré laissa inédites, et dont les manuscrits révèlent un traitement moins méthodique.

Remerciements

Nos sincères remerciements vont à tous ceux qui ont aimablement mis des sources à notre disposition pour étude ou qui ont aidé autrement, notamment aux bibliothécaires et collectionneurs privés à travers le monde (avec un merci particulier au personnel musical de la Bibliothèque nationale de France) et à de nombreuses personnes, dont Helen Abbott, Thierry et Pierrette Bodin, Mimi Segal Daitz, Denis Herlin, Ken Johansen, Peter Jost, Edmond Lemaître (et aux Éditions Durand), Roger Nichols, Robert Orledge et Herbert Schneider, et à Angela Newport, Valeria Schiavone et Diego Ropele pour leur aide avec les textes toscans. Les collègues interprètes et enseignants nous ont fait profiter de leur soutien enthousiaste, de leurs compétences et de leurs inestimables réactions musicales lors de stages et de concerts ; nous remercions en particulier Mary Dibbern, Amber Evans, Guy Flechter, François Le Roux, Robert Macfarlane, Rosalind Martin, Kurt Ollmann, Christopher Underwood et Darlene Wiley. Basé à la Royal Academy of Music, Londres, le projet éditorial a été soutenu par un Project Grant de l'Arts and Humanities Research Council (Royaume-Uni) ; nous y remercions tout spécialement Nicole Tibbels pour son inestimable collaboration enthousiaste et ses lumières sur les questions pratiques et linguistiques, Richard Stokes pour son aimable autorisation de reproduire ses traductions anglaises des textes chantés, et les étudiants en chant de troisième cycle de l'Academy, ainsi que David Gorton, Neil Heyde et Timothy Jones.

Londres, 2014 *Roy Howat et Emily Kilpatrick*
(Traduction : Dennis Collins)

---

[1] Ces numéros furent ajoutés aux mélodies dans l'ordre du premier recueil d'Hamelle en 1896, au moment de la candidature de Fauré à l'Institut. Par souci de commodité, la présente édition les donne entre parenthèses (comme pour l'op. 21 : voir note 11 ci-dessous). Pour une discussion plus détaillée de cette question éditoriale et d'autres dans les premières mélodies de Fauré, voir la **bibliographie sélective**.

[2] Lettre du juillet 1922, dans Fauré-Fremiet (éd.), *Gabriel Fauré : Lettres intimes*, p. 282.

[3] Lettre à Julien Koszul de juin 1870, dans Nectoux (éd.), *Gabriel Fauré : Correspondance*, p. 26.

[4] Les documents qui subsistent laissent à penser que Fauré pourrait n'avoir conservé que des brouillons de quelques mélodies anciennes après avoir offert des manuscrits de présentation soigneusement annotés (notamment de *Mai* et *S'il est un charmant gazon*), ces derniers n'étant donc plus accessibles des années plus tard quand se présenta la possibilité de les publier.

[5] Nectoux (éd.), *Gabriel Fauré : Correspondance*, p. 19-20 (lettre non datée) ; Hugo accorda son autorisation dans une réponse datée du 29 mai 1864. *Puisqu'ici-bas* fut publié en 1879 comme duo vocal (voir *Mélodies complètes*, vol. 2) ; si *L'Aube naît* fut mis en musique, il n'en reste aujourd'hui pas de trace.

[6] Nectoux (éd.), *Gabriel Fauré : Correspondance*, p. 26.

[7] En 1911, Fauré avoua : « Je n'ai jamais non plus réussi à mettre du Victor Hugo en musique, et rarement du Leconte de Lisle, parce que leurs vers à tous deux sont trop pleins, trop riches, trop complets pour que la musique puisse s'y adapter utilement. » (« Sous la Musique que faut-il mettre ? », *Musica* 101, février 1911, p. 38). Peut-être Fauré (comme maint compositeur d'un certain âge) se montrait-il excessivement critique vis-à-vis de ses œuvres de jeunesse, compte tenu du charme naturel et de la légèreté de touche qui imprègnent ces mélodies.

[8] Baudelaire n'avait auparavant été mis en musique que par ses amis chansonniers. Fauré, Duparc et Chabrier furent également les cofondateurs, en 1871, de la Société nationale de musique, dont le but explicite était de promouvoir la nouvelle musique française. Bien que *Chant d'automne* soit attesté pour la première fois en 1878 (dans une lettre de Fauré à Marie Clerc : « J'ai dédié le *Chant d'automne* à Madame M. Camille Clerc : ai-je bien fait ? » ; Nectoux (éd.), *Gabriel Fauré : Correspondance*, p. 83), la formulation de Fauré, qui s'explique manifestement par une publication imminente, semble indiquer que c'est une mélodie qu'elle connaît depuis longtemps plutôt que quelque chose de nouveau.

[9] Pour plus de détails, voir notre article « Wagnérisme de Fauré : *Pénélope* (1913) et les mélodies », dans Marie-Cécile Leblanc et Danièle Pistone (éd.), *Wagner, 1913-2013, Ruptures et Continuité*, Paris, Presses de la Sorbonne-Nouvelle, à paraître en 2015.

[10] « J'ai accompli ce travail d'Hercule de mettre en musique des vers de Choudens (Paul) ! oui, chère Madame, Lucette [sic] va marcher dans la vie avec une escorte de quatre bémols et de douze doubles croches par mesure. [...] Maintenant que je suis en règle avec Choudens j'espère que l'édition du volume de mélodies va marcher rondement. » Nectoux (éd.), *Gabriel Fauré : Correspondance*, p. 83 (lettre du 3 octobre 1878 à Marie Clerc).

[11] Il ne reste pas de trace du contrat dans les archives des Éditions Durand ; il fut probablement signé en 1879. Le numéro d'opus 21 fut attribué au cycle pour la première fois en 1897, Hamelle s'étant approprié le numéro d'opus 17 en 1880 pour son édition (1881) des *Romances sans paroles* pour piano de Fauré, composées de nombreuses années auparavant.

[12] *Nell* de Leconte de Lisle s'inspire de *Handsome Nell* de Robert Burns, une ode à son amour d'adolescent, Nellie Kilpatrick.

[13] Fauré réussit à résister cette fois à une apparente tentative d'Hamelle visant à sentimentaliser ces titres : « Je tiens beaucoup au titre *Le Voyageur* parce que c'est celui que le poète a donné à sa poésie. Quant à l'autre mélodie, j'y bien réfléchi, le titre de *Juin* ne saurait lui convenir aussi bien que le titre de *Nell*. Juin, et le charme qui se dégage de sa floraison et de son soleil, n'est que pris en terme de comparaison avec l'ardeur que l'amour de Nell a allumée au cœur du poète. C'est bien Nell qui est le sujet et non pas juin. Pourquoi ne mettrions-nous pas *– à Nell –* ? » Nectoux (éd.), *Gabriel Fauré : Correspondance*, p. 99.

[14] Nectoux, *Gabriel Fauré : les voix du clair-obscur*, p. 194.

[15] Les mélodies sont tirées de deux recueils, *Le Pays de roses* et *Les Ailes d'or*, qui comportent tous deux des sections ainsi intitulées.

[16] Maurice Ravel, « Les Mélodies de Gabriel Fauré », *La Revue musicale* 3, octobre 1922, dans Arbie Orenstein (éd.), *Maurice Ravel : Lettres, écrits, entretiens*, Paris, Flammarion, 1990, p. 323.

[17] La transposition en *ut* mineur pour le premier recueil pourrait résulter de la préférence de l'éditeur pour une tonalité « plus facile ».

[18] La première entrée vocale de *Notre amour* le montre dès le départ : un tempo trop modéré laisse une syllabe faible trop exposée sur la note aiguë. Aucune source manuscrite ne confirme ces indications métronomiques, ajoutées plus de quinze dans après la première publication (voir le **commentaire critique**). Parmi les coquilles analogues dans l'œuvre de Fauré, on peut citer la première de ses *Pièces brèves* pour piano, dont la première édition donnait par erreur pour indication 69 au lieu de 96.

[19] Abraham (éd.), *Un art de l'interprétation*, p. 138 ; Bannerman (éd.), *The Singer as Interpreter*, p. 83.

[20] La publication du premier recueil en 1879 changeait la première entrée vocale du *Papillon et la fleur*, à la mesure 10, pour commencer sur le temps avec une formule à $\frac{6}{8}$ sans ambiguïté (voir **commentaire critique**) ; le but essentiel était probablement de garantir une entrée vocale sûre plutôt que de repenser la syllabification, étant donné que les oppositions rythmiques $\frac{3}{4}$-$\frac{6}{8}$ se poursuivent ensuite pendant une bonne partie de la mélodie (y compris mesure 11). La décision de Fauré de rétablir la version originale de la mesure 10 dans toutes les éditions ultérieures était certainement délibérée, car elle obligeait à corriger les planches gravées du premier recueil.

[21] Pour une étude détaillée de cette question, voir Kilpatrick, « Moot point : Editing poetry and punctuation in Fauré's early songs ».

Allgemeines Vorwort

In seinen Liedern bringt Fauré wahrhaftig die Blüte seiner Schöpferkraft zum Vorschein. – Maurice Ravel[1]

Kein Komponist hat einen wesentlicheren und vielfältigeren Beitrag zum französischen Liedrepertoire geleistet als Gabriel Fauré. Angefangen beim charmanten *Le Papillon et la fleur* aus dem Jahr 1861 bis hin zum meisterhaften, sechzig Jahre später komponierten Zyklus *L'Horizon chimérique* durchzog die Komposition von *Mélodies* sein musikalisches Schaffen. Die Bedeutung seines Beitrags wurde lange Zeit durch die unstete Veröffentlichungsgeschichte beeinträchtigt: Viele der über verschiedene Verleger und Sammelpublikationen verteilten Lieder wurden durch gravierende Druckfehler und widersprüchliche Lesarten innerhalb der unterschiedlichen Druckfassungen entstellt. Diese erste kritische Gesamtausgabe liefert einen sowohl verlässlichen als auch flexiblen Notentext mit Stücken aus der bekannten dreibändigen Sammlung mit sechzig Liedern (verlegt 1908 von Hamelle) sowie anderen separat veröffentlichten Liedern und Zyklen, darunter drei zu Faurés Lebzeiten unveröffentlichte Lieder und vier Lieder für mehr als eine Stimme. Ein separater Band mit Faurés *Vokalisen* (EP 11385) beinhaltet vierundvierzig erstmals veröffentlichte Vokalisen sowie die 1907 veröffentlichte *Vocalise-Étude*.

Mit ihrem sowohl praktischen als auch wissenschaftlichen Schwerpunkt möchte die vorliegende Ausgabe eine kreative, sichere und sachkundige Aufführung ermöglichen. Sie basiert auf dem Studium hunderter Manuskripte und gedruckter Quellen und wurde international im Rahmen von Meisterklassen, Workshops, Seminaren, Konzerten und Aufnahmen unter Teilnahme professioneller Sänger/-innen, Studierender, Lehrender, Coaches und Spezialisten auf den Prüfstand gestellt. Hierin orientierten sich die Herausgeber am Vorgehen des Komponisten, der seine eigenen Ausgaben auf Grundlage von Aufführungserfahrungen erstellte. Berücksichtigt wurden zudem interpretatorische Einsichten von Musikern, die mit Fauré zusammenarbeiteten, sowie dessen dokumentierte Präferenzen bezüglich der Aufführung.

Quellen und editorische Herangehensweise

Die Hauptverleger der Lieder Faurés waren Choudens (1869–1879), Hamelle (1880–1904), Heugel (1905–1910) und Durand (1915–1921); mehrere seiner Lieder wurden zu unterschiedlichen Zeiten auch von Hartmann, Durand & Schœnewerk, Fromont und dem Londoner Unternehmen Metzler publiziert (hinzu kommen einige von den französischen Originalausgaben abhängige amerikanische Ausgaben). Die meisten seiner Lieder wurden einzeln veröffentlicht, bevor man sie in Sammlungen vereinte. 1879 erschien die erste Sammlung (Choudens), die zweite 1897 (Hamelle) und die dritte im Jahr 1908 (Hamelle).[2] Diese Sammlungen wurden, wie auch die meisten Einzeldrucke, in Tonarten für die hohe und mittlere Stimmlage herausgegeben, einige Lieder wurden in zusätzlichen Transpositionen separat veröffentlicht. Im Gegensatz zu der Vielzahl gedruckter Ausgaben ist die Quellenlage bei den Manuskripten weniger ergiebig. Viele der derzeit ausfindig gemachten Manuskripte sind – insbesondere was die früheren Lieder betrifft – frühe Entwürfe, Widmungsautographe oder Zwischenfassungen.

Der editorische Umgang mit solch unterschiedlichen Quellen erfordert große Sorgfalt. Trotz aller wertvollen Korrekturen, Verifizierungen und Lesarten, die die Manuskripte bieten, müssen sie mit Vorsicht genossen werden, insbesondere dann, wenn sie kein direktes Glied einer zur Veröffentlichung führenden Quellenkette waren. Mittlerweile ist es trotz der Fülle der Quellen häufig unmöglich, eine bestimmte Quelle als den endgültigen oder definitiven Notentext des Komponisten anzusehen und diesem zu folgen. Jede Quelle birgt sowohl wesentliche Informationen als auch Probleme und Verfälschungen (was vor allem die erwähnten früheren Lieder betrifft). Um die im Laufe vieler Jahre vorgenommenen Korrekturen Faurés so getreu wie möglich zu erfassen, mussten hier die besten Quellen ihrer logischen Priorität und ihres musikalischen Sinns entsprechend kombiniert werden. Stets berücksichtigt wurde dabei die Kohärenz einzelner Lieder, Gruppierungen, Zyklen und Sammlungen, ferner sämtliche Kenntnisse über Faurés Kompositions-, Korrektur- und Aufführungsgewohnheiten sowie alle weiteren verfügbaren Indizien. *Ossia*-Versionen sind angegeben, wenn eindeutig mehr als eine Lesart realisierbar ist. Dazu zählen einige frühe Lesarten, die gewisse Aspekte der kompositorischen Absicht Faurés verdeutlichen, beispielsweise Elemente, die mitunter von späteren Korrekturen verdeckt wurden, um die Musik vor unsachgemäßer Aufführung zu „schützen". Ausführliche Erläuterungen finden sich im **Kritischen Bericht**.

Tonarten

Es gibt keinerlei Anzeichen dafür, dass Fauré die Transposition seiner Lieder konkret oder prinzipiell ablehnte.[3] Mehrere seiner Lieder existieren in mehr als einer autographen Tonart (darunter einige Transpositionen, die nach der Veröffentlichung vorgenommen wurden), andere erschienen in einer oder mehreren Tonarten, die von den überlieferten Manuskripten abweicht, während es bei den Liedern, deren Manuskripte verschollen sind, manchmal unmöglich ist, anhand der gedruckten Quellen eine Originaltonart oder eine vom Komponisten bevorzugte Tonart zu identifizieren. (Selbst in den Erstausgaben Hamelles sind Kennzeichnungen der „Originaltonart" nicht immer verlässlich.)[4] Als lebenslang ausübender Musiker, Begleiter und ausgebildeter Chorleiter war es Fauré gewohnt, mit verschiedenen Stimmen zu arbeiten. Überlieferte Konzertprogramme bezeugen, dass er seine Lieder regelmäßig mit Sänger/-innen verschiedener Stimmgattungen aufführte, wobei die Umstände – darunter einige wichtige Premieren – häufig das Transponieren von Stücken erforderten. Wie jeder Komponist hatte Fauré für einige Lieder spezifische Präferenzen in Bezug auf Tessitur und Tonartencharakter. Entsprechende Belege sind in dieser Gesamtausgabe zitiert und wurden in dieser Edition berücksichtigt.

Die Herausgeber würdigen insofern die pragmatische Herangehensweise Faurés und machen seine Lieder innerhalb angemessener geschmacklicher Grenzen und im wissenschaftlichen Rahmen für möglichst viele Sänger/-innen zugänglich. Die in den genannten Sammlungen enthaltenen Tonarten für die hohe und mittlere Stimmlage wurden größtenteils beibehalten. Änderungen wurden nur vorgenommen, wenn eine Quelle eine stringentere Option liefert oder auf eine Präferenz Faurés hindeutet, gelegentlich aber auch, um realistischer zwischen hoher und mittlerer Stimmlage zu unterscheiden. Weiterhin wurde die Spielbarkeit auf dem Klavier berücksichtigt. Einige wenige Lieder wurden in eine bestimmte Tonart transponiert, wenn musikalischer Sinn, Tessitur und die Quellenauswertung Anlass dazu gaben. Für die wenigen nur in einer Tonart veröffentlichten oder zu Faurés Lebzeiten noch nicht publizierten Lieder haben die Herausgeber die Transposition nach bestem Wissen bestimmt. Einige wenige ausgewählte Stücke, deren Quellen zusätzliche hilfreiche Tonarten liefern, sind online unter www.fabermusic.com/editionpetersresources in einer dritten Tonart abrufbar. Die vorliegende Ausgabe führt für jedes Lied die bekannte(n) Originaltonart(en) an; war kein Manuskript auffindbar oder unterscheiden sich die gedruckten Originaltonarten, stehen Letztere in runden Klammern, wobei die in den Sammlungen Hamelles angegebenen Originaltonarten **fett** gedruckt sind.

Aufführung

Zeitzeugenberichte über Faurés bevorzugte Spielweise und Interpretation lassen darauf schließen, dass er in seinen Liedern den Vorwärtsfluß in den Mittelpunkt stellte und eine strenge Abneigung gegen unnötiges Verlangsamen, Rubato und sentimentale Affektiertheit hegte.[5] Sein Tempoverständnis entsprach dem natürlichen Tempo des gesprochenen Gedichts. Faurés gute Kollegin, die berühmte Mezzosopranistin Claire Croiza, betonte, welche Bedeutung er dem Gedicht und dessen Artikulation im Lied beimaß. Croiza erinnerte außerdem:

> Fauré war das personifizierte Metronom. [...] Vor allem das Verlangsamen entstellt ihn [...]. Mehr als bei jedem anderen muss der Ausdruck bei Fauré im Rahmen des vorgegebenen Metrums gefunden werden [...]. Einmal hörte ich, wie ein Sänger *Après un rêve* vortrug und dabei [fast] buchstäblich starb. Beim Essen mit Fauré am selben Abend fragte ich ihn: „Welches Tempo haben Sie tatsächlich für *Après un rêve* vorgesehen, Maître?" Und er sagte: *„Sans ralentir, sans ralentir!"*.[6]

Obwohl Croiza die Intensität tragischer Momente betont (*Chanson du pêcheur* oder *Prison*), warnt sie immer wieder davor, Faurés melancholischere Lieder mit Wehmut zu interpretieren: Die Finesse und Zurückhaltung dieses Stils erreiche man nicht durch Übertreiben und Karikieren dessen, was der Komponist bereits wohl ausbalanciert habe.[7] Besonders unter Faurés frühen Liedern bringt ein offenkundig melancholisches Gedicht wie *Tristesse* bisweilen ein gewisses Maß an Parodie oder Selbstironie mit sich,[8] das Fauré mit leichter Hand quittiert. Zahlreiche Schilderungen seiner Familie und Kollegen über dessen lebendigen Humor und die Fröhlichkeit, die ihm bis in seine späten Jahre erhalten blieb, lassen offensichtliche Parallelen erkennen.[9]

Editorische Gestaltung

Sofern erforderlich, wurden *ossia*-Lesarten von ihren Originaltonarten transponiert. Alle fraglichen musikalischen Varianten wurden mit Fußnoten versehen. Binde- und Haltebögen (sowie vervollständigte Bindebögen) der Herausgeber sind gestrichelt, andere editorische Zusätze stehen in eckigen Klammern. In runden Klammern notierte Warnungsakzidenzien wurden den Quellen entnommen. Rund eingeklammert sind zudem überflüssige Atemzeichen, die sich lediglich in einigen Quellen finden, sowie nützliche Dynamikangaben und andere Angaben aus Sekundärquellen (Ausführungen siehe **Kritischer Bericht**).

London, 2014
Roy Howat und Emily Kilpatrick
(Übersetzung: Lore Horlamus)

---

[1] Maurice Ravel, *Les Mélodies de Gabriel Fauré*, La Revue musicale 3 (Oktober 1922), in: Arbie Orenstein (Hrsg.), *Maurice Ravel: Lettres, écrits, entretiens* (Paris: Flammarion 1990), S. 325.

[2] Die Veröffentlichung der dritten Sammlung im Jahr 1908 erfolgte zeitgleich mit der Neuausgabe der ersten und zweiten Sammlung durch Hamelle (1887 hatte dieser die erste Sammlung von Choudens abgekauft und davon 1890 eine Fassung für die hohe Stimmlage herausgegeben), wobei eine gewisse inhaltliche Umverteilung erfolgte; siehe **Kritischer Bericht**.

[3] Eingehende Erörterungen dessen und anderer für die vorliegende Ausgabe wesentlicher editorischer Aspekte finden sich in den von den Herausgebern dieser Gesamtausgabe verfassten Artikeln *Editorial Challenges in the Early Songs of Gabriel Fauré* und *Gabriel Fauré's Middle-Period Songs*.

[4] Diese finden sich nur in der zweiten und dritten Sammlung Hamelles ab op. 18. Auch war die Tonhöhe zu damaliger Zeit in Europa noch nicht standardisiert – sie unterschied sich über die Ländergrenzen hinweg mitunter um einen Halbton oder mehr –, obwohl sie während Faurés Berufsleben in Frankreich (durch einen Parlamentsbeschluss im Jahr 1859 auf $a' = 435$ Hz festgelegt wurde, also etwas tiefer als der heutige Standard-Kammerton, der bei 440 Hz oder etwas höher liegt.

[5] Verschiedene dieser Zeitzeugenberichte von Familie und Musikerkollegen Faurés zitiert Roy Howat in: *The Art of French Piano Music* (London und New Haven: Yale UP 2009), S. 247 und im Allgemeinen in den Kapiteln 17, 18 und 21.

[6] Zitiert nach Abraham (Hrsg.), *Un Art de l'interprétation*, S. 199 und 212 und teilweise nach Bannerman (Hrsg.), *The Singer as Interpreter*, S. 82; Letztere bringt eine spezifische Quelle an, welche die Anweisung „*(sans ralentir)*" in Takt 46 der vorliegenden Ausgabe veranlasst hat. Eine Violinistin und Kollegin Faurés, Hélène Jourdan-Morhange, bekräftigte diese Eigenschaft mit einer Anekdote über eine (nicht namentlich genannte) Sängerin, die an Phrasenenden innehielt und schmachtete: Eines Tages von Fauré bei einem Nachmittagskonzert begleitet, war sie „schockiert, sich vom Klavier angetrieben auf einer wellenlosen Straße wiederzufinden... auf der Autobahn der Zukunft!" (Jourdan-Morhange, *Mes amis musiciens*, S. 22f.).

[7] Vgl. Bannerman (Hrsg.), *The Singer as Interpreter*, S. 84–88 und Abraham, *Un Art de l'interprétation*, S. 31, 40 und 212.

[8] Vladimir Jankélévitch (*Gabriel Fauré et ses mélodies*, S. 49) machte eine ähnliche Beobachtung: „Dennoch ist nichts davon tragisch zu sehen. Fauré war immun gegenüber der Welle der Neurasthenie, die mit Duparc und Chausson über Frankreich hereinzubrechen begann [...] und die Melancholie in *Tristesse* ist nicht allzu ernst."

[9] Die Schwiegertochter des Komponisten erinnerte ihn so: „Als fröhlicher Südländer neigte Fauré zu Scherzen" (*Brève rencontre avec Blanche Fauré-Fremiet*, in: *Journal de Vichy*, 28. Juni 1958). Hélène Jourdan-Morhange beschrieb ihn als jemanden, der im Geiste stets ein „Straßenjunge" [*l'esprit gavroche*] geblieben sei (*Mes amis musiciens*, S. 24). In einigen Erinnerungen, die Fauré mit Ende Siebzig niederschrieb, schildert er mit unverstellter Freude die Jugendstreiche, die er mit seinen Klassenkameraden den Lehrern der École Niedermeyer spielte (*Souvenirs*, in: *La Revue musicale* 4/11, spezielle Fauré-Ausgabe, 1. November 1922, S. 3–9).

Vorwort zu Band 1

Dieser Band umfasst Faurés frühe Lieder bis zu op. 27 aus dem Jahr 1882, darunter zwanzig Lieder aus der originalen „ersten Sammlung" (in ihrer ursprünglichen Gestalt enthielt diese die *Barcarolle* Op. 7 no. 3), drei zu Faurés Lebzeiten unveröffentlichte Lieder (Nr. 2, 5 und 7 der vorliegenden Ausgabe) und die ersten vier Opusgruppen aus der historischen „zweiten Sammlung", darunter Faurés erster Liederzyklus *Poème d'un jour*. Eine Erläuterung der Geschichte dieser Sammlungen und Gruppierungen findet sich im **Kritischen Bericht**.

In Anbetracht der Tatsache, dass die meisten vor op. 18 entstandenen Lieder selbst dutzende Jahre nach ihrer Komposition in willkürlicher Reihenfolge veröffentlicht wurden, lag hier eine Hauptaufgabe darin, diese Lieder Faurés möglichst zuverlässig zu ordnen. Auch in der historischen ersten Sammlung sind sie (mit Ausnahme der ersten beiden Lieder) nicht chronologisch angeordnet, und dass dem Band später die Opusnummern 1–8 hinzugefügt wurden, entbehrt einer musikwissenschaftlichen Logik.[1] Mehr als die Hälfte dieser Lieder kann lediglich einem Zeitraum von zwei bis fünf Jahren zugeschrieben werden (vgl. **Chronologie** auf S. 128–129). Wie unten ausgeführt, scheint auch *Poème d'un jour* trotz seiner höheren Opusnummer vor den Liedern der Gruppe op. 18 komponiert worden zu sein.

Die hier für die ersten dreiundzwanzig Lieder aufgestellte Reihenfolge legt – mit nur einer Ausnahme – logische, auf der dichterischen Vorlage basierende Gruppierungen im Rahmen der bekannten Chronologie fest. Dadurch wird zugleich eine erstaunlich schlüssige stilistische Entwicklung innerhalb der frühen Lieder Faurés deutlich. Die einzige Ausnahme innerhalb der chronologischen Reihenfolge bildet *L'Absent*, Faurés letztes Victor-Hugo-Lied, das zumindest nach *Lydia*, *Hymne* und *Seule!* entstanden sein muss. Da selbst diese Information keine genaue chronologische Einordnung ermöglicht, wurde in diesem einen Fall der Gruppierung des Dichters Vorrang vor einer strikten Chronologie eingeräumt.

Die Lieder

In *Le Papillon et la fleur* zeigt der 16-jährige Fauré bereits die ungezwungene melodische Grazie und rhythmische Lebendigkeit, die viele seiner Lieder charakterisiert. „[M]ein allererstes Lied", so erinnerte sich Fauré, „schrieb ich im Speisesaal [der École Niedermeyer], inmitten der Kochdämpfe [...] und Saint-Saëns war mein erster Interpret".[2] Die Karikatur auf der Titelseite des überlieferten Manuskripts zeichnete wahrscheinlich Saint-Saëns (siehe Faksimile S. IV), der neue Klavierlehrer der Schule und des jungen Faurés (die zwei Komponisten sollten lebenslange Freunde bleiben). Auch *Puisque j'ai mis ma lèvre* (1862) stammt aus Faurés Zeit an der École Niedermeyer. Die mandolinenartige Begleitung lässt spätere Lieder wie *Clair de lune* und *Mandoline* vorausahnen, vor allem aber hat das Stück eine hörbare und beachtenswerte Ähnlichkeit mit dem zweiten Klavierstück der *Consolations* von Liszt (dies erklärt vielleicht, warum Fauré dieses Lied nicht veröffentlichen ließ). Zwei weitere Hugo-Romanzen, *Mai* und *S'il est un charmant gazon*, stammen aus der Zeit zwischen 1862 und Anfang 1864. Letztere wurde erst 1875 als *Rêve d'amour!* veröffentlicht, ein Titel, den der Verleger Choudens dem Stück zu Faurés Unbehagen verlieh.[3] Ein frühes Widmungsautograph zeigt das Lied in einem lebhaften Tempo, mit einer luftigeren Klaviertextur und einem kompakteren Schluss. All dies zeugt von einer schlanken, originellen musikalischen Bearbeitung des Gedichts. Diese Fassung unterscheidet sich hinlänglich von der lange Zeit veröffentlichten Version, um hier in Gänze als brauchbare Alternative abgedruckt zu werden.[4]

Diese frühen Hugo-Vertonungen erwähnt Paul Meurice, seines Zeichens Faktotum Victor Hugos, in einem an den Dichter gerichteten Brief von Anfang 1864:

> Ein junger Mann, Schüler der Niedermeyer-Schule, M. Gabriel Fauré, hat einige Ihrer Gedichte vertont; er ist bereit, Sie für die Rechte zu bezahlen, aber ich weiß, dass mehrere Stücke bereits vorbehalten sind, und ich sende Ihnen die Titel jener Gedichte, die er ausgewählt hat, damit Sie mir bitte mitteilen mögen, ob diese ausgeschlossen sind: *La Fleur et le papillon* [sic], *Puisque mai tout en fleurs*, *S'il est un charmant gazon*, *Puisqu'ici-bas toute âme*, *L'aube naît*, *Puisque j'ai mis ma lèvre*.[5]

Um 1865 (Fauré hatte in diesem Jahr eine Organistenstelle an der Kirche Saint-Sauveur in Rennes angenommen), versuchte er sich an einem sehr anders gearteten Gedicht Hugos, *Tristesse d'Olympio*. Dieser Vertonung, bei deren einziger Überlieferung es sich augenscheinlich um eine Abschrift handelt, liegt ein Auszug aus einem längeren dramatischen Gedicht zugrunde. Sie besteht aus einer deklamatorischen Einleitung und einem ruhelosen strophischen *Allegro* in der Tradition einer Schubertschen *Szene*. *Dans les ruines d'une abbaye* folgte wahrscheinlich kurz darauf; 1869 wurde es zusammen mit *Le Papillon et la fleur* als erste Liedausgabe des Komponisten veröffentlicht.

Bei der einzig auffindbaren Quelle von *L'Aurore* (ca. 1868–1870) handelt es sich erneut um eine nicht-autographe Abschrift mit einigen Nachbesserungen von Faurés Hand. In seiner kompositorischen Anlage ähnelt das Stück *Lydia* (entstanden um dieselbe Zeit) und dem späteren *Green* (aus op. 58), während der Mittelteil in seiner auffälligen Klangfolge eine Ähnlichkeit mit zwei späteren Liedern aufweist: *Après un rêve* aus dem Jahr 1877 und *Prison* von 1894. Warum Fauré dieses reizvolle Lied nicht veröffentlichte, ist ungewiss, obwohl es – wie bei *Tristesse d'Olympio* – darauf zurückzuführen sein könnte, dass er nur einen kleinen Teil von Hugos deutlich längerem Gedicht vertont hatte.

Faurés letzte Solo-Vertonung eines Hugo-Gedichts ist mit einem finsteren Ereignis verbunden: Das mit „3 avril 1871" datierte *L'Absent* wurde während des Aufruhrs der Pariser Commune komponiert. Mit der Gedichtvorlage aus Hugos Sammlung *Les Châtiments*, einer wutentbrannten Reaktion auf den Staatsstreich Napoleon III. im Jahr 1851, kann das Lied als äußerst passende Erwiderung interpretiert werden, die an das gewalttätige Ende des daraus resultierenden Zweiten Kaiserreichs erinnert. Zu dieser Zeit hatte Fauré mit *Lydia* (berühmt ist der Anfang im lydischen Modus) bereits seinen ersten Exkurs in die Dichtung Leconte de Lisles unternommen. Wie Jean-Michel Nectoux beobachtete,[6] handelt es sich dabei höchstwahrscheinlich um die „petite mélodie", die Fauré in einem Brief vom Juni 1870 Julien Koszul zusammen mit seiner „Romanze" *S'il est un charmant gazon* zu schicken versprach. Die explizite stilistische Unterscheidung, die Fauré darin vornimmt, markiert einen Wendepunkt zwischen den leichteren *Romanzen* der 1860er und den konzentrierteren, gewagteren *Mélodies*, die folgten.[7]

Faurés drei Vertonungen Charles Baudelaires demonstrieren eine neue dramatische Intensität und strukturelle Kühnheit, die zusammen genommen den vielleicht größten stilistischen Sprung in seinem Lebenswerk darstellen. Diese ausgewählten Gedichte können als durch und durch Baudelairsche Trilogie der Liebe (*Hymne*), des Verstands (*La Rançon*) und der Sterblichkeit (*Chant d'automne*) interpretiert werden, letzteres als eine Antwort auf das „salut d'immortalité" in *Hymne*. Obwohl *Hymne* 1871 und die anderen beiden Lieder erst 1879 veröffentlicht wurden, deutet ihre enge musikalische Verwandtschaft darauf hin, dass sie alle zwischen 1870 und 1871 komponiert wurden. Dies wiederum weist auf eine mögliche geheime Absprache mit Faurés Freunden Henri Duparc und Emmanuel Chabrier hin, deren erste Baudelaire-Vertonungen ebenso von 1870 stammen; das Duparc gewidmete *La Rançon* stellt das einzige Lied dar, das Fauré jemals einem anderen bedeutenden Komponisten widmete.[8] Diese ursprünglich über die erste Sammlung verteilten drei Lieder sind als anspruchsvolle musikalische Umsetzung der reichen und komplexen Poesie Baudelaires oft unterschätzt worden. Ihre chronologische Anordnung in der vorliegenden Ausgabe verdeutlicht die bemerkenswerte Verwandtschaft und den Zusammenhang dieser Lieder, insbesondere aufgrund der strukturellen und stilistischen Elemente, die ihnen gemein sind (die steigenden chromatischen Linien, die das erste und dritte Lied durchdringen und die strukturell ähnlichen Übergänge nach Dur im zweiten und dritten Lied).[9]

Auf diese dramatischen Höhen folgen vier Lieder mit wiederum sehr kontrastierenden Texten: die völlig andersartige Dichtung Théophile Gautiers *Les Matelots*, die an die einfachere Strophenform der früheren *Romanzen* anknüpft; auf das zutiefst grüblerische *Seule!* folgt das wehmütige *Chanson du pêcheur (Lamento)* sowie *Tristesse*, ein unverblümt sentimentaler Text, der, durch Faurés leicht ironisierenden Walzerrhythmus, nach einem *Café-concert* duftet. *Chanson du pêcheur* ist der großen Mezzosopranistin Pauline Viardot gewidmet, ihres Zeichens Protegé Chopins, Komponistin und Salonnière, die Saint-Saëns Fauré in den frühen 1870er Jahren bekannt gemacht hatte. Bald wurde Fauré regelmäßiges Mitglied ihres Musikerkreises – 1877 sollte er sich kurzzeitig mit ihrer Tochter Marianne verloben – und mit seinen folgenden Liedern, *Aubade* und *Barcarolle*, vertonte er Gedichte der mit Viardot befreundeten Louis Pomey und Marc Monnier.

Mitte der 1870er Jahre wagte er sich an die Lyrik Sully Prudhommes (*Ici-bas* und *Au bord de l'eau*), was seine Liedkompositionen um einen wendigeren Dialog zwischen Stimme und Klavier bereicherte. *Ici-bas* stammt spätestens aus dem Jahr 1874, *Au bord de l'eau* wahrscheinlich aus dem Sommer 1875, den Fauré mit Camille und Marie Clerc verbrachte, beide Freundinnen und Unterstützerinnen seiner Musik: Ein frühes Fragment des Liedes steht auf dem Rücken einer Manuskriptseite seiner ersten Violinsonate, die er hauptsächlich in jenem Sommer komponierte.

In den späten 1870er Jahren wählte Fauré zwei toskanische Gedichte, frei übersetzt von seinem Sängerfreund Romain Bussine. *Après un rêve* (1877) wurde zu Faurés wohl bekanntestem Lied, die *Sérénade toscane* erweckt die Vorstellung einer wahren Tenor-Serenade. Mit der vorliegenden Ausgabe sind beide Lieder erstmals komplett mit toskanischem Originaltext singbar (eine Option, die auch die Originalausgaben lieferten, jedoch mit einer derart fehlerhaften Silbentrennung, dass zumindest *Sérénade toscane* in dieser Form nicht singbar ist).

Sylvie, die Vertonung eines Textes von Paul de Choudens (ein aufstrebender, gleichwohl mittelmäßiger Lyriker, Sohn des Verlegers Faurés), zeugt von dem Kompromiss, den Fauré einging, um die Veröffentlichung einer ersten Sammlung zwanzig seiner Lieder zu beschleunigen.[10] Besagter Band erschien wie erwartet im Dezember 1879 im Verlag Choudens – paradoxerweise nur einen Monat, nachdem Fauré seinen ersten Vertrag mit Julien Hamelle unterschrieben hatte, unter anderem für seine drei Lieder op. 18. Zu diesem Zeitpunkt hatte er möglicherweise bereits das Triptychon *Poème d'un jour* an den Verleger Durand & Schœnewerk verkauft; das Manuskript weist den gestrichenen Vermerk „op. 17" auf.[11] Obwohl die Lieder in Faurés Manuskript in Tonarten für die hohe Stimmlage stehen (Des-Dur, fis-Moll und Ges-Dur), veröffentlichten Durand & Schœnewerk den Zyklus zunächst in einer Transposition für die mittlere Stimmlage. Die entsprechenden Tonarten hatte Fauré für diesen Zweck im Manuskript notiert. Als schließlich 1894 eine Version für die hohe Stimmlage erschien, wurden die letzten beiden Lieder vermutlich versehentlich erneut nach f-Moll und F-Dur transponiert. In vorliegender Neuausgabe für die hohe Stimmlage erscheinen sie in ihren Originaltonarten. Wie auch *Sylvie*, seine toskanischen Lieder und Pomeys *Aubade* erhielt Fauré diese Gedichte wahrscheinlich direkt vom Autor, Charles Grandmougin; für sie ist keine publizierte Quelle bekannt.

Mit op. 18 vereinte Fauré erstmals bewußt verschiedene Dichter in einer eigens definierten Opusgruppe: ein Muster, das er einige Jahrzehnte beibehielt. Mit *Nell* kehrte er glücklich zu Leconte de Lisle zurück,[12] der lyrische Fluss des Liedes kontrastiert mit den deutlich düstereren Stücken *Le Voyageur* und *Automne*.[13] Bei letzten beiden handelt es sich um Faurés erste von zwölf Vertonungen der Lyrik Silvestres, ein weiterer Dichter, mit dem er persönlich bekannt war (1881 planten beide eine opéra-comique, *Lizarda*, die jedoch nicht zustande kam).[14] Neun vertonte Gedichte Silvestres (aus den Jahren 1878–1884) finden sich verteilt über die Opusgruppen 18, 23, 27 und 39, eine weitere Silvestre-Vertonung im *Madrigal* op. 35 für SATB. Auch die meisten dieser Texte erhielt Fauré mit großer Wahrscheinlichkeit vom Dichter selbst. Obwohl selten tiefgehend, so sprach die in Form, Charakter und Thematik vielfältige Lyrik Silvestres den gewandten und kreativen Melodiker an, zu dem Fauré mittlerweile geworden war. Bezeichnenderweise hatte Silvestre diese ersten neun Vertonungen als *Vers pour être chantés* [Verse zum Singen] konzipiert.[15]

Auch die zwischen 1879 und 1881 komponierten Lieder des op. 23 schließen zwei Silvestre-Vertonungen ein: das gefühlvolle *Le Secret*, das Maurice Ravel als „eines der schönsten Lieder Faurés"[16] bezeichnete, und das überschwängliche *Notre amour*, eines seiner leichtesten und lebhaftesten Lieder. Mit *Les Berceaux* kehrte Fauré zum letzten Mal zur Lyrik Sully Prudhommes zurück. Wie auch in *Ici-bas* und *Au bord de l'eau* erkundet er darin den aktiven Dialog zwischen Stimme und Klavier: Beim Erreichen des Höhepunkts des Stückes wird das Klavier gewissermaßen dazu herausgefordert, die letzte Gesangssilbe gleichsam durch eine brechende Welle zu ertränken. Zwei weitere Silvestre-Vertonungen aus dem Jahr 1882 bilden op. 27. Mit *Chanson d'amour* verwandelte Fauré ein weniger bemerkenswertes Gedicht Silvestres in eine Spielwiese für musikalisches und dichterisches *Enjambment*, während er in *La Fée aux chansons* reuevoll einige seiner Erfahrungen als Gesangspädagoge erkannt haben mag und einfließen ließ.

Hinweise zur Ausgabe und Aufführung

Tonarten

Die meisten Lieder sind hier in den Tonarten abgedruckt, die in den Sammlungen Choudens'/Hamelles festgesetzt wurden. Für *Mai*, *Au bord de l'eau*, „Toujours" und „Adieu" (*Poème d'un jour*) sowie *La Fée aux chansons* wurden die Tonarten der Fassungen für die hohe Stimmlage jedoch den handschriftlichen Quellen entnommen. Der Fall von *Poème d'un jour* wurde weiter oben bereits dargelegt; was *La Fée aux chansons* betrifft, so scheint das von Fauré ursprünglich vorgesehene E-Dur besser für die hohe Stimmlage und Klavier geeignet zu sein als das verbreitete F-Dur. Analog wurden für *Chant d'automne* und *Le Voyageur* die Originaltonarten für hohe Stimme festgesetzt (cis-Moll bzw. a-Moll statt des c-Molls bzw. g-Molls in den historischen Sammlungen). Diese haben nicht nur eine sehr instrumentenspezifische Lage, auch versah Fauré die Klavierstimme in *Chant d'automne* mit einigen tonartenspezifischen Fingersätzen.[17] *Dans les ruines d'une abbaye*, *Ici-bas* und *Au bord de l'eau* lagen in ihren traditionellen Fassungen für die hohe und mittlere Stimmlage einen Halbton auseinander. Für ersteres Lied wurde in der vorliegenden Ausgabe (statt des etablierten As-Dur) G-Dur als Tonart für die mittlere Stimmlage gewählt; für *Au bord de l'eau* wurde statt des lange Zeit gedruckten cis-Moll das d-Moll aus Faurés frühem Entwurf als Tonart für die hohe Stimmlage übernommen (als Tonart für die mittlere Stimmlage wurde c-Moll, die Tonart aller drei vollständigen Manuskripte, beibehalten). Für *Ici-bas*, mit seiner an sich hohen Tessitur, wurde das seit 1890 als Tonart für die mittlere Stimmlage gedruckte fis-Moll hier als Tonart für die hohe Stimmlage gewählt statt des etablierten g-Molls, und e-Moll als Tonart für die mittlere Stimmlage festgesetzt (auch liegt die Klavierstimme in dieser Kreuztonart besser). Die in der vorliegenden Ausgabe für *Sérénade toscane* gewählte Tonart für die mittlere Stimmlage, a-Moll (statt des etablierten b-Molls), wurde aus einer Einzelausgabe von 1901 übernommen, was das Lied mehr in den Stimmumfang von Mezzosopran und Bariton verlagert. Die Manuskripttonarten von *L'Aurore* und *Tristesse d'Olympio* wurden hier für die Fassungen für die hohe beziehungsweise mittlere Stimmlage übernommen, während die Transpositionen von den Herausgebern gewählt wurden; *Puisque j'ai mis ma lèvre* ist in seinen beiden Manuskripttonarten abgedruckt.

Tempo, Metrum und Rhythmus

Neben den Bemerkungen im obigen **Allgemeinen Vorwort** können Kenntnisse über Faurés Gewohnheiten und Aufführungspräferenzen einige Eigenarten bezüglich Notation und Edition seiner frühen Lieder beleuchten. Seine Verwendung von *Allegretto* kommt üblicherweise der von *Allegro* sehr nahe, geht jedoch mit einer lockereren Struktur und einem leichteren Charakter einher. Seine häufige Verwendung von *Andante* – oft relativiert durch *quasi allegretto* oder gar *quasi adagio* – bezeichnet moderate, fließende Tempi im heutigen Sinne und verkörpert das *andante* wörtlich als „gehend", das *adagio* als „gemächlich" – und das *quasi adagio* in der Tat als „fast gemächlich". Dies betrifft vor allem *Lydia*, *Chant d'automne*, „Rencontre" und *Nell* sowie *Seule!* und *L'Absent*. Für die letzten beiden wurde in vorliegender Ausgabe das in den Manuskripten und ersten Ausgaben dieser Lieder vorhandene 𝄵 reproduziert (anstelle des in nachfolgenden Ausgaben gedruckten 𝄴), was deren spezifische Halbtaktigkeit und Vorwärtsbewegung unterstreicht. Die Struktur und der fließende Charakter von *Lydia* und *Chanson d'amour* (wo keine Manuskripte überliefert sind) hat die Herausgeber zum entsprechenden [𝄴] veranlasst. Im Fall von *Lydia* stützt sich diese Entscheidung auch auf die kompositorische Ähnlichkeit mit *L'Aurore*, dessen Achtel ähnlich wie die Viertel in *Lydia* fließen.

Faurés Tempoüberschriften erklären sich häufig am besten, wenn sie vor dem Hintergrund der Melodielinien und des zugrunde liegenden harmonischen Rhythmus' und nicht gemessen an geschäftigeren Begleitfigurationen verstanden werden. In *Aubade* beispielsweise verlangt die zweiteilige Tempovorschrift eine recht lebhaften Beginn des Klaviers, damit der Sänger die langen Phrasen besser halten kann. Dies gilt umso mehr für *Chant d'automne*, dessen Eingangstempo *Andante* rückblickend entscheidend durch die spätere metrische Entsprechung bis in die Coda definiert wird.

Da Fauré die Tempoangaben immer wieder modifizierte, enthalten viele Lieder unterschiedliche Angaben in ihren Fassungen für die hohe, mittlere beziehungsweise tiefe Stimmlage. Während die meisten davon unterschiedliche Bezeichnungen für ein und dasselbe musikalische Konzept darstellen, (wie *Allegretto* versus *Allegro non troppo* in *Le Papillon et la fleur* und *Dans les ruines d'une abbaye*), ist der Sachverhalt bei *Ici-bas* komplexer: In den frühen Quellen und späteren Sammlungen für die hohe Stimmlage mit *Andantino* überschrieben, erschien es in der Sammlung für mittlere Stimmlage seit 1879 unter der Überschrift *Adagio*, einhergehend mit einer Verdichtung der Klavierstimme. Vorrang wurde hier der *Andantino*-Version gegeben, da sie Faurés ursprünglicher Konzeption und dem (eher wehmütigen als tragischen) Gedicht entspricht; die alternative Lesart ist in Fußnoten angeben. Das einzige Lied aus der ursprünglichen ersten Sammlung, welches mit einer Metronomangabe versehen wurde, ist *Barcarolle* (welches wie im **Kritischen Bericht** angemerkt, später in Hamelles zweite Sammlung verschoben wurde). Für einige Lieder wirken die ursprünglichen Metronomangaben unhaltbar langsam. Insbesondere scheint ♩ = 66 in *Nell* ein Druckfehler für 96 zu sein, während die Angaben in *Chanson d'amour* und *Notre amour* dem spielerischen, gar atemlosen Charakter der Lieder nicht gerecht werden.[18] In solchen Fällen sind die Metronomvorgaben aus den Quellen durch Vorschläge der Herausgeber in eckigen Klammern ergänzt.

Dass Fauré der stetigen Vorwärtsbewegung große Bedeutung beimaß, wird auch deutlich durch die gelegentliche Tempoaufnahme (nach einem kurzen *ritard.*) kurz vor einer Kadenz oder einem Hauptschlag, anstatt direkt darauf, so etwa in seinen handschriftlichen *a tempo*-Angaben in *Mai* (Takte 26 und 59) und *L'Aurore*. In Ersterem ist dies eine Vorwärtsbewegung, die über ein Textkomma hinaus geht – zweifelsohne verfolgte Fauré damit auch den Zweck, ein gemächliches Atmen an dieser Stelle zu verhindern. Eine ähnliche Geste, ein Bindebogen über einem Satzzeichen, findet sich (in lediglich einigen Quellen) in *Au bord de l'eau* und *Chanson d'amour*. Obwohl Fauré dies in *Au bord de l'eau* bekräftigt, indem er wenige Noten darauf ein Atemzeichen setzt (Takte 15 und 31 während einer lieblichen Imitation in der Basslinie), zitiert Claire Croiza Fauré mit der Aussage, später davon zugunsten des Atmens am Satzzeichen abgerückt zu sein.[19] Dass Fauré solche Fragen im Laufe seiner langen und bewegten Komponistenlaufbahn so unterschiedlich handhabte, zeigt die von Anfang an variable Konzeption dieser Lieder (weiter unten dazu mehr).

Faurés Musik steckt voller rhythmischer Akzentverschiebungen in Form von Hemiolen (klingende 3/4- oder 3/2-Metren innerhalb einer 6/8-oder 3/4-Taktstruktur), ein in den Volksweisen seiner Heimatregion Südfrankreich verwurzeltes kompositorisches Mittel, von dem er insbesondere in seinen *Barcarolles* für Klavier Gebrauch machte. Diese Vorliebe wird schon im allerersten Gesangseinsatz in *Le Papillon et la fleur* erkennbar, wo ein Großteil der Silbentrennung wider den 6/8-Rhythmus des Klaviers faktisch im 3/4-Rhythmus erklingt.[20] Diese Besonderheit findet sich auch ebenso teilweise in *Au bord de l'eau* und in den Eröffnungszeilen von *Notre amour*. Interpreten der Lieder Faurés müssen mit solchen rhythmischen Akzentverschiebungen stets rechnen und angesichts der beweglichen Betonungs- und Rhythmusmuster der Sprache wissen, dass schwache Silben auf scheinbar starken Zählzeiten in der gesungen französischen Prosodie nicht *per se* falsch sind.

Musikalische Quellen

Die zwanzig Lieder der ursprünglichen ersten Sammlung – Nr. 1, 3–4, 6 und 8–23 der vorliegenden Ausgabe – lagen den Herausgebern in Form verschiedener früher Fassungen mit einem zum Teil verwirrenden Spektrum an Varianten vor, welche auf die verschiedenen Verleger, Stiche, Tonarten und überarbeiteten Neuausgaben im Laufe Faurés Lebens zurückzuführen sind. Tendenziell finden sich in jeder neuen Quelle neue Revisionen neben Verfälschungen oder Aufhebungen früherer Revisionen, so dass keine einzige Quelle als maßgeblich stimmige Version angesehen werden kann. Manuskripte des Komponisten konnten lediglich für vierzehn Lieder des vorliegenden Bandes ausfindig gemacht werden. Das einzige davon für den Druck verfasste Manuskript war *Poème d'un jour*, obwohl noch einige andere Handschriften eine Rolle in der zur Veröffentlichung führenden Quellenkette gespielt haben könnten. Einige sind auf bis zu zehn Jahre vor Veröffentlichung zurückzudatieren und dokumentieren ein Lied in einem früheren Stadium oder stellen vermutlich nur einen von vielen Kompositionsentwürfen dar: Drei autographe Reinschriften von *Au bord de l'eau* zum Beispiel, alle von etwa 1875–1876, unterscheiden sich durchweg in Hinblick auf die Struktur und gewisse Nuancen des Stückes. Obwohl sie im Wesentlichen von den publizierten Versionen abgelöst wurden, helfen diese Manuskripte, Druckfehler zu beseitigen oder Details bezüglich der Stimmführung und des Layouts zu klären. Auch enthalten sie zahlreiche aufschlussreiche Varianten, die zum Teil aus der ersten Entwurfsphase stammen. Die wichtigsten von ihnen sind in den *ossia*-Lesarten der vorliegenden Ausgabe dargestellt; auch eine vollständige alternative Fassung (von *S'il est un charmant gazon*) konnte aufgefunden werden.

All dies zeugt in einem gewissen Grad davon, dass die frühen Lieder Faurés keineswegs starr konzipiert waren. Ihre Veränderlichkeit ist ein wichtiges Merkmal, das in der vorliegenden Ausgabe akzeptiert, in der Tat aufgegriffen wurde. Während die stimmigste Lesart jedes einzelnen Liedes als Hauptnotentext gedruckt wurde, sind realisierbare Varianten in *ossia*-Notenlinien oder Fußnoten angegeben. Bot eine andere Quelle wesentliche Korrekturen, so wurden diese in den Notentext aufgenommen; einige weniger grundlegende, jedoch nützliche Hinweise aus Sekundärquellen sind in Klammern notiert.

Unter Berücksichtigung obiger Ausführungen sollten die überarbeiteten Neuausgaben der ersten beiden Hamelle-Sammlungen aus dem Jahr 1908 im Prinzip die verlässlichste Quelle für die zu Faurés Lebzeiten veröffentlichten Lieder des Komponisten darstellen: Sie wurden in dieser Zeit auch nicht revidiert. Dieses Ideal durchkreuzen leider wiederholt unterschiedliche Tempi, Silbentrennungen sowie Dynamik- und Artikulationsvorschriften in den Fassungen für die hohe und mittlere Stimmlage. Das betrifft insbesondere die erste Sammlung, deren erste Ausgabe für die hohe Stimmlage von 1890 größtenteils auf Notentexten basiert, die in der Quellenkette weiter zurück liegen. Dadurch gingen viele sorgfältige Revisionen Faurés verloren, die in die ursprüngliche Publikation des Bandes (hauptsächlich für die mittlere Stimmlage) von 1879 mit eingegangen waren. Stattdessen weist die Ausgabe von 1890 für die hohe Stimmlage verschiedenste vermutlich in letzter Minute eingeflossene behelfsmäßige, aber auch einige unverzichtbare Revisionen auf. Aufgrund dieser Diskrepanzen, die nie behoben wurden, waren die Herausgeber der vorliegenden Ausgabe gezwungen, für jedes Lied durch sorgfältige Erstellung oder Revision aus den Bänden für die hohe und mittlere Stimmlage die vorrangige Quelle auszuwählen. Welcher der beiden Fassungen auch der Vorrang gegeben wurde, so musste diese stets durch andere Quellen ergänzt werden, um zu einem Notentext zu gelangen, der Faurés über Jahrzehnte hinweg sorgfältig vorgenommenen Revisionen berücksichtigt und gleichzeitig die Geschlossenheit des Notentextes bewahrt.

In dem Bemühen, den Fluss und die Umsetzbarkeit seiner Textverteilung immer weiter zu verbessern, variiert die Silbentrennung in Faurés früheren Liedern von Quelle zu Quelle. Während viele seiner Änderungen potentiell ungeschickte oder unidiomatische Betonungen betreffen, sind andere als Reaktion darauf zu verstehen, dass Interpreten die Flexibilität von Rhythmus und Betonung einer ursprünglichen Fassung nicht durchdrangen. In der vorliegenden Ausgabe sind die interessanteren dieser Varianten als *ossia* notiert; bedeutende Beispiele finden sich gegen Ende von *La Rançon* (mit einem gelungeneren *Enjambement* auf Kosten einer ausgedehnten schwachen Silbe) sowie in den Takten 28–30 in *Seule!* (mehr auf Betonungen ausgerichtet als die späteren, sichereren Lesarten). Durch eine aufmerksame Interpretation kann vielen der immanenten Gefahren begegnet werden.

Text

Häufig wandelte Fauré den Text der von ihm vertonten Gedichte ab, änderte die Satzstellung oder entfernte Zeilen und Strophen, um das Gedicht seinen musikalischen Entwürfen anzupassen. Mit seinen üblicherweise musikalisch wohl begründeten Nachbearbeitungen verfolgte Fauré das Ziel, den Text so melodisch und singbar wie möglich zu gestalten. Diese Änderungen sind in der vorliegenden Ausgabe berücksichtigt und darüber hinaus parallel zu den Originaltexten auf S. XXVIII–XLI in Klammern aufgeführt.

Komplexer sind Änderungen der Satzzeichen sowie Großschreibung: Innerhalb der vielen Manuskripte und gedruckten Quellen wurden viele Satzzeichen übergangen, unzählige andere ersetzt und gelegentlich neue hinzugefügt. Ebenso wurden Schemata für die Großschreibung unterschiedlich gehandhabt: Manchmal entsprechen sie der lyrischen Vorlage, mitunter weichen sie stark davon ab. Sofern solche Diskrepanzen zwischen den Quellen eines Liedes scheinbar durch ein Versehen des Komponisten oder Stechers zustande kamen, folgt die vorliegende Ausgabe stillschweigend der Quelle, die die Zeichensetzung und Großschreibung des Gedichtes beibehält. Ist in den musikalischen Quellen keine Zeichensetzung vorhanden oder sind Alternativen unbrauchbar, so haben die Herausgeber der vorliegenden Ausgabe die Interpunktion des gedruckten Gedichts übernommen und dies im **Kritischen Bericht** angegeben.

Häufig weisen die musikalischen Quellen jedoch plausible oder für die Interpretation nützliche Änderungen der Satzzeichen oder Formatierung des Gedichts auf, die eine Absicht des Komponisten erkennen lassen. Dazu zählt die Vereinfachung von Passagen mit vielen Satzzeichen, das Ersetzen von Ausrufezeichen, Kommata, Semikola oder Punkten und das Einfügen von Semikola oder Punkten, um das Ende von Strophen oder musikalischen Abschnitten zu präzisieren; ferner die Verwendung von Ausrufezeichen als Hinweis auf dynamische Intensität sowie das Einfügen von Kommata als Atemhinweis oder als Hinweis darauf, Silben nicht zu verschmelzen (viele derartige Fälle finden sich insbesondere in *Mai* und *L'Absent*). Nicht nur haben die Herausgeber die seitens Fauré vorgenommenen Wortänderungen berücksichtigt, auch waren sie bemüht, absichtliche und systematische Änderungen der Interpunktion und Großschreibung zu erkennen und beizubehalten, sofern dies keine syntaktischen oder musikalischen Probleme verursachte.[21] Diese grundsätzlich nicht im **Kritischen Bericht** aufgeführten Varianten sind einfach erkennbar, vergleicht man den Notentext mit den in ihrer ursprünglichen Form abgedruckten Gedichten auf den Seiten XXVIII–XLI. Lieder, die Fauré nicht veröffentlichen ließ, lassen weniger methodische Aufarbeitung erkennen, weshalb hier in größerem Umfang auf Satzzeichen und Großschreibung dfer Gedichte zurückgegriffen wurde.

Danksagungen

Der herzliche Dank der Herausgeber gilt all jenen, die uns für die wissenschaftliche Untersuchung freundlicherweise Quellen zur Verfügung gestellt oder auf praktische Weise Unterstützung geleistet haben, einschließlich der Bibliothekare und privaten Sammler auf der ganzen Welt (mit besonderem Dank an die Mitarbeiter der Musikabteilung der Bibliothèque nationale de France) sowie unzähligen Einzelpersonen: insbesondere Helen Abbott, Thierry und Pierrette Bodin, Mimi Segal Daitz, Denis Herlin, Ken Johansen, Peter Jost, Edmond Lemaître (und Éditions Durand), Roger Nichols, Robert Orledge und Herbert Schneider sowie Angela Newport, Valeria Schiavone und Diego Ropele für ihre Hilfe hinsichtlich der toskanischen Texte. Musiker- und Lehrerkollegen sowie Studenten unterstützten uns in Workshops und Konzerten mit ihrem Enthusiasmus, ihrer Fachkompetenz und ihrem unschätzbaren musikalischen Feedback; der besondere Dank der Herausgeber gilt Mary Dibbern, Amber Evans, Guy Flechter, François Le Roux, Robert Macfarlane, Rosalind Martin, Kurt Ollmann, Christopher Underwood und Darlene Wiley. Der Standort dieses Editionsprojekts, die Royal Academy of Music, London, wurde durch eine Projektförderung des Arts and Humanities Research Councils (GB) unterstützt; der spezielle Dank gilt hier Nicole Tibbels für ihre grenzenlos enthusiastische Mitarbeit sowie ihre Einsichten bezüglich praktischer und linguistischer Fragen, ferner Richard Stokes für die freundliche Genehmigung des Nachdrucks seiner englischen Übersetzungen der Liedtexte, den Gesangsstudenten im Aufbaustudium der Royal Academy sowie David Gorton, Neil Heyde und Timothy Jones.

London, 2014 *Roy Howat und Emily Kilpatrick*

(Übersetzung: Lore Horlamus)

[1] Im Zuge der Kandidatur Faurés für das Institut de France vergab Hamelle diese Opusnummern 1896 für die bestehende Reihenfolge der ersten Sammlung. Zu Referenzzwecken sind sie in der vorliegenden Ausgabe in runden Klammern aufgeführt (so wie auch bei op. 21: siehe Fußnote 11 unten). Literaturhinweise zu ausführlicheren Erörterungen dieser und anderer editorischer Aspekte der frühen Lieder Faurés finden sich in der **Auswahlbibliographie**.

[2] Brief vom 14. Juli 1922, in: Fauré-Fremiet (Hrsg.), *Gabriel Fauré : Lettres intimes*, S. 282.

[3] Brief an Julien Koszul Juni 1870, in: Nectoux (ed.), *Gabriel Fauré : Correspondance*, S. 26.

[4] Überliefertes Quellenmaterial deutet darauf hin, dass Fauré möglicherweise nur Rohentwürfe einiger früher Lieder bewahrte, nachdem er die mit sorgfältigen Hinweisen und Korrekturen versehenen Widmungsautographen verschenkt hatte (insbesondere von *Mai* und *S'il est un charmant gazon*), sodass letzteres nicht mehr verfügbar war, als sich die Gelegenheit der Veröffentlichung bot.

[5] In: Nectoux (ed.), *Gabriel Fauré : Correspondance*, S. 19–20 (undatierter Brief); in einer Antwort vom 29. Mai 1864 erteilte Hugo seine Zustimmung. *Puisqu'ici-bas* wurde 1879 als Gesangsduett veröffentlicht (vgl. *Complete Songs*, Bd. 2); sollte *L'Aube naît* vertont worden sein, so ist dieses nicht überliefert.

[6] Nectoux (ed.), *Gabriel Fauré: Correspondance*, S. 26.

[7] 1911 äußerte Fauré, die Gedichte Victor Hugos nie (und jene Leconte de Lisles nur selten) zu seiner Zufriedenheit vertont zu haben: „[I]hre Gedichte [...] sind zu gehaltvoll, zu wortreich, zu vollendet, als dass eine erfolgreiche musikalische Bearbeitung möglich wäre." („Sous la Musique que faut-il mettre?", in: *Musica* 101, Februar 1911, S. 38). Dies (wie die Äußerungen vieler älterer Komponisten) als Abwertung seiner eigenen frühen Werke zu deuten, scheint angesichts des natürlichen Charmes und der Leichtigkeit dieser Lieder nicht abwegig.

[8] Baudelaire wurde zuvor von seinen *Chansonnier*-Freunden vertont. Fauré, Duparc und Chabrier gehörten 1871 zu den Mitbegründern der Société nationale de musique, die ausdrücklich errichtet wurde, um die französische Musik zu fördern. Obwohl Fauré *Chant d'automne* erstmals 1878 erwähnte (in einem Brief an Marie Clerc: „Ich habe *Chant d'automne* Mme M. Camille Clerc gewidmet – war das richtig?"; in: Nectoux (ed.), *Gabriel Fauré: Correspondance*, S. 83), deutet seine offensichtlich auf die bevorstehende Veröffentlichung zurückzuführende Formulierung darauf hin, dass M. Clerc das Lied bereits bekannt war.

[9] Weitere Einzelheiten finden sich in: Roy Howat und Emily Kilpatrick, *Wagnérisme de Fauré : Pénélope (1913) et les mélodies*, in: Marie-Cécile Leblanc und Danièle Pistone (Hrsg.), *Wagner, 1913–2013, Ruptures et Continuité*, Paris, Presses de la Sorbonne-Nouvelle: im Erscheinen 2015.

[10] „Mit der Vertonung der Verse Choudens' (Paul) habe ich eine Herkulesarbeit verrichtet! Ja, liebe Madame, Lucette [vermutlich ein Spaß] wird nun mit einer Eskorte von vier Erniedrigungszeichen und zwölf Sechzehnteln pro Takt durchs Leben gehen. [...] Jetzt, da ich mich mit Choudens gut gestellt habe, hoffe ich, dass die Veröffentlichung der Liedersammlung reibungslos vonstatten geht." (Brief vom Oktober 1878 an Marie Clerc, leicht abgewandelte Übersetzung aus: Nectoux (ed.), *Gabriel Fauré: Correspondance*, S. 83)

[11] In den Archiven der Éditions Durand ist der Vertrag nicht mehr auffindbar; er wurde wahrscheinlich 1879 unterzeichnet. Die Opusnummer 21 wurde dem Zyklus erstmals 1897 zugewiesen, da Hamelle die Nummer 17 im Jahr 1880 für Faurés *Romances sans paroles* (veröffentlicht 1881) vergeben hatte, einem viele Jahre zuvor komponierten Klavierstück.

[12] Leconte de Lisles *Nell* geht auf Robert Burns' *Handsome Nell* zurück, eine Ode an dessen Jugendfreundin Nellie Kilpatrick.

[13] Fauré widersetzte sich dieses Mal erfolgreich dem offensichtlichen Versuch Hamelles, die Titel dieser Lieder zu verkitschen: „Ich bevorzuge vielmehr den Titel *Le Voyageur*, da dies derjenige ist, den der Dichter seinem Gedicht verliehen hat. Was das andere Lied betrifft, so habe ich mir überlegt, dass der Titel *Juin* nicht so gut passt wie der Titel *Nell*. Der Juni, der die Blütenpracht und den Sonnenschein bringt, wird allein als Vergleich für das Feuer, das Nells Liebe im Herzen des Dichters angefacht hat, herangezogen. Doch es geht um Nell, nicht um den Juni. Warum nennen wir es nicht – *für Nell* – ?" (Brief an Hamelle, 24. Juni 1880, in : Nectoux (ed.), *Gabriel Fauré : Correspondance*, S. 99).

[14] Nectoux, *Gabriel Fauré: les voix du clair-obscur*, S. 194.

[15] Die Vertonungen stammen aus den beiden Sammlungen *Le Pays de roses* und *Les Ailes d'or*, die beide auf diese Weise betitelte Abschnitte enthalten.

[16] Ravel „Les Mélodies de Gabriel Fauré", *La Revue musicale* 3 (Oktober 1922), in Arbie Orenstein (Hrsg.), *Maurice Ravel : Lettres, écrits, entretiens*, Paris, Flammarion, 1990, S. 323.

[17] Die Änderung nach c-Moll resultiert möglicherweise aus einer Präferenz des Verlegers für eine „einfachere" Tonart.

[18] Die einsetzende Gesangsstimme in *Notre amour* verdeutlicht diesen Punkt von Anbeginn des Liedes: Durch ein zu moderates Tempo wird eine schwache Silbe auf dem höchsten Ton zu sehr betont. Es existieren keine handschriftlichen Quellen, die diese mehr als fünfzehn Jahre nach der ersten Veröffentlichung hinzugefügten Metronomangaben bestätigen (vgl. **Kritischer Bericht**). Zu Druckfehlern dieser Art zählen Faurés *Pièces brèves* für Klavier, für die das Tempo in der ersten Ausgabe mit 69 statt 96 angegeben war.

[19] Abraham (Hrsg.), *Un Art de l'interprétation*, S. 138; Bannerman (Hrsg.), *The Singer as Interpreter*, S. 83.

[20] Mit Erscheinen der ersten Sammlung im Jahr 1879 wurde der erste Gesangseinsatz in *Le Papillon et la fleur*, Takt 10, so geändert, dass er in einem eindeutigen $\frac{6}{8}$-Metrum auf den Schlag erfolgt (siehe **Kritischer Bericht**). Da die Polyrhythmie von $\frac{3}{4}$- und $\frac{6}{8}$-Metren im restlichen Lied größtenteils unverändert beibehalten wurde (einschließlich in Takt 11), ist dies wohl weniger durch eine neu erwägte Silbentrennung als durch die Gewährleistung eines sicheren Gesangseinsatzes zu begründen. Dass Fauré für alle späteren Ausgaben wieder die ursprüngliche Lesart von Takt 10 drucken ließ, war zweifellos eine bewusste Entscheidung, da zu diesem Zweck die Druckplatten für die erste Sammlung geändert werden mussten.

[21] Eine eingehendere Auseinandersetzung mit diesem Thema findet sich in: Kilpatrick: *Moot point: Editing poetry and punctuation in Fauré's early songs*.

Index of Songs / Table des mélodies / Liederverzeichnis

			Key *Tonart*	Page *Seite*
1.	*Le Papillon et la fleur*	Victor Hugo	C	1
2.	*Puisque j'ai mis ma lèvre*	Victor Hugo	B♭	5
3.	*Mai*	Victor Hugo	F	10
4a.	*S'il est un charmant gazon* (I)	Victor Hugo	E♭	14
4b.	*S'il est un charmant gazon* (II) (*Rêve d'amour*)	Victor Hugo	E♭	18
5.	*Tristesse d'Olympio*	Victor Hugo	e	22
6.	*Dans les ruines d'une abbaye*	Victor Hugo	G	28
7.	*L'Aurore*	Victor Hugo	F	32
8.	*L'Absent*	Victor Hugo	a	34
9.	*Lydia*	Leconte de Lisle	F	38
10.	*Hymne*	Charles Baudelaire	F	41
11.	*La Rançon*	Charles Baudelaire	c	46
12.	*Chant d'automne*	Charles Baudelaire	a	49
13.	*Les Matelots*	Théophile Gautier	E♭	56
14.	*Seule !*	Théophile Gautier	e	59
15.	*Chanson du pêcheur (Lamento)*	Théophile Gautier	f	62
16.	*Tristesse*	Théophile Gautier	c	66
17.	*Aubade*	Louis Pomey	F	70

			Key *Tonart*	Range *Umfang*	Page *Seite*
18.	*Barcarolle*	Marc Monnier	f		73
19.	*Ici-bas !*	Sully Prudhomme	e		76
20.	*Au bord de l'eau*	Sully Prudhomme	c		78
21.	*Après un rêve*	Romain Bussine	c		81
22.	*Sérénade toscane*	Romain Bussine	a		84
23.	*Sylvie*	Paul de Choudens	F		88
24–26.	*Poème d'un jour*	Charles Grandmougin			
	24. *Rencontre*		B		93
	25. *Toujours*		e		97
	26. *Adieu*		E		100
27.	*Nell* (Op. 18 no. 1)	Leconte de Lisle	E♭		102
28.	*Le Voyageur* (Op. 18 no. 2)	Armand Silvestre	f		105
29.	*Automne* (Op. 18 no. 3)	Armand Silvestre	b		108
30.	*Les Berceaux* (Op. 23 no. 1)	Sully Prudhomme	b♭		111
31.	*Notre amour* (Op. 23 no. 2)	Armand Silvestre	D		114
32.	*Le Secret* (Op. 23 no. 3)	Armand Silvestre	D♭		118
33.	*Chanson d'amour* (Op. 27 no. 1)	Armand Silvestre	F		120
34.	*La Fée aux chansons* (Op. 27 no. 2)	Armand Silvestre	D		123

Poetic texts / Textes poétiques des mélodies / Liedtexte

The French texts follow the layout, wording and punctuation of the poetic sources, as listed in the **Critical Commentary**.
Fauré's textual modifications are shown in [ ]; omitted words and lines are shown in ( ); […] indicates omitted stanzas.
The English and German translations, derived from the song texts, tacitly incorporate Fauré's amendments.

Le texte français suit les sources poétiques, citées dans le **commentaire critique**, y compris dans leur disposition et leur ponctuation.
Les modifications textuelles de Fauré sont placées entre crochets ; les mots et vers omis, entre parenthèses ; les strophes omises sont indiquées par […].
Les traductions anglaises et allemandes, faites à partir des textes des mélodies, incorporent tacitement les changements de Fauré.

Die französischen Texte stimmen in Layout, Wortlaut und Interpunktion mit der im **Kritischen Bericht** aufgeführten dichterischen Vorlage überein.
Faurés Änderungen am Text sind in [ ] angegeben; ausgelassene Wörter oder Zeilen stehen in ( ); […] signalisiert ausgelassene Strophen.
In den englischen und deutschen Übersetzungen der Liedtexte wurden Faurés Änderungen stillschweigend übernommen.

English translations by Richard Stokes / Deutsche Übersetzung von Klaus Strobel

1. {Le Papillon et la fleur}
Victor Hugo

La pauvre fleur disait au papillon céleste :
  Ne fuis pas !
Vois comme nos destins sont différents. Je reste,
  Tu t'en vas !

Pourtant nous nous aimons, nous vivons sans les hommes
  Et loin d'eux,
Et nous nous ressemblons, et l'on dit que nous sommes
  Fleurs tous deux !

Mais, hélas ! l'air t'emporte et la terre m'enchaîne.
  Sort cruel !
Je voudrais embaumer ton vol de mon haleine
  Dans le ciel !

Mais non, tu vas trop loin ! – Parmi des fleurs sans nombre
  Vous fuyez,
Et moi je reste seule à voir tourner mon ombre
  À mes pieds !

Tu fuis, puis tu reviens, puis tu t'en vas encore
  Luire ailleurs.
Aussi me trouves-tu toujours à chaque aurore
  Toute en pleurs !

Oh ! [Ah !] pour que notre amour coule des jours fidèles,
  Ô mon roi,
Prends comme moi racine, ou donne-moi des ailes
  Comme à toi ! [Comme toi !]

2. Puisque j'ai mis ma lèvre
Victor Hugo

Puisque j'ai mis ma lèvre à ta coupe encor pleine ;
Puisque j'ai dans tes mains posé mon front pâli ;
Puisque j'ai respiré parfois la douce haleine
De ton âme, parfum dans l'ombre enseveli ;

Puisqu'il me fut donné de t'entendre me dire
Les mots où se répand le cœur mystérieux ;
Puisque j'ai vu pleurer, puisque j'ai vu sourire
Ta bouche sur ma bouche et tes yeux sur mes yeux ;

Puisque j'ai vu briller sur ma tête ravie
Un rayon de ton astre, hélas ! voilé toujours ;
Puisque j'ai vu tomber dans l'onde de ma vie
Une feuille de rose arrachée à tes jours,

Je puis maintenant dire aux rapides années :
– Passez ! passez toujours ! je n'ai plus à vieillir !
Allez-vous-en avec vos fleurs toutes fanées ;
J'ai dans l'âme une fleur que nul ne peut cueillir !

Votre aile en le heurtant ne fera rien répandre
Du vase où je m'abreuve et que j'ai bien rempli.
Mon âme a plus de feu que vous n'avez de cendre !
Mon cœur a plus d'amour que vous n'avez d'oubli !

1. {The butterfly and the flower}
Victor Hugo

The humble flower said to the heavenly butterfly:
  Do not flee!
See how our destinies differ. Fixed to earth am I,
  You fly away!

Yet we love each other, we live without men
  And far from them,
And we are so alike, it is said that both of us
  Are flowers!

But alas! The breeze bears you away, the earth
                                holds me fast.
  Cruel fate!
I would perfume your flight with my fragrant breath
  In the sky!

But no, you flit too far! Among countless flowers
  You fly away,
While I remain alone, and watch my shadow circle
  Round my feet!

You fly away, then return; then take flight again
  To shimmer elsewhere.
And so you always find me at each dawn
  Bathed in tears!

Ah, that our love might flow through faithful days,
  O my king,
Take root like me, or give me wings
  Like yours!

2. Since I've pressed my lips
Victor Hugo

Since I've pressed my lips to your still brimming cup;
Since on your brow I've laid my pale brow;
Since at times I have caught the sweet breath
Of your soul, fragrance in the shrouded shade;

Since I've been favoured to hear you utter
Words poured from a mysterious heart;
Since I've seen tears, since I've seen smiles,
Your mouth on my mouth, your eyes on mine;

Since catching on my delighted face
A ray of light from your star, still veiled, alas!
Since watching fall into the stream of my life
A rose leaf from your days;

I can now say to the swift years:
– Roll on, roll ever on! I can age no more!
Away with you and your withered flowers;
In my soul I've a flower that none can gather!

Should your wing jolt it, nothing will spill
From the vessel where I drink and which I have filled.
My soul has more fire than you have ashes!
My heart has more love than you oblivion!

1. {Der Schmetterling und die Blume}
Victor Hugo

Die arme Blume sagte zum himmlischen Schmetterling:
  Flüchte nicht!
Schau wie verschieden unsere Schicksale sind. Ich bleibe,
  Du gehst fort!

Dennoch lieben wir uns, wir leben ohne die Menschen
  Und weit weg von ihnen.
Und wir gleichen uns, und man sagt, wir seien
  Beide Blumen!

Aber leider trägt dich die Luft fort und die Erde
                                kettet mich fest.
  Grausames Schicksal!
Ich möchte deinen Flug mit meinem Atem erfüllen
  Am Himmel.

Aber nein, du gehst zu weit! – Zwischen zahllose Blumen
  Flieht ihr,
Und ich bleibe allein, um meinen Schatten zu verfolgen
  Zu meinen Füßen!

Du fliehst, kommst dann zurück, dann gehst du erneut
  Woanders leuchten.
Darum findest du mich an jedem Morgen immer
  In Tränen aufgelöst!

Ah! damit unsere Liebe treue Tage erlebe,
  O mein König,
Schlage, wie ich, Wurzeln oder gib mir Flügel
  Wie deine!

2. Weil ich meine Lippen legte
Victor Hugo

Weil ich meine Lippen legte auf deinen noch vollen Kelch;
Weil meine blasse Stirn geruht in deinen Händen;
Weil ich manches Mal einsog den süßen Atem
Deiner Seele, Duft im Schatten verborgen;

Weil mir's gegeben ward von dir zu hören
Worte, in denen sich eröffnet das rätselhafte Herz;
Weil ich die Tränen sah und auch das Lächeln
Mund an Mund und deine Augen in den meinen;

Weil ich sah auf meinem sel'gen Haupte
Einen Strahl von deinem Stern, ach, stets verborgen;
Weil ich sah, wie in die Welle meines Lebens fiel
Ein Rosenblatt, gepflückt aus deinen Tagen;

Nun kann ich sagen zu den schnellen Jahren:
– Zieht hin! Zieht immer hin! Ich brauche nicht
                                mehr zu altern!
Gehet fort mit euren welken Blüten;
Mein Herz birgt eine Blume, die niemand pflücken kann!

Ihr Flügelschlag wird nichts entweichen lassen
Aus dem Gefäß, das gut gefüllt mich labt.
Mehr Feuer noch hat meine Seele als ihr Asche!
Mehr Liebe hat mein Herz als ihr Vergessenheit!

(Übersetzung: KERN AG, Sprachendienste)

3. [Mai]
Victor Hugo

Puisque mai tout en fleurs dans les prés nous réclame,
Viens ! ne te lasse pas de mêler à ton âme
La campagne, les bois, les ombrages charmants,
Les larges clairs de lune au bord des flots dormants,
Le sentier qui finit où le chemin commence,
Et l'air et le printemps et l'horizon immense,
L'horizon que ce monde attache humble et joyeux
Comme une lèvre au bas de la robe des cieux !
Viens ! et que le regard des pudiques étoiles
Qui tombe sur la terre à travers tant de voiles,
Que l'arbre pénétré de parfums et de chants,
Que le souffle embrasé de midi dans les champs,
Et l'ombre et le soleil, et l'onde et la verdure,
Et le rayonnement de toute la nature
Fassent épanouir, comme une double fleur,
La beauté sur ton front et l'amour dans ton cœur !

3. [May]
Victor Hugo

Since full-flowering May calls us to the meadows,
Come! do not tire of mingling with your soul
The countryside, the woods, the charming shade,
Vast moonlights on the banks of sleeping waters,
The path ending where the road begins,
And the air, the spring and the huge horizon,
The horizon which this world fastens, humble and joyous,
Like a lip to the hem of heaven's robe!
Come! and may the gaze of the chaste stars,
Falling to earth through so many veils,
May the tree steeped in scent and song,
May the burning breath of noon in the fields,
And the shade and the sun, and the tide and verdure,
And the radiance of all nature –
May they cause to blossom, like a double flower,
Beauty on your brow and love in your heart!

3. [Mai]
Victor Hugo

Da der Mai, der auf den Wiesen ganz in Blut steht,
    nach uns verlangt,
Komm! werde nicht müde, deine Seele zu vereinigen mit
Der Landschaft, den Wäldern, den bezaubernden
    Schatten
Dem weiten Mondschein am Ufer schlafender Fluten,
Dem Pfad der endet wo der Weg beginnt,
Und der Luft und dem Frühling und dem
    unendlichen Horizont
Dem Horizont, den diese Welt demütig und
    vergnügt zusammenhält
Wie eine Lippe am Saum des Himmelskleides!
Komm! Und daß der Blick schamhafter Sterne,
Der durch so viele Schleier zur Erde fällt,
Daß der von Düften und Gesängen durchdrungene
    Baum,
Daß der versengende Hauch am Mittag in den Feldern,
Und der Schatten und die Sonne und die Welle des
    Grüns
Und die Strahlung der ganzen Natur
Wie eine doppelte Blume aufblühen lassen
Die Schönheit auf deiner Stirn und die Liebe in
    deinem Herzen!

4. Nouvelle chanson sur un vieil air [S'il est un charmant gazon]
Victor Hugo

S'il est un charmant gazon
    Que le ciel arrose,
Où brille [naisse] en toute saison
    Quelque fleur éclose,
Où l'on cueille à pleine main
Lis [Lys], chèvrefeuille et jasmin,
J'en veux faire le chemin
    Où ton pied se pose !

S'il est un sein bien aimant
    Dont l'honneur dispose,
Dont le ferme [tendre] dévouement
    N'ait rien de morose,
Si toujours ce noble sein
Bat pour un digne dessein,
J'en veux faire le coussin
    Où ton front se pose !

S'il est un rêve d'amour,
    Parfumé de rose,
Où l'on trouve chaque jour
    Quelque douce chose,
Un rêve que Dieu bénit,
Où l'âme à l'âme s'unit,
Oh ! j'en veux faire le nid
    Où ton cœur se pose !

4. New song on an old air [If there be a lovely lawn]
Victor Hugo

If there be a lovely lawn
    Watered by the sky,
Where each new season
    Blossoming flowers spring up,
Where lily, woodbine, and jasmine
Can be gathered liberally,
I would strew the way with them
    For your feet to tread!

If there be a loving breast
    Wherein honour dwells,
Whose tender devotion
    Never is morose,
If this noble breast always
Beats with worthy intent,
I would make of it a pillow
    Where your head can rest!

If there be a dream of love
    With the scent of roses,
Where each day may be found
    Some sweet new delight,
A dream blessed by the Lord
Where soul unites with soul,
Oh! I shall make of it the nest
    Where your heart will rest!

4. Neues Lied über eine alte Weise [Wenn es einen reizenden Rasen gibt]
Victor Hugo

Wenn es einen reizenden Rasen gibt,
    Den der Himmel besprengt,
Wo zu jeder Jahreszeit
    Irgendeine Blume aufblüht,
Wo man mit voller Hand pflückt
Lilie, Geißblatt und Jasmin,
Dann möchte ich daraus den Weg machen
    Auf den dein Fuß sich setzt!

Wenn es eine innig liebende Brust gibt,
    Über welche die Ehre verfügt,
Deren zarte Ergebenheit
    Nichts Verdrießliches hat,
Wenn diese edle Brust immer
Für eine würdige Absicht schlägt,
Möchte ich daraus das Kissen machen,
    Auf das sich deine Stirn legt.

Wenn es einen Liebestraum gibt
    Nach Rosen duftend,
Wo man jeden Tag
    Etwas Liebliches findet,
Einen Traum, den Gott segnet,
Wo sich Seele mit Seele vereint,
Oh! Dann möchte ich das Nest daraus machen,
    In das dein Herz sich legt.

5. Tristesse d'Olympio
Victor Hugo

Les champs n'étaient point noirs, les cieux n'étaient
    pas mornes,
Non, le jour rayonnait dans un azur sans bornes
    Sur la terre étendue,
L'air était plein d'encens et les prés de verdures
Quand il revit ces lieux où par tant de blessures
    Son cœur s'est répandu !

[...]

Hélas ! se rappelant ses douces aventures,
Regardant, sans entrer, par-dessus les clôtures,
    Ainsi qu'un paria,

5. The sadness of Olympio
Victor Hugo

The fields were not black, the skies were not bleak;
No, daylight blazed in infinite blueness
    Above the earth,
The air was filled with incense, the meadows with
    greenness,
When he set eyes on those places again where
    through so many wounds
    His heart poured forth!

[...]
Alas! recalling his sweet adventure,
Gazing, without entering, over the fences
    Like an outcast,

5. Olympios Trauer
Victor Hugo

Die Felder waren nicht schwarz, der Himmel war
    nicht düster;
Nein, der Tag strahlte in einem grenzenlosen Blau
    Über der ausgedehnten Erde,
Die Luft war voll Weihrauch und die Wiese voll Grün,
Als er diesen Ort wiedersah, wo durch so viele
    Verletzungen
    Sein Herz sich ergossen hat!

[...]
Ach! sich seiner süßen Abenteuer erinnernd,
Ohne einzutreten über die Zäune schauend,
    Wie ein Ausgestoßener,

XXX

Il erra tout le jour. Vers [À] l'heure où la nuit tombe,
Il se sentit le cœur triste comme une tombe,
    Alors il s'écria :
	He wandered all day long. Towards nightfall,
	His heart felt as heavy as a tomb,
	    Then he cried out:
		Irrte er den ganzen Tag bis zur Stunde, da die
		    Nacht einbricht,
		Er fühlte sich traurigen Herzens wie ein Grab,
		    Da rief er aus:

– «Ô douleur ! j'ai voulu, moi, dont l'âme est troublée, Savoir si l'urne encor conservait la liqueur, Et voir ce qu'avait fait cette heureuse vallée De tout ce que j'avais laissé là de mon cœur !	"O grief! I, whose soul is troubled, wished To know if the urn still contained the liquor, And to see what this happy vale had made Of all I had left there of my heart!	„O Schmerz! ich wollte, ich, dessen Seele verstört ist, Wissen, ob die Urne noch die Lösung bewahrt, Und sehen, was dieses glückliche Tal gemacht hat Aus allem, was ich von meinem Herzen hiergelassen habe
«Que peu de temps suffit pour changer toutes choses ! Nature au front serein, comme vous oubliez ! Et comme vous brisez dans vos métamorphoses Les fils mystérieux où nos cœurs sont liés !	How quickly everything can change! O nature, how you forget with your unfurrowed brow! And how you and your metamorphoses sever The mysterious threads whereby our hearts are bound!	Wie wenig Zeit genügt, um alles zu ändern! Natur mit beschaulicher Stirn, wie Euch vergessen! Und wie Ihr in Euren Verwandlungen zerreißen Die mysteriösen Fäden, wo unsere Herzen verbunden sind!
[…]	[…]	[…]

«Eh bien ! oubliez-nous, maison, jardin, ombrages !
Herbe, use notre seuil ! ronce, cache [cachez] nos pas !
Chantez, oiseaux ! ruisseaux, coulez ! croissez, feuillages !
Ceux que vous oubliez ne vous oublieront pas.
	So then! let house, garden and shade forget us!
	Grasses, wear out our threshold! Brambles, hide
	    our steps!
	Sing, O birds; stream, O brooklets! Grow, O leaves!
	Those you forget shall not forget you.
		Nun gut! vergeßt uns, Haus, Garten, Schatten!
		Gras, nutze unsere Schwelle! Brombeerstrauch,
		    versteck' unseren Schritt!
		Singt, Vögel! Bäche, fließt! wachst, Blätter!
		Die ihr vergeßt, vergessen euch nicht.

«Car vous êtes pour nous l'ombre de l'amour même ! Vous êtes l'oasis qu'on rencontre en chemin ! Vous êtes, ô vallon, la retraite suprême Où nous avons pleuré nous tenant par la main ! »	Because you are for us the shadow of love itself! You are the oasis we encountered on the way! You are, O valley, the dearest shelter Where we wept and held hands!"	Denn ihr seid für uns der Schatten der Liebe selbst! Ihr seid die Oase, auf die man unterwegs trifft! Ihr seid, o kleines Tal, der höchste Zufluchtsort Wo wir, uns an den Händen gefaßt, geweint haben!
[…]	[…]	[…]

6. Dans les ruines d'une abbaye / 6. In the ruins of an abbey / 6. In den Ruinen einer Abtei
Victor Hugo

Seuls tous deux, ravis, chantants !
    Comme on s'aime !
Comme on cueille le printemps
    Que Dieu sème !
	Alone, together, enraptured, singing!
	    How we love each other!
	How we reap the springtime
	    That God sows!
		Wir zwei allein, entzückt, singend!
		    Wie wir uns lieben!
		Wie wir den Frühling ernten,
		    Den Gott sät.

Quels rires étincelants
    Dans ces ombres
Pleines jadis [Jadis pleines] de fronts blancs,
    De cœurs sombres !
	What sparkling laughter
	    In these shadows
	Once full of pale faces
	    And sombre hearts!
		Welch strahlendes Lachen
		    In diesen Schatten,
		Einst voll von weißen Häuptern,
		    Von dunklen Herzen!

On est tout frais mariés.
    On s'envoie
Les charmants cris variés
    De la joie.
	We are newly married.
	    We send each other
	Charming and varied
	    Cries of joy.
		Wir sind ganz frisch vermählt,
		    Wir schicken uns
		Die verschiedensten entzückenden
		    Freudenrufe zu.

Purs ébats [Frais échos] mêlés au vent
    Qui frissonne !
Gaîtés que le noir couvent
    Assaisonne !
	Fresh echoes mingling with
	    The shivering wind!
	Gaiety that the black convent
	    Heightens!
		Kühle Echos vermengt mit dem Wind,
		    Der fröstelt,
		Heiterkeit, die das schwarze Kloster
		    Würzt.

On effeuille des jasmins
    Sur la pierre
Où l'abbesse joint ses [les] mains
    En prière.
	We pluck the jasmine flowers
	    On the stone
	Where the abbess joins her hands
	    In prayer.
		Wir entlauben den Jasmin
		    Auf dem Stein,
		Wo die Äbtissin ihre Hände vereint
		    Zum Gebet.

[…]	[…]	[…]

On se cherche, on se poursuit,
    On sent croître
Ton aube, amour, dans la nuit
    Du vieux cloître.
	We seek each other, chase each other,
	    We feel your dawn
	Grow in the night, O love,
	    Of the old cloister.
		Wir suchen uns, wir verfolgen uns,
		    Wir fühlen wachsen
		Dein Morgengrauen, Liebe, in der Nacht
		    Des alten Klosters.

On s'en va se becquetant,
    On s'adore,
On s'embrasse à chaque instant,
    Puis encore,
	On we go, kissing and cuddling,
	    Adoring one another,
	Embracing each other every moment,
	    Then again,
		Wir gehen schnäbelnd fort,
		    Wir beten uns an,
		Wir küssen uns jeden Augenblick,
		    Dann nochmals,

Sous les piliers, les arceaux,
    Et les marbres.
C'est l'histoire des oiseaux
    Dans les arbres.
	Beneath the pillars, beneath the vault,
	    And the marbles;
	Just like all the birds
	    In the trees.
		Unter den Pfeilern, den Arkaden
		    Und dem Marmor;
		Dies ist die Geschichte von Vögeln
		    In den Bäumen.

7. {L'Aurore}
Victor Hugo

L'aurore s'allume,
L'ombre épaisse fuit ;
Le rêve et la brume
Vont où va la nuit ;
Paupières et roses
S'ouvrent demi-closes ;
Du réveil des choses
On entend le bruit.

Tout chante et murmure,
Tout parle à la fois,
Fumée et verdure,
Les nids et les toits ;
Le vent parle aux chênes,
L'eau parle aux fontaines ;
Toutes les haleines
Deviennent des voix !

Tout reprend son âme,
L'enfant son hochet,
Le foyer sa flamme,
Le luth son archet ;
Folie ou démence,
Dans le monde immense,
Chacun recommence
Ce qu'il ébauchait.

[…]

8. {L'Absent}
Victor Hugo

– Sentiers où l'herbe se balance,
Vallons, coteaux, bois chevelus,
Pourquoi ce deuil et ce silence ?
– Celui qui venait ne vient plus.

– Pourquoi personne à ta fenêtre,
Et pourquoi ton jardin sans fleurs,
Ô maison ! où donc est ton maître ?
– Je ne sais pas, il est ailleurs.

– Chien, veille au logis. – Pourquoi faire ?
La maison est vide à présent.
– Enfant, qui pleures-tu ? – Mon père.
– Femme, qui pleures-tu ? – L'absent.

– Où s'en [donc] est-il allé ? – Dans l'ombre.
– Flots qui gémissez sur l'écueil,
D'où venez-vous ? – Du bagne sombre.
– Et qu'apportez-vous ? – Un cercueil.

9. Lydia
Leconte de Lisle

Lydia, sur tes roses joues,
Et sur ton col frais, et plus [si] blanc
(Que le lait,) roule étincelant
L'or fluide que tu dénoues.

Le jour qui luit est le meilleur ;
Oublions l'éternelle tombe ;
Laisse tes baisers de colombe
Chanter sur tes lèvres [ta lèvre] en fleur.

Un lis [lys] caché répand sans cesse
Une odeur divine en ton sein ;
Les délices, comme un essaim,
Sortent de toi, jeune déesse !

Je t'aime et meurs, ô mes amours !
Mon âme en baisers m'est ravie.
Ô Lydia, rends-moi la vie,
Que je puisse mourir toujours !

7. {The dawn}
Victor Hugo

The dawn lights up,
Thick shadows flee;
Dream and mist
Go where night goes;
Eyelids and roses
Open half-closed;
The sound of things wakening
Can be heard.

All things sing and murmur,
All things speak at once,
Smoke and verdure,
Nests and roofs;
The wind speaks to the oaks,
Water speaks to the springs;
The breath of all things
Becomes voice!

All things recapture their soul,
The child finds its rattle,
The hearth its flame,
The lute its bow;
Madness or lunacy –
In this vast world,
Everyone begins afresh
What he was sketching out.

[…]

8. {The absent one}
Victor Hugo

– Paths of swaying grass,
Valleys, hillsides, leafy woods,
Why this mourning and this silence?
– He who came here comes no more.

– Why is no one at your window,
And why is your garden without flowers,
O house, where is your master?
– I do not know: he is elsewhere.

– Dog, guard the home. – For what reason?
The house is empty now.
– Child, who is it you mourn? – My father.
– Woman, who is it you mourn? – The absent one.

– Where has he gone? – Into the shadow.
– Waves that moan against the reefs,
From where do you come? – The dark convict prison.
– And what do you carry? – A coffin.

9. Lydia
Leconte de Lisle

Lydia, onto your rosy cheeks
And your neck so fresh and pale,
The liquid gold that you unbind
Cascades glittering down.

The day that dawns is the best;
Let us forget the eternal tomb.
Let your dove-like kisses
Sing on your flowering lips.

A hidden lily unceasingly sheds
A heavenly fragrance in your breast;
Delights without number
Stream from you, young goddess!

I love you and die, O my love!
My soul is ravished by kisses.
O Lydia, give me back my life again,
That I may ever die!

7. {Die Morgenröte}
Victor Hugo

Die Morgenröte entflammt,
Der dichte Schatten flieht;
Der Traum und der Nebel
Gehen, wohin die Nacht geht;
Lider und Rosen
Öffnen sich halbgeschlossen;
Vom Erwachen der Dinge
Hört man das Geräusch.

Alles singt und murmelt,
Alles spricht auf einmal,
Rauch und Grün,
Die Nester und die Dächer;
Der Wind spricht zu den Eichen;
Das Wasser spricht zu den Brunnen;
Aller Atem
Wird zu Stimmen!

Alles erlangt wieder seine Seele zurück,
Das Kind seine Klapper,
Der Herd seine Flamme,
Die Laute ihren Bogen;
Torheit oder Wahnsinn
In der unermeßlich großen Welt,
Beginnt jeder wieder,
Was er angefangen hat.

[…]

8. {Der Abwesende}
Victor Hugo

– Pfade, wo Gräser sich wiegen,
Kleine Täler, sanfte Hügel, buschiges Gehölz,
Warum diese Trauer und diese Stille?
– Derjenige, der immer kam, der kommt nicht mehr.

– Warum ist niemand an deinem Fenster,
Und warum ist dein Garten ohne Blumen,
O Haus! Wo ist denn dein Herr?
– Ich weiß es nicht. Er ist woanders.

– Hund, wache über das Haus. – Um was zu tun?
Das Haus ist jetzt leer.
– Kind, um wen weinst du? – Um meinen Vater.
– Frau, um wen weinst du? – Um den Abwesenden.

– Wo ist er hingegangen? – In den Schatten.
– Fluten die ihr auf den Klippen ächzt,
Woher kommt ihr? – Aus dem düsteren Bagno.
– Und was bringt ihr? – Einen Sarg.

9. Lydia
Leconte de Lisle

Lydia, auf deinen rosa Wangen
Und auf deinem frischen und so weißen Hals
Rollt glitzernd
Das flüssige Gold, welches du löst.

Der Tag, der leuchtet, ist der beste:
Vergessen wir das ewige Grab.
Laß deine Küsse eines Täubchens
Auf deiner erblühenden Lippe singen.

Eine verborgene Lilie verbreitet ständig
Einen göttlichen Duft in deiner Brust;
Die Wonnen, wie ein Schwarm,
Kommen aus dir, junge Göttin!

Ich liebe dich und sterbe, o meine Lieben!
Meine Seele aus Küssen ist entzückt.
O Lydia, gib mir das Leben zurück,
Damit ich immer sterben kann.

10. Hymne
Charles Baudelaire

À la très-chère, à la très-belle
Qui remplit mon cœur de clarté,
À l'ange, à l'idole immortelle,
Salut en immortalité !

Elle se répand dans ma vie
Comme un air imprégné de sel,
Et dans mon âme inassouvie
Verse le goût de l'éternel.

[…]

Comment, amour incorruptible,
T'exprimer avec vérité ?
Grain de musc qui gis, invisible,
Au fond de mon éternité !

À la très-bonne [-chère], à la très-belle
Qui fait ma joie et ma santé [Qui remplit mon cœur de clarté],
À l'ange, à l'idole immortelle,
Salut en immortalité !

10. Hymn
Charles Baudelaire

To the dearest one, the fairest one,
Who fills my heart with light,
To the angel, the immortal idol –
I pledge undying love!

She permeates my life
Like a briny breeze,
And into my unsated soul
Pours the taste of the eternal.

[…]

How, incorruptible love,
Can I express you faithfully?
Grain of musk lying unseen
In the depths of my eternity!

To the best one, the fairest one,
Who is my joy and my health
To the angel, the immortal idol –
I pledge undying love!

10. Hymne
Charles Baudelaire

An die sehr Liebe, an die sehr Schöne,
Die mein Herz mit Licht erfüllt
An den Engel, an das unsterbliche Bild,
Gruß in Unsterblichkeit!

Sie verbreitet sich in meinem Leben
Wie von Salz getränkte Luft,
Und in meine ungestillte Seele
Gießt sie den Vorgeschmack der Ewigkeit.

[…]

Wie, unvergängliche Liebe,
Dich in Wahrheit ausdrücken?
Moschuskorn, welches unsichtbar ruht
Auf dem Grund meiner Ewigkeit!

An die sehr Gute, an die sehr Schöne,
Die mein Herz mit Licht erfüllt
An den Engel, an das unsterbliche Bild,
Gruß in Unsterblichkeit!

11. La Rançon
Charles Baudelaire

L'homme a, pour payer sa rançon,
Deux champs au tuf profond et riche,
Qu'il faut qu'il remue et défriche
Avec le fer de la raison ;

Pour obtenir la moindre rose,
Pour extorquer quelques épis,
Des pleurs salés de son front gris,
Sans cesse il faut qu'il les arrose.

L'un est l'Art, et l'autre l'Amour.
– Pour rendre le juge propice,
Lorsque de la stricte justice
Paraîtra le terrible jour,

Il faudra lui montrer des granges
Pleines de moissons, et de fleurs
Dont les formes et les couleurs
Gagnent le suffrage des Anges.

11. The ransom
Charles Baudelaire

Man, that his ransom may be paid,
Has two fields of soil, rich and deep,
Which he must till and rake
With the blade of reason;

To grow the merest rose,
To reap but meagre ears of corn,
He must water them night and morn
With salt tears from his ashen brow.

One field is Art, the other Love.
– To propitiate the judge,
When the terrible day
Of strict justice dawns,

He will have to show him barns abrim
With harvested crops and flowers,
Whose forms and colours gain
The approval of the seraphim.

11. Das Lösegeld
Charles Baudelaire

Der Mensch hat, um sein Lösegeld zu zahlen,
Zwei Felder tiefen und reichen Tuffs,
Den er umgraben und roden muß
Mit der Pflugschar des Verstandes.

Um die kleinste Rose zu bekommen,
Um einige Ähren zu erzwingen,
Mit salzigen Tränen seiner grauen Stirn
Muß er sie unaufhörlich gießen.

Eines ist die Kunst, das andere die Liebe.
– Um den Richter günstig zu stimmen,
Wenn des strengen Gerichts
Schrecklicher Tag erscheint.

Muß man ihm Scheunen zeigen
Voll Ernte und Blumen,
Deren Formen und Farben
Die Stimmen der Engel gewinnen.

12. Chant d'automne
Charles Baudelaire

Bientôt nous plongerons dans les froides ténèbres ;
Adieu, vive clarté de nos étés trop courts !
J'entends déjà tomber avec des chocs funèbres
 [un choc funèbre]
Le bois retentissant sur le pavé des cours.

[…]

J'écoute en frémissant chaque bûche qui tombe ;
L'échafaud qu'on bâtit n'a pas d'écho plus sourd.
Mon esprit est pareil à la tour qui succombe
Sous les coups du bélier infatigable et lourd.

Il me semble, bercé par ce choc monotone,
Qu'on cloue en grande hâte un cercueil quelque part…
Pour qui ? – C'était hier l'été ; voici l'automne !
Ce bruit mystérieux sonne comme un départ.

II

J'aime de vos longs yeux la lumière verdâtre,
 Douce beauté, mais tout aujourd'hui [aujourd'hui tout] m'est amer,
Et rien, ni votre amour, ni le boudoir, ni l'âtre,
Ne me vaut le soleil rayonnant sur la mer.

[…]

12. Song of autumn
Charles Baudelaire

Soon we shall plunge into cold shadows;
Farewell, vivid light of our too-short summers!
Already I hear the funereal thud
Of echoing logs on the courtyard floor.

[…]

I listen, trembling, to the fall of each log;
A gallows being built makes no duller sound.
My spirit is like the tower that falls
To the remorseless blows of the battering-ram.

Rocked by those monotone blows, it seems
Somewhere in haste they are nailing a coffin.
But whose? Yesterday summer; autumn now!
This eerie sound rings like some farewell.

II

I love the emerald glow of your wide eyes,
My sweet, but all today is bitter for me,
And nothing, not your love, the boudoir, or the hearth
Can compare with the sunlight on the sea.

[…]

12. Herbstgesang
Charles Baudelaire

Bald tauchen wir in die kalte Finsternis;
Leb wohl, lebendiger Lichtschein unserer zu kurzen Sommer!
Ich höre schon mit unheimlichen Schlägen fallen
Das Holz, das auf das Pflaster der Höfe kracht.

[…]

Ich höre erschauernd jedes fallende Scheit;
Das Schafott, das man baute, hat kein dumpferes Echo.
Mein Geist ist wie der Turm, der einstürzt
Unter den unermüdlichen und schweren Schlägen des Sturmbocks.

Es scheint mir, gewiegt durch den einförmigen Schlag,
Daß man irgendwo in großer Hast einen Sarg zusammennagelt.
Für wen? – Gestern war Sommer, heute ist nun Herbst!
Dieser geheimnisvolle Lärm klingt wie ein Abschied.

II

Ich liebe mit sehnsuchtsvollem Blick das grünliche Licht,
Sanfte Schönheit, aber heute erscheint mir alles bitter,
Und nichts, weder eure Liebe, noch das Gemach, noch der Herd
Ersetzt mir die über dem Meer scheinende Sonne.

[…]

13. Les Matelots
Théophile Gautier

Sur l'eau bleue et profonde
Nous allons voyageant,
Environnant le monde
D'un sillage d'argent,
Des îles de la Sonde,
De l'Inde au ciel brûlé,
Jusqu'au pôle gelé…

[…]

Nous pensons à la terre
Que nous fuyons toujours,
À notre vieille mère,
À nos jeunes amours ;
Mais la vague légère
Avec son doux refrain,
Endort notre chagrin.

[…]

Existence sublime !
Bercés par notre nid,
Nous vivons sur l'abîme
Au sein de l'infini ;
Des flots rasant la cime,
Dans le grand désert bleu
Nous marchons avec Dieu !

14. {Seule !}
Théophile Gautier

Dans un baiser l'onde au rivage
    Dit ses douleurs ;
Pour consoler la fleur sauvage,
    L'aube a des pleurs ;
Le vent du soir conte sa plainte
    Au vieux cyprès ;
La tourterelle au térébinthe
    Ses longs regrets.

Aux flots dormants, quand tout repose !
    Hors la douleur,
La lune parle, et dit la cause
    De sa pâleur.
Ton dôme blanc, Sainte-Sophie,
    Parle au ciel bleu,
Et, tout rêveur, le ciel confie
    Son rêve à Dieu.

Arbre ou tombeau, colombe ou rose,
    Onde ou rocher,
Tout, ici-bas, a quelque chose
    Pour s'épancher…
Moi, je suis seule, et rien au monde
    Ne me répond,
Rien que ta voix morne et profonde,
    Sombre Hellespont !

15. Lamento (La Chanson du pêcheur)
Théophile Gautier

    Ma belle amie est morte :
    Je pleurerai toujours ;
    Sous la tombe elle emporte
    Mon âme et mes amours.
    Dans le ciel, sans m'attendre,
    Elle s'en retourna ;
    L'ange qui l'emmena
    Ne voulut pas me prendre.
    Que mon sort est amer !
Ah ! sans amour, s'en aller sur la mer !

---

13. The sailors
Théophile Gautier

We journey
On the deep blue sea,
Encircling the world
With a silver wake.
From the Sunda Islands,
From India's burning sky,
As far as the frozen pole…

[…]

We think of the land
We are leaving behind,
Of our old mother,
Of our young loves.
But the light wave
With its sweet refrain
Lulls our sorrow to sleep.

[…]

Sublime existence,
Rocked in our crow's-nest,
We live on the abyss
At the heart of the infinite,
Skimming the crests of waves.
In the great blue desert
We go with God!

14. {Alone!}
Théophile Gautier

In a kiss, the wave to the shore
    Voices its grief;
To console the wild flower
    Dawn has its tears;
The evening breeze tells its sorrow
    To the ancient cypress,
The turtle-dove to the terebinth
    Its endless regrets.

To the sleeping waves, when all is quiet
    But pain,
The moon speaks, explaining why
    It is pale.
Your white dome, Santa Sophia,
    Speaks to the blue sky,
And, lost in dreams, the sky confides
    Its dream to God.

Tree or tomb, dove or rose,
    Wave or rock,
Everything here below
    Has something to pour out.
But I am alone, and nothing on earth
    Ever responds to me,
Nothing but your deep and gloomy voice,
    Sombre Hellespont!

15. Lament (Song of the fisherman)
Théophile Gautier

    My dearest love is dead:
    I shall weep for evermore;
    To the tomb she takes with her
    My soul and all my love.
    Without waiting for me
    She has returned to Heaven;
    The angel who took her away
    Did not wish to take me.
    How bitter is my fate!
Alas! to set sail loveless across the sea!

---

13. Die Matrosen
Théophile Gautier

Über dem blauen und tiefen Wasser
Fahren wir reisend,
Umschließen die Welt
Mit einem silbernen Kielwasser,
Von den Sundainseln,
Von Indien mit dem verbrannten Himmel
Bis zum vereisten Pol…

[…]

Wir denken an die Erde
Der wir ständig entfliehen,
An unsere alte Mutter,
An unsere jungen Lieben;
Aber die leichte Welle
Mit ihrem lieblichen Refrain
Wiegt unseren Kummer in den Schlaf.

[…]

Erhebendes Dasein!
Gewiegt durch unser Nest,
Leben wir über dem Abgrund
Am Busen der Unendlichkeit;
Die Krone der Wellen streifend,
In der großen blauen Wüste
Gehen wir mit Gott!

14. {Allein!}
Théophile Gautier

In einem Kuß erzählt die Welle dem Ufer
    Ihre Schmerzen;
Um die wilde Blume zu trösten,
    Hat die Morgendämmerung Tränen;
Der Abendwind erzählt seine Klage
    Den alten Zypressen,
die Turteltaube der Terebinthe
    Ihr langes Leid.

Zu den schlafenden Fluten, wenn alles ruht
    Ohne Schmerz,
Spricht der Mond und erzählt den Grund
    Seiner Blässe.
Deine weiße Kuppel, Heilige Sophie,
    Spricht zum blauen Himmel,
Und, ganz verträumt, vertraut der Himmel
    Seinen Traum dem Gotte an.

Baum oder Grab, Taube oder Rose,
    Welle oder Felsen,
Alles hier unten hat etwas,
    Um sich anzuvertrauen…
Ich, ich bin allein, und nichts auf der Welt
    Antwortet mir,
Nichts als deine bedrückte und tiefe Stimme,
    Dunkler Hellespont.

15. Lamento (Lied des Fischers)
Théophile Gautier

    Meine schöne Freundin ist tot,
    Ich werde immer weinen;
    Ins Grab nimmt sie
    Meine Seele und mein Leben mit.
    In den Himmel, ohne mich zu erwarten,
    Ging sie wieder fort;
    Der Engel, der sie wegbrachte,
    Wollte mich nicht mitnehmen.
    Wie bitter mein Schicksal ist!
Ach! Ohne Liebe über das Meer zu fahren!

XXXIV

La blanche créature	The pure white soul	Das weiße Geschöpf
Est couchée au cercueil.	Lies in her coffin.	Liegt im Sarg.
Comme dans la nature	How everything in nature	Wie mir in der Natur
Tout me paraît en deuil !	Seems to mourn!	Alles zu trauern scheint!
La colombe oubliée	The forsaken dove	Die vergessene Taube
Pleure et songe à l'absent ;	Weeps, dreaming of its absent mate;	Weint und denkt an den Abwesenden;
Mon âme pleure et sent	My soul weeps and feels	Meine Seele weint und spürt,
Qu'elle est dépareillée.	Itself adrift.	Daß ihr viel genommen ist.
Que mon sort est amer !	How bitter is my fate!	Wie bitter mein Schicksal ist!
Ah ! sans amour, s'en aller sur la mer !	Alas! to set sail loveless across the sea!	Ah! Ohne Liebe über das Meer zu fahren!
Sur moi la nuit immense	The immense night above me	Über mir die unendliche Nacht
S'étend [Plane] comme un linceul ;	Is spread like a shroud;	Schwebt wie ein Leichentuch;
Je chante ma romance	I sing my song	Ich singe meine Romanze,
Que le ciel entend seul.	Which heaven alone can hear.	Welche allein der Himmel hört.
Ah ! comme elle était belle	Ah! how beautiful she was,	Ah! Wie schön sie war;
Et comme [combien] je l'aimais !	And how I loved her!	Und wie ich sie liebte!
Je n'aimerai jamais	I shall never love a woman	Ich werde niemals wieder
Une femme autant qu'elle.	As I loved her.	Eine Frau so sehr lieben wie sie.
Que mon sort est amer !	How bitter is my fate!	Wie bitter mein Schicksal ist!
Ah ! sans amour, s'en aller sur la mer !	Alas! to set sail loveless across the sea!	Ah! Ohne Liebe über das Meer zu fahren!

16. Tristesse
Théophile Gautier

16. Sadness
Théophile Gautier

16. Traurigkeit
Théophile Gautier

Avril est de retour.	April has returned.	April ist zurück.
La première des roses,	The first of the roses	Die erste der Rosen
De ses lèvres mi-closes	From half-open lips	Lacht mit ihren halbgeschlossenen Lippen
Rit au premier beau jour ;	Smiles at the first fine day;	An dem ersten schönen Tag.
La terre bienheureuse	The happy earth	Die glückselige Erde
S'ouvre et s'épanouit.	Opens and blooms:	Öffnet sich und erblüht;
Tout aime, tout jouit.	All is love and ecstasy.	Alles liebt, alles freut sich.
Hélas ! j'ai dans le cœur une tristesse affreuse.	Alas! a dreadful sadness afflicts my heart.	Ach! Ich habe eine schreckliche Traurigkeit im Herzen!
Les buveurs en gaîté,	The merry drinkers	Die fröhlichen Trinker
Dans leurs chansons vermeilles,	With their crimson songs	In ihren feurigen Liedern
Célèbrent sous les treilles	Drink, beneath trellises,	Rühmen unter der Weinlaube
Le vin et la beauté ;	To wine and beauty;	Den Wein der Schönheit;
La musique joyeuse,	The joyous music	Die fröhliche Musik
Avec leur rire clair	With their bright laughter	Verbreitet sich zusammen mit ihrem klaren Lachen
S'éparpille dans l'air.	Scatters in the air.	In der Luft.
Hélas ! j'ai dans le cœur une tristesse affreuse.	Alas! a dreadful sadness afflicts my heart.	Ach! Ich habe eine schreckliche Traurigkeit im Herzen!
En déshabillés blancs [déshabillé blanc],	In scanty white dresses	Im weißen Negligé
Les jeunes demoiselles	Young girls	Gehen die jungen Damen
S'en vont sous les tonnelles	Pass beneath the arbours	In die Lauben
Au bras de leurs galants [leur galant] ;	On their lovers' arms;	Am Arm ihres Kavaliers;
La lune langoureuse	The languishing moon	Der schmachtende Mond
Argente leurs baisers	Silvers their long	Versilbert ihre langen Küsse.
Longuement appuyés.	Insistent kisses.	
Hélas ! j'ai dans le cœur une tristesse affreuse.	Alas! a dreadful sadness afflicts my heart.	Ach! Ich habe eine schreckliche Traurigkeit im Herzen!
Moi, je n'aime plus rien,	But I love nothing any more,	Ich liebe nichts mehr,
Ni l'homme, ni la femme,	Neither man nor woman,	Weder Mann noch Frau,
Ni mon corps, ni mon âme,	Neither my body nor my soul,	Weder meinen Körper noch meine Seele,
Pas même mon vieux chien.	Nor even my old dog;	Selbst meinen alten Hund nicht.
Allez dire qu'on creuse,	Send for them to dig	Geht und ordnet an, daß man gräbt
Sous le pâle gazon,	Beneath the pallid turf	Unter dem blassen Rasen
Une fosse sans nom.	A nameless grave.	Eine Grube ohne Namen.
Hélas ! j'ai dans le cœur une tristesse affreuse.	Alas! a dreadful sadness afflicts my heart.	Ach! Ich habe eine schreckliche Traurigkeit im Herzen!

17. Aubade
Louis Pomey

17. Dawn song
Louis Pomey

17. Morgenständchen
Louis Pommey

L'oiseau dans le buisson	The bird in the thicket	Der Vogel im Gebüsch
A salué l'aurore,	Has greeted the dawn,	Hat die Morgenröte begrüßt,
Et d'un pâle rayon	And the horizon is tinged	Und mit einem blassen Strahl
L'horizon se colore,	With a pale ray –	Schließt sich der Horizont.
Voici le frais matin !	A fresh morning has broken!	Da ist der frische Morgen!
Pour voir les fleurs à la lumière,	To see the flowers all around	Um die Blumen im Licht
S'ouvrir de toute part,	Opening to the light,	Von überall sich öffnen zu sehen,
Entr'ouvre ta paupière,	Open your eyes a little,	Öffne dein Lid,
Ô vierge au doux regard !	O maiden with the gentle look.	O Jungfrau mit dem lieblichen Blick!

La voix de ton amant
A dissipé ton rêve,
Je vois ton rideau blanc
Qui tremble et se soulève,
D'amour signal charmant!
Descends sur ce tapis de mousse,
La brise est tiède encor,
Et la lumière est douce,
Accours, ô mon trésor!

18. Barcarolle
Marc Monnier

Gondolier du Rialto,
Mon château
    C'est la lagune,
Mon jardin c'est le Lido,
Mon rideau,
    Le clair de lune.

Gondolier du Grand-Canal,
Pour fanal
    J'ai la croisée
Où s'allument tous les soirs
Tes yeux noirs,
    Mon épousée!

Ma gondole est aux heureux;
Deux à deux
    Je les promène,
Et les vents légers et frais
Sont discrets
    Sur mon domaine.

J'ai passé dans les amours,
Plus de jours
    Et de nuits folles,
Que Venise n'a d'îlots,
Que ses flots
    N'ont de gondoles.
[…]

19. Ici-bas
Sully Prudhomme

Ici-bas tous les lilas meurent,
Tous les chants des oiseaux sont courts,
Je rêve aux étés qui demeurent
    Toujours…

Ici-bas les lèvres effleurent
Sans rien laisser de leur velours,
Je rêve aux baisers qui demeurent
    Toujours…

Ici-bas tous les hommes pleurent
Leurs amitiés ou leurs amours,
Je rêve aux couples qui demeurent
    Toujours…

20. Au bord de l'eau
Sully Prudhomme

S'asseoir tous deux au bord du flot qui passe,
    Le voir passer;
Tous deux, s'il glisse un nuage en l'espace,
    Le voir glisser;
À l'horizon, s'il fume un toit de chaume,
    Le voir fumer;
Aux alentours si quelque fleur embaume,
    S'en embaumer;
[…]
Entendre au pied du saule où l'eau murmure
    L'eau murmurer;
Ne pas sentir, tant que ce rêve dure,
    Le temps durer;

Your lover's voice
Has dispersed your dream;
I see your white veil
Tremble and lift –
That charming sign of love!
Come down to this mossy carpet,
The breeze is still balmy
And the light is soft.
Make haste, my precious love!

18. Barcarolle
Marc Monnier

Gondolier of the Rialto,
My castle
    is the lagoon,
My garden is the Lido,
My curtain
    the moonlight.

Gondolier of the Grand Canal,
My beacon
    is the casement window,
Where every night
Your dark eyes shine anew,
    my bride.

My gondola is for the happy,
I take them out
    two by two,
And the fresh, light breezes
Are discreet
    in my domain.

I have spent more days
And intoxicated nights
    in loving
Than Venice has islands,
Than its waves
    have gondolas.
[…]

19. In this world
Sully Prudhomme

In this world all the flowers wither,
The sweet songs of the birds are brief;
I dream of summers that will last
    Always…

In this world lips touch but lightly,
And no taste of sweetness remains;
I dream of a kiss that will last
    Always…

In this world every man is mourning
His lost friendship or his lost love;
I dream of fond lovers abiding
    Always…

20. By the water
Sully Prudhomme

To sit together on the bank of a flowing stream,
    To watch it flow;
Together, if a cloud glides by,
    To watch it glide;
On the horizon, if smoke rises from thatch,
    To watch it rise;
If nearby a flower smells sweet,
    To savour its sweetness;
[…]
To listen at the foot of the willow, where water
    murmurs,
    To the murmuring water;
Not to feel, while this dream passes,

Die Stimme deines Liebhabers
Hat deinen Traum vertrieben,
Ich sehe deinen weißen Schleier,
Der zittert und sich lüftet
Aus Liebe, bezauberndes Zeichen!
Komm herunter auf diesen Teppich aus Moos,
Der Wind ist noch lind
Und das Licht ist mild;
Eile herbei, o mein Schatz!

18. Barcarolle
Marc Monnier

Gondoliere vom Rialto,
Mein Schloß
    Ist die Lagune,
Mein Garten ist der Lido,
Mein Schleier
    Der Mondenschein.

Gondoliere vom Großen Kanal,
Als Laterne
    Habe ich das Fenster,
Wo jeden Abend
Deine schwarzen Augen aufleuchten,
    Meine Gattin!

Meine Gondel gehört den Glücklichen,
Immer zu zweien
    Fahre ich sie spazieren,
Und die leichten und frischen Winde
Sind diskret
    Über meinem Bereich.

Ich habe zwischen den Sich-Liebenden
Mehr verrückte Tage
    Und Nächte verbracht
Als Venedig Inseln hat,
Als seine Fluten
    Gondeln haben.
[…]

19. Auf Erden
Sully Prudhomme

Hier auf Erden sterben alle Flieder,
Alle Lieder der Vögel sind kurz;
Ich träume von Sommern, die bleiben
    Für immer…

Hier auf Erden berühren die Lippen nur flüchtig
Ohne etwas von ihrer Zartheit zu lassen;
Ich träume von Küssen, die bleiben
    Für immer…

Hier auf Erden beweinen alle Menschen
Ihre Freundschaften oder ihre Liebe;
Ich träume von Paaren, die bleiben
    Für immer…

20. Am Ufer des Wassers
Sully Prudhomme

Sich zu zweit ans Ufer eines vorbeifließenden
    Stromes setzen;
    Ihn vorbeifließen sehen;
Alle beide, wenn eine Wolke im Raum gleitet,
    Sie gleiten sehen;
Am Horizont, wenn ein Strohdach qualmt,
    Es qualmen sehen;
In der Gegend, wenn irgendeine Blume duftet,
    Sich mit Duft erfüllen;
[…]
Am Fuß der Weide, wo das Wasser plätschert,
    Das Wasser plätschern hören;
Nicht spüren, solange dieser Traum dauert,

Mais n'apportant de passion profonde
    Qu'à s'adorer,
Sans nul souci des querelles du monde,
    Les ignorer;
Et seuls, heureux [tous deux] devant tout ce qui lasse,
    Sans se lasser,
Sentir l'amour, devant tout ce qui passe,
    Ne point passer!

The passing of time;
But feeling no deep passion,
    Except to adore each other,
With no cares for the quarrels of the world,
    To know nothing of them;
And alone together, seeing all that tires,
    Not to tire of each other,
To feel that love, in the face of all that passes,
    Shall never pass!

Wie die Zeit andauert;
Sondern lediglich der gegenseitigen Bewunderung
    Leidenschaft entgegenbringend,
    Sich bewundern;
Ohne jede Sorge um den Zank der Welt,
    Nichts von ihm wissen;
Und allein, zu zweit vor allem, was ermattet,
    Ohne zu ermatten,
Die Liebe, vor allem, was vergeht,
    Nicht vergehen spüren.

21. Après un rêve
Romain Bussine

Dans un sommeil que charmait ton image
Je rêvais le bonheur, ardent mirage,
Tes yeux étaient plus doux, ta voix pure et sonore,
Tu rayonnais comme un ciel éclairé par l'aurore;

Tu m'appelais et je quittais la terre
Pour m'enfuir avec toi vers la lumière,
Les cieux pour nous entr'ouvraient leurs nues,
Splendeurs inconnues, lueurs divines entrevues,

Hélas! triste réveil des songes,
Je t'appelle, ô nuit, rends moi tes mensonges!
Reviens, radieuse,
Reviens, ô nuit mystérieuse!

21. After a dream
Romain Bussine

In sleep made sweet by a vision of you
I dreamed of happiness, fervent illusion,
Your eyes were softer, your voice pure and ringing,
You shone like a sky that was lit by the dawn;

You called me and I departed the earth
To flee with you toward the light,
The heavens parted their clouds for us,
We glimpsed unknown splendours, celestial fires.

Alas, alas, sad awakening from dreams!
I summon you, O night, give me back your delusions;
Return, return in radiance,
Return, O mysterious night!

21. Nach einem Traum
Romain Bussine

In einem Schlafe, der deinem Bild schmeichelte
Träumte ich von Glück, glühende Täuschung,
Deine Augen waren lieblicher, deine Stimme rein
    und klangvoll,
Du strahltest wie ein von der Morgenröte erhellter
    Himmel;

Du riefst mich, und ich verließ die Erde,
Um mit dir ins Licht zu entfliehn,
Der Himmel öffnete seine Wolken für uns,
Unbekannter Glanz, flüchtig gesehener göttlicher
    Schein.

Ach! ach, trauriges Erwachen aus den Träumen.
Ich rufe dich, o Nacht, gib mir Deine Lügen zurück;
Komm zurück, strahlende,
Komm zurück, o geheimnisvolle Nacht!

21. {Après un rêve}
Anon. Tuscan, coll. Niccolò Tommaseo

Levati, sol, che la luna è levata;
Leva dagli occhi miei tanto dormire.
Il traditor del sonno m'ha ingannata;
Il meglio [bello] amante m'ha fatto sparire.

Se lo ritrovo quell' amor giocondo,
Io mai più mi farò tradir del sonno.
Se lo ritrovo quell' amor gentile,
Mai più dal sonno mi farò tradire.

Lève-toi, soleil, car la lune est levée;
Empêche mes yeux de tant dormir.
Le traître sommeil m'a perdue,
Et m'a fait disparaître le bel amant.

Si je retrouve cet amour joyeux,
Je ne me laisserai plus trahir par le sommeil.
Si je retrouve cet amour si doux,
Plus jamais le sommeil ne ma trahira.

(Traduction: Dennis Collins)

Rise, sun, for the moon is high;
Take from my eyes all this slumber.
Treacherous sleep has deceived me;
Has cheated me of my handsome lover.

If I find that playful love again,
I never again shall let sleep betray me.
If I find that sweet love again,
Never again by sleep shall I be tricked.

(Translation: Roy Howat)

Sonne, geh auf, denn der Mond steht hoch;
Nimm aus meinen Augen den vielen Schlaf.
Trügerischer Schlaf hat mich getäuscht;
Mich um den schmucken Liebsten betrogen.

Falls ich wiederfinde diese heitere Liebe,
Laß ich mich nie mehr vom Schlaf hintergehen.
Falls ich wiederfinde diese wunderbare Liebe,
Laß ich mich nie mehr vom Schlaf überlisten.

(Übersetzung: Anne Steeb/Bernd Müller)

22. Sérénade toscane
Romain Bussine

Ô toi que berce un rêve enchanteur,
Tu dors tranquille en ton lit solitaire,
Éveille-toi, regarde le chanteur,
Esclave de tes yeux, dans la nuit claire !

Éveille-toi, mon âme, ma pensée,
Entends ma voix par la brise emportée,
Entends ma voix chanter !
Entends ma voix pleurer dans la rosée !

Sous ta fenêtre en vain ma voix expire,
Et chaque nuit je redis mon martyre,
Sans autre abri que la voûte étoilée,
Le vent brise ma voix et la nuit est glacée ;

Mon chant s'éteint en un accent suprême,
Ma lèvre tremble en murmurant, je t'aime,
Je ne peux plus chanter !
Ah ! daigne te montrer ! daigne apparaître !

Si j'étais sûr que tu ne veux paraître
Je m'en irais, pour t'oublier, demander au sommeil
De me bercer jusqu'au matin vermeil,
De me bercer jusqu'à ne plus t'aimer !

22. Tuscan serenade
Romain Bussine

You whom a lovely dream lulls,
You sleep quietly in your lonely bed,
Awake, gaze at the singer,
Enslaved by your eyes in the moonlit night!

Awake, my soul, my thoughts,
Hear my voice borne on the breeze:
Hear my voice sing,
Hear my voice weep in the dew!

Beneath your window my voice fades in vain,
And each night I tell my torment anew,
With no shelter but the starlit vault:
The wind drowns my voice and the night is chill.

My song dies on a final cadence.
My lips quiver as they murmur: I love you,
I can no longer sing!
Ah! deign to show yourself! Deign to appear!

If I was sure you did not wish to appear,
I would go away to forget you, I would ask of sleep
To cradle me until the rosy dawn,
To cradle me till I loved you no more!

22. Toskanische Serenade
Romain Bussine

O du, die ein bezaubernder Traum wiegt,
Du schläfst ruhig in deinem einsamen Bett,
Wach auf, sieh' den Sänger,
Den Sklaven deiner Augen, in der hellen Nacht.

Wach auf, meine Seele, mein Denken,
Höre meine durch den Wind getragene Stimme,
Höre meine Stimme singen,
Höre meine Stimme weinen im Tau!

Unter deinem Fenster verhallt meine Stimme
    vergebens,
Und jede Nacht wiederhole ich mein Leiden,
Ohne anderen Unterstand als das Sternengewölbe,
Der Wind bricht meine Stimme und die Nacht ist eiskalt.

Mein Gesang erstirbt mit einem letzten Ton,
Meine Lippe zittert während sie murmelt: ich liebe dich,
Ich kann nicht mehr singen!
Ah! wage dich zu zeigen! Wage zu erscheinen!

Wenn ich sicher wäre, daß du nicht erscheinen willst,
Würde ich gehen, um dich zu vergessen, den Schlaf
    bitten,
Mich bis zum purpurroten Morgen zu wiegen,
Mich zu wiegen, bis ich dich nicht mehr liebe.

22. [Sérénade toscane]
Anon. Tuscan, coll. Niccolò Tommaseo

O tu che dormi e riposata stai
'N testo bel letto senza pensamento,
Risvegliati un pochino, e sentirai
Tuo servo che per te fa un gran lamento.
Risvegliati, madonna, in tempo, un'ora:
Lo sentirai cantar che l'è di fuora.

Non posso più cantar:
Stanotte son dormito a ciel sereno,
E son dormito all'ombra d'una noce
Dove non era nè paglia nè fieno.

Non posso più cantar, che non ho voce,
E m'entra in bocca, e non mi lassa dire,
Non posso più cantar, che tira vento!

L'ho ben paura di perdarlo il tempo.
Fossi sicur, non andere' a dormire.
Fossi sicuro, a dormir 'n andarei:
Chesto bel tempo non lo perdarei.

Ô toi qui dors, calme
Et insouciante dans ce beau lit,
Réveille-toi un instant et tu entendras
La longue plainte de ton serviteur.
Réveille-toi, ma dame, à cet instant, une heure :
Tu l'entendras chanter, il est dehors.

Je ne peux plus chanter :
Cette nuit, j'ai dormi sous la voûte étoilée,
J'ai dormi à l'ombre d'un noyer
Sans paille ni foin.

Je ne peux plus chanter, je n'ai plus de voix,
Elle entre dans ma bouche mais je reste muet,
Je ne peux plus chanter, le vent se lève !

J'ai grande peur de perdre mon temps.
Si j'en étais sûr, je n'irais pas dormir.
Si j'en étais sûr, dormir je n'irais pas :
Ce temps si beau je ne le perdrais pas.

(Traduction : Diego Ropele)

Oh you who sleep, at rest
In this beautiful bed without a care,
Awaken a little, and you will hear
The great lamentations of your servant.
Awake, my lady, in time, for an hour:
You will hear him sing, for he is outside.

I can sing no more:
Last night I slept under the clear sky,
I slept in the shade of a nut-tree
Where there was neither straw nor hay.

I can sing no more, for I have no voice,
It enters my mouth, but does not let me speak,
I can sing no more, for the wind is blowing!

I am much afeared that time is fleeing.
Were I sure, I would not go to sleep.
Were I sure, to sleep I would not go:
I would not lose this beautiful moment.

(Translation: Roy Howat/Emily Kilpatrick
with Angela Newport/Valeria Schiavone)

Oh Du, die Du schläfst und ruhst
Sorgenlos, in diesem prächtigen Bett,
Erwache ein wenig, um Deinen Ergebenen zu hören,
Der für Dich ein Klagelied singt.
Erwache mein Fräulein, denn schon bald, in einer Stunde:
Wirst Du ihn draußen für Dich singen hören.

Ich kann nicht mehr singen:
Heute Nacht habe ich unter klarem Himmel geschlafen,
Im Schatten eines Nussbaumes,
Wo es weder Stroh noch Heu gab.

Ich kann nicht mehr singen, denn ich habe keine Stimme,
Die Worte im Mund, doch ich kann sie nicht aussprechen,
Ich kann nicht mehr singen, denn es windet!

Ich habe Angst sie zu verlieren – die Zeit.
Wäre ich sicher, würde ich nicht schlafen gehen.
Wäre ich sicher, schlafen gehen würde ich nicht:
Denn diese selige Zeit ließe ich mir nicht entgehen.

(Übersetzung: KERN AG, Sprachendienste)

XXXVIII

23. Sylvie
Paul de Choudens

Si tu veux savoir[,] ma belle,
Où s'envole à tire d'aile,
L'oiseau qui chantait sur l'ormeau ?
Je te le dirai, ma belle,
Il vole vers qui l'appelle
    Vers celui-là
    Qui l'aimera !

Si tu veux savoir, ma blonde,
Pourquoi sur terre et sur l'onde
La nuit tout s'anime et s'unit ?
Je te le dirai, ma blonde,
C'est qu'il est une heure au monde
    Où, loin du jour,
    Veille l'amour !

Si tu veux savoir, Sylvie,
Pourquoi j'aime à la folie
Tes yeux brillants et langoureux ?
Je te le dirai, Sylvie,
C'est que sans toi dans la vie
    Tout pour mon cœur
    N'est que douleur !

24–26. Poème d'un jour
Charles Grandmougin
Rencontre

J'étais triste et pensif quand je t'ai rencontrée ;
Je sens moins, aujourd'hui, mon obstiné tourment.
Ô dis-moi, serais-tu la femme inespérée,
Et le rêve idéal poursuivi vainement ?

Ô, passante aux doux yeux, serais-tu donc l'amie
Qui rendrait le bonheur au poète isolé,
Et vas-tu rayonner, sur mon âme affermie,
Comme le ciel natal sur un cœur d'exilé ?

Ta tristesse sauvage, à la mienne pareille,
Aime à voir le soleil décliner sur la mer !
Devant l'immensité ton extase s'éveille,
Et le charme des soirs à ta belle âme est cher.

Une mystérieuse et douce sympathie
Déjà m'enchaîne à toi comme un vivant lien,
Et mon âme frémit, par l'amour envahie,
Et mon cœur te chérit sans te connaître bien.

Toujours

Vous me demandez de me taire,
De fuir loin de vous pour jamais,
Et de m'en aller, solitaire,
Sans me rappeler qui j'aimais !

Demandez plutôt aux étoiles
De tomber dans l'immensité,
À la nuit de perdre ses voiles,
Au jour de perdre sa clarté !

Demandez à la mer immense
De dessécher ses vastes flots,
Et, quand les vents sont en démence,
D'apaiser ses sombres sanglots !

Mais n'espérez pas que mon âme
S'arrache à ses âpres douleurs,
Et se dépouille de sa flamme
Comme le printemps de ses fleurs !

---

23. Sylvie
Paul de Choudens

If you wish to know, my sweet,
Where the bird is hastening
That was singing in the elm,
I shall tell you, my sweet,
It flies to the one who calls it,
    To the one
    Who will love it!

If you wish to know, my fair one,
Why on land and sea
All things at night revive and merge,
I shall tell you, my fair one:
There is one hour in the world,
    When far from day
    Love stands watch!

If you wish to know, Sylvie,
Why I love to distraction
Your bright and yearning eyes,
I shall tell you, Sylvie,
That without you in my life,
    My heart feels
    Naught but pain!

24–26. One Day's Poem
Charles Grandmougin
Meeting

I was sad and pensive when I met you,
Today I feel less my persistent pain;
O tell me, could you be the long hoped-for woman,
And the ideal dream pursued in vain?

O passer-by with gentle eyes, could you be the friend
To restore the lonely poet's happiness,
And will you shine on my steadfast soul
Like native sky on an exiled heart?

Your timid sadness, like my own,
Loves to watch the sun set on the sea!
Such boundless space awakes your rapture,
And your fair soul prizes the evenings' charm.

A mysterious and gentle sympathy
Already binds me to you like a living bond,
And my soul quivers, overcome by love,
And my heart, without knowing you well, adores you.

Forever

You ask me to be silent,
To flee far from you for ever
And to go my way alone,
Forgetting whom I loved!

Rather ask the stars
To fall into infinity,
The night to lose its veils,
The day to lose its light!

Ask the boundless sea
To drain its mighty waves,
And the raging winds
To calm their dismal sobbing!

But do not expect my soul
To tear itself from bitter sorrow,
Nor to shed its passion
As springtime sheds its flowers!

---

23. Sylvie
Paul de Choudens

Wenn du wissen willst, meine Schöne,
Wohin pfeilschnell fliegt
Der Vogel, der auf der Ulme sang?
Werde ich es dir sagen, meine Schöne,
Er fliegt zu dem, der ihn ruft,
    Zu jenem,
    Der ihn lieben wird!

Wenn du wissen willst, meine Blonde,
Warum auf Erden und auf der Welle
Sich nachts alles belebt und vereint?
Werde ich es dir sagen, meine Blonde,
Weil es eine Stunde auf der Welt gibt,
    Zu der weit vom Tage
    Die Liebe wacht!

Wenn du wissen willst, Sylvie,
Warum ich wahnsinnig liebe
Deine glänzenden und schmachtenden Augen?
Werde ich es dir sagen, Sylvie,
Es ist, weil im Leben ohne dich
    Alles für mein Herz
    Nur Schmerz ist.

24–26. Gedicht eines Tages
Charles Grandmougin
Begegnung

Ich war traurig und nachdenklich als ich dich kennengelernt habe,
Heute fühle ich meine hartnäckige Qual weniger,
O sage mir, bist du die unerwartete Frau
Und der vergeblich verfolgte ideale Traum?

O Passantin mit den lieblichen Augen, bist du etwa die Freundin,
Die das Glück dem einsamen Dichter zurückgibt
Und wirst du über meiner bestärkten Seele strahlen
Wie der heimatliche Himmel über dem Herz eines Verbannten?

Deine wilde Traurigkeit, gleich der meinen,
Liebt es, die Sonne über dem Meer herabsinken zu sehen!
Vor der Unermeßlichkeit erwacht deine Verzückung,
Und der Zauber der Abende ist deiner schönen Seele teuer.

Eine geheimnisvolle und liebliche Sympathie
Bindet mich schon an dich wie ein lebendiges Band,
Und meine Seele schaudert, von der Liebe übermannt,
Und mein Herz liebt dich zärtlich ohne dich gut zu kennen.

Immerfort

Ihr verlangt von mir zu schweigen,
Für immer weit weg von Euch zu fliehen
Und fortzugehen, einsam,
Ohne mich zu erinnern, wen ich liebte!

Verlangt eher von den Sternen,
In die Unermeßlichkeit zu fallen,
Von der Nacht, ihre Schleier zu verlieren,
vom Tag, seine Helligkeit zu verlieren!

Verlang vom undendlich großen Meer,
Seine ausgedehnten Fluten auszutrocknen,
Und wenn die Winde ihren Wahnsinn treiben,
Ihr düsteres Schluchzen beruhigen!

Aber hofft nicht, daß meine Seele
Sich von ihren herben Schmerzen losreißt
Und sich ihrer Flamme entledigt,
Wie der Frühling sich seiner Blumen!

Adieu

Comme tout meurt vite, la rose
    Déclose,
Et les frais manteaux diaprés
    Des prés ;
Les longs soupirs, les bien-aimées,
    Fumées !

On voit, dans ce monde léger,
    Changer
Plus vite que les flots des grèves,
    Nos rêves,
Plus vite que le givre en fleurs,
    Nos cœurs !

À vous l'on se croyait fidèle,
    Cruelle,
Mais hélas ! les plus longs amours
    Sont courts !
Et je dis en quittant vos charmes,
    Sans larmes,
Presqu'au moment de mon aveu :
    Adieu !

Farewell

How swiftly all things die, the rose
    In bloom,
And the cool dappled mantle
    Of the meadows;
Long-drawn sighs, loved ones,
    All smoke!

In this fickle world we see our dreams
    Change
More swiftly than waves
    On the shore,
Our hearts change more swiftly
    Than frosted flowers!

To you I thought I would be faithful,
    Cruel one,
But alas! the longest loves
    Are short!
And I say, taking leave of your charms,
    Without tears,
Almost at the moment of my avowal,
    Farewell!

Lebewohl

Wie alles schnell stirbt, die Rose
    Halbgeschlossen,
Und die frischen schillernden Mäntel
    Der Wiesen;
Die langen Seufzer, die Vielgeliebten,
    Rauch!

Man sieht in dieser leichten Welt
    Sich verändern,
Schneller als die Fluten der Ufer,
    Unsere Träume,
Schneller als der Reif der Blumen,
    Unsere Herzen!

Euch glaubte man sich treu,
    Grausame,
Aber ach! die längsten Lieben
    Sind kurz!
Und ich sage beim Verlassen Eures Zaubers
    Ohne Tränen,
Fast im Moment meines Geständnisses,
    Lebewohl!

27. Nell
Leconte de Lisle

Ta rose de pourpre, à ton clair soleil,
    Ô Juin, étincelle enivrée ;
Penche aussi vers moi ta coupe dorée :
    Mon cœur à ta rose est pareil.

Sous le mol abri de la feuille ombreuse
    Monte un soupir de volupté :
Plus d'un ramier chante au bois écarté,
    Ô mon cœur, sa plainte amoureuse.

Que ta perle est douce au ciel parfumé [enflammé],
    Étoile de la nuit pensive !
Mais combien plus douce est la clarté vive
    Qui rayonne en mon cœur charmé !

La chantante mer, le long du rivage,
    Taira son murmure éternel,
Avant qu'en mon cœur, chère amour, ô Nell,
    Ne fleurisse plus ton image !

27. Nell
Leconte de Lisle

Your crimson rose in your bright sun
    Glitters, June, in rapture;
Incline to me also your golden cup:
    My heart is like your rose.

From the soft shelter of shady leaves
    Rises a languorous sigh;
More than one dove in the secluded wood
    Sings, O my heart, its love-lorn lament.

How sweet is your pearl in the blazing sky,
    Star of meditative night!
But sweeter still is the vivid light
    That glows in my enchanted heart!

The singing sea along the shore
    Shall cease its eternal murmur,
Before in my heart, dear love, O Nell,
    Your image shall cease to bloom!

27. Nell
Leconte de Lisle

Deine purpurne Rose in deiner hellen Sonne,
    O Juni, funkelt berauscht,
Neige auch zu mir deinen goldenen Becher;
    Mein Herz gleicht deiner Rose.

Unter dem weichen Schutz des schattigen Blattes
    Steigt ein wollüstiges Seufzen auf;
Mehr als eine Ringeltaube singt im abgelegenen Wald
    O mein Herz, ihre Liebesklage.

Wie lieblich deine Perle im flammenden Himmel ist,
    Stern gedankenvoller Nacht!
Aber um wieviel lieblicher ist die lebendige Helligkeit
    Die in meinem entzückten Herzen strahlt!

Das singende Meer, entlang des Ufers,
    Wird sein ewiges Plätschern verstummen lassen,
Bevor in meinem Herzen, teure Liebe, o Nell,
    Dein Bild nicht mehr blüht!

28. Le Voyageur
Armand Silvestre

Voyageur, où vas-tu, marchant
Dans l'or vibrant de la poussière ?
– Je m'en vais au soleil couchant,
Pour m'endormir dans la lumière.

Car j'ai vécu n'ayant qu'un Dieu,
L'astre qui luit et qui féconde,
Et c'est dans son linceul de feu
Que je veux m'en aller du monde !

– Voyageur, presse donc le pas :
L'astre vers l'horizon décline...
 – Que m'importe, j'irai plus bas
L'attendre au pied de la colline.

Et lui montrant mon cœur ouvert,
Saignant de son amour fidèle,
Je lui dirai : J'ai trop souffert :
Soleil ! emporte-moi loin d'elle !

28. The wanderer
Armand Silvestre

Wanderer, where are you bound,
Walking in the golden dust?
– I am going towards the sunset,
To fall asleep in the light.

For I have lived with only one God,
The sun which shines and makes fertile.
It is shrouded in his fire
That I wish to leave the world!

– Wanderer, you must hurry, then:
The sun slips towards the horizon...
– What do I care, I shall descend further
And wait at the foot of the hill.

And showing the sun my open heart,
Bleeding with faithful love,
I shall say: I have suffered too much:
Sun! Take me away from her!

28. Der Reisende
Armand Silvestre

Reisender, wohin gehst du, schreitend
Im zitternden Gold des Staubes!
– Ich gehe fort in die untergehende Sonne,
Um im Lichte einzuschlafen.

Denn ich habe mit nur einem Gott gelebt,
Dem Stern, der leuchtet und der befruchtet,
Und in seinem feurigen Leichentuch,
Will ich von der Welt gehen!

– Reisender, beschleunige doch den Schritt:
Der Stern sinkt zum Horizont herab...
– Was bedeutet mir das schon, ich werde tiefer gehen,
Ihn am Fuß des Hügels erwarten.

Indem ich ihm mein offenes Herz zeige,
Das vor treuer Liebe blutet,
Werde ich ihm sagen: Ich habe zuviel gelitten;
Sonne! bringe mich weit weg von ihr.

29. Chanson d'Automn
[Automne]
Armand Silvestre

Automne au ciel brumeux, aux horizons navrants,
Aux rapides couchants, aux aurores pâlies,
Je regarde couler, avec [comme] l'eau des torrents
                              [du torrent],
    Tes jours faits de mélancolies [mélancolie].

Sur l'aile des regrets mes esprits emportés,
– Comme s'il se pouvait que notre âge renaisse ! –
Parcourent, en rêvant, les coteaux enchantés
    Où jadis sourit ma jeunesse.

Je sens, au clair soleil du souvenir vainqueur,
Refleurir en bouquet les roses déliées
Et monter à mes yeux des larmes, qu'en mon cœur,
    Mes vingt ans avaient oubliées !

30. [Les Berceaux]
Sully Prudhomme

Le long du quai les grands vaisseaux,
Que la houle incline en silence,
Ne prennent pas garde aux berceaux
Que la main des femmes balance.

Mais viendra le jour des adieux ;
Car il faut que les femmes pleurent,
Et que les hommes curieux
Tentent les horizons qui leurrent.

Et ce jour-là les grands vaisseaux,
Fuyant le port qui diminue,
Sentent leur masse retenue
Par l'âme des lointains berceaux.

31. Notre amour
Armand Silvestre

Notre amour est chose légère
Comme les parfums que le vent
Prend aux cimes de la fougère
Pour qu'on les respire en rêvant.
– Notre amour est chose légère.

Notre amour est chose charmante,
Comme les chansons du matin
Où nul regret ne se lamente,
Où vibre un espoir incertain.
– Notre amour est chose charmante.

Notre amour est chose sacrée
Comme les mystères des bois
Où tressaille une âme ignorée,
Où les silences ont des voix.
– Notre amour est chose sacrée.

Notre amour est chose infinie,
Comme le chemin [les chemins] des couchants
Où la mer, aux cieux réunie,
S'endort sous les soleils penchants.
(– Notre amour est chose infinie.)

Notre amour est chose éternelle
Comme tout ce qu'un Dieu vainqueur
A touché du feu de son aile.
Comme tout ce qui vient du cœur,
– Notre amour est chose éternelle.

29. Autumn Song
[Autumn]
Armand Silvestre

Autumn of misty skies and heartbreaking horizons,
Of swift sunsets and pale dawns,
I watch flow by, like torrential water,
    Your days imbued with melancholy.

My thoughts, borne away on the wings of regret,
– As though our time could come round again! –
Roam in reverie the enchanted hills,
    Where long ago my youth once smiled.

In the bright sun of triumphant memory
I feel untied roses reflower in bouquets,
And tears rise to my eyes, which in my heart
    At twenty had been forgotten!

30. [The cradles]
Sully Prudhomme

Along the quay the great ships,
Listing silently with the surge,
Pay no heed to the cradles
Rocked by women's hands.

But the day of parting will come,
For it is decreed that women shall weep,
And that men with questing spirits
Shall seek enticing horizons.

And on that day the great ships,
Leaving the dwindling harbour behind,
Shall feel their hulls held back
By the soul of the distant cradles.

31. Our love
Armand Silvestre

Our love is light and gentle,
Like fragrance fetched by the breeze
From the tips of ferns
For us to breathe while dreaming.
– Our love is light and gentle.

Our love is enchanting,
Like morning songs,
Where no regret is voiced,
Quivering with uncertain hopes.
– Our love is enchanting.

Our love is sacred,
Like woodland mysteries,
Where an unknown soul throbs
And silences are eloquent.
– Our love is sacred.

Our love is infinite
Like sunset paths,
Where the sea, joined with the skies,
Falls asleep beneath slanting suns.
(–Our love is infinite.)

Our love is eternal,
Like all that a victorious God
Has brushed with his fiery wing,
Like all that comes from the heart,
– Our love is eternal.

29. Herbstlied
[Herbst]
Armand Silvestre

Herbst des nebligen Himmels, der betrübenden
                            Horizonte,
Der raschen Abende, der erblaßten Morgenröte,
Ich beobachte wie das Wasser der Ströme verrinnen
    Deine Tage von Schwermut.

Auf dem Flügel des Bedauerns durchlaufen meine
                            fortgetragenen Gedanken,
– Als wenn unser Alter wiedergeboren werden könnte! –
Träumend die verzauberten Hügel
    Wo einst meine Jugend lächelte.

Ich fühle in der hellen Sonne der siegreichen Erinnerung
Die schlanken Rosen als Strauß neu erblühen
Und meine Augen Tränen steigen, die in meinem Herzen
    Meine zwanzig Jahre vergessen hatten!

30. [Die Wiegen]
Sully Prudhomme

Entlang des Kais die großen Schiffe,
Die die Dünung still neigt,
Geben nicht auf die Wiegen acht,
Die die Hände der Frauen schaukeln.

Sondern der Tag des Abschieds wird kommen,
Denn die Frauen müssen weinen,
Und die neugierigen Männer
Durch die lockenden Horizonte gereizt werden.

Und an diesem Tag fühlen die großen Schiffe,
Während sie den kleiner werdenden Hafen fliehen,
Ihre Masse zurückgehalten
Von der Seele der entfernten Wiegen.

31. Unsere Liebe
Armand Silvestre

Unsere Liebe ist eine leichtfertige Sache,
Wie die Düfte, die der Wind
Den Spitzen des Farnes entlockt,
Damit man sie träumend atmet.
– Unsere Liebe ist eine leichte Sache.

Unsere Liebe ist eine bezaubernde Sache,
Wie die Morgenlieder,
In denen kein Bedauern klagt,
Wo eine ungewisse Hoffnung vibriert.
– Unsere Liebe ist eine bezaubernde Sache.

Unsere Liebe ist eine heilige Sache,
Wie die Geheimnisse der Wälder,
Wo eine unbekannte Seele erschauert,
Wo das Schweigen Stimmen hat.
– Unsere Liebe ist eine heilige Sache.

Unsere Liebe ist eine unendliche Sache,
Wie der Weg der untergehenden Sonne,
Wo das Meer, mit dem Himmel vereint,
Unter den sich neigenden Sonnen einschläft.
(– Unsere Liebe ist eine undendliche Sache.)

Unsere Liebe ist eine ewige Sache,
Wie alles, was ein siegreicher Gott
Mit dem Feuer seines Flügels berührt hat,
Wie alles, was von Herzen kommt.
– Unsere Liebe ist eine ewige Sache.

32. Mystère {Le Secret}
Armand Silvestre

Je veux que le matin l'ignore
Le nom que j'ai dit à la nuit,
Et qu'au vent de l'aube, sans bruit,
Comme une larme il s'évapore.

Je veux que le jour le proclame
L'amour qu'au matin j'ai caché,
Et sur mon cœur ouvert penché,
Ainsi qu'un [Comme un] grain d'encens l'enflamme.

Je veux que le couchant l'oublie
Le secret que j'ai dit au jour
Et l'emporte, avec mon amour,
Aux plis de sa robe pâlie!

33. Chanson d'amour
Armand Silvestre

J'aime tes yeux, j'aime ton front,
Ô ma rebelle, ô ma farouche.
J'aime tes yeux, j'aime ta bouche
Où mes baisers s'épuiseront.

J'aime ta voix, j'aime l'étrange
Grâce de tout ce que tu dis,
Ô ma rebelle, ô mon cher ange,
Mon enfer et mon paradis!

J'aime tout ce qui te fait belle,
De tes pieds jusqu'à tes cheveux,
Ô toi vers qui montent mes vœux,
Ô ma farouche, ô ma rebelle!

34. La Fée aux chansons
Armand Silvestre

Il était une fée,
D'herbes folles [herbe folle] coiffée,
Qui courait les buissons,
Sans s'y laisser surprendre,
En Avril, pour apprendre
Aux oiseaux leurs chansons.

Lorsque geais et linottes
Faisaient de fausses notes,
En récitant leurs chants,
La fée, avec constance,
Gourmandait d'importance
Ces élèves méchants.

Sa petite main nue,
D'un brin d'herbe menue
Cueilli dans les halliers,
Pour stimuler leur zèle [leurs zèles].
Fouettait sur leurs ailes
Ces mauvais écoliers.

Par un matin d'automne,
Elle vient et s'étonne
De voir les bois déserts.
Avec les hirondelles,
Ses amis infidèles
Avaient fui par [dans] les airs.

Et, tout l'hiver, la fée,
D'herbe morte coiffée,
Et comptant les instants,
Sous les forêts immenses,
Compose des romances
Pour le prochain printemps.

32. Mystery {The secret}
Armand Silvestre

Would that the morn were unaware
Of the name I told to the night,
And that in the dawn breeze, silently,
It would vanish like a tear.

Would that the day might proclaim it,
The love I hid from the morn,
And poised above my open heart,
Like a grain of incense kindle it.

Would that the sunset might forget,
The secret I told to the day,
And would carry it and my love away
In the folds of its faded robe!

33. Love song
Armand Silvestre

I love your eyes, I love your brow,
O my rebel, O my wild one,
I love your eyes, I love your mouth
Where my kisses shall dissolve.

I love your voice, I love the strange
Charm of all you say,
O my rebel, O my dear angel,
My inferno and my paradise.

I love all that makes you beautiful
From your feet to your hair,
O you the object of all my vows,
O my wild one, O my rebel.

34. The song fairy
Armand Silvestre

There was a fairy
Crowned with rank weeds
Who ran through the bushes
Without being caught,
In April, to teach
The birds their songs.

When jays and linnets
Sang wrong notes
As they recited their songs,
The fairy, tirelessly,
Sternly rebuked
Those naughty pupils.

Her little bare hand,
With a tiny blade of grass
Plucked from the thickets,
To stimulate their zeal
Would whip the wings
Of those bad scholars.

One autumn morning
She comes and is amazed
To find the woods deserted.
With the swallows,
Her unfaithful friends
Had flown away on the wind.

And all winter long, the fairy,
Crowned with dead grass
And counting time
In the vast forests
Composes songs
For the coming Spring!

32. Das Geheimnis
Armand Silvestre

Ich will, daß der Morgen nicht weiß
Den Namen, den ich der Nacht gesagt habe,
Und daß er sich ohne Lärm im Wind der
                                Morgendämmerung
Wie eine Träne verflüchtigt.

Ich will, daß der Tag sie verkündet,
Die Liebe, die ich vor dem Morgen versteckt habe,
Und daß er, über mein offenes Herz gebeugt,
Sie wie ein Weihrauchkorn entflamme.

Ich will, daß der Abend es vergißt,
Das Geheimnis, das ich dem Tag gesagt habe,
Und es mit meiner Liebe mitnimmt
In den Falten seines erblaßten Kleides.

33. Liebeslied
Armand Silvestre

Ich liebe deine Augen, ich liebe deine Stirn,
O meine Rebellin, o meine Grausame,
Ich liebe deine Augen, ich liebe deinen Mund,
Wo sich meine Küsse erschöpfen werden.

Ich liebe deine Stimme, ich liebe das Fremde,
Dank allem was du sagst,
O meine Rebellin, o mein lieber Engel,
Meine Hölle und mein Paradies!

Ich liebe alles was dich schön macht,
Von deinen Füßen bis zu deinen Haaren,
O du, zu der meine Schwüre steigen,
O meine Grausame, o meine Rebellin.

34. Die Fee mit den Liedern
Armand Silvestre

Es war eine Fee,
Mit wilden Gräsern auf dem Kopf,
Die durch das Strauchwerk lief,
Ohne sich überraschen zu lassen,
Im April, um zu lehren
Den Vögeln ihre Lieder.

Wenn Häher und Hänflinge
Falsche Noten hervorbrachten,
Während sie ihren Gesang vortrugen,
Hat die Fee mit Beharrlichkeit
Tüchtig zurechtgewiesen
Diese bösen Schüler.

Ihre kleine nackte Hand
Mit einem feinen Grashalm,
Im Dickicht gepflückt,
Um ihren Eifer anzuspornen,
Peitschte die Flügel
Dieser schlechte Schüler.

An einem Herbstmorgen
Kommt sie und ist erstaunt,
Den Wald verlassen zu sehen.
Mit den Schwalben,
Sind ihre untreuen Freunde
In die Lüfte geflohen.

Und den ganzen Winter, die Fee,
Mit welken Gräsern auf dem Kopf
Und die Augenblicke zählend
In den unendlichen Wäldern,
Komponiert ihre Romanzen
Für den nächsten Frühling.

Select Bibliography / Bibliographie sélective / Auswahlbibliographie

Abraham, Hélène (ed.). *Un Art de l'interprétation: Claire Croiza: les cahiers d'une auditrice.*
    Paris: Office de centralisation d'ouvrages, 1954

Bannerman, Betty (ed. & trans.). *The Singer as Interpreter: Claire Croiza's Master Classes.* London: Gollancz, 1989

Bernac, Pierre. *The Interpretation of French Song.* Translations of song texts by Winifred Radford. London: Gollancz, 1970

Duchen, Jessica. *Gabriel Fauré.* London: Phaidon, 2000

Fauré-Fremiet, Philippe (ed.). *Gabriel Fauré: Lettres intimes.* Paris: Grasset, 1951

Grubb, Thomas. *Singing in French: A Manual of French Diction and French Vocal Repertoire.* New York: Schirmer, 1979

Howat, Roy and Emily Kilpatrick. "Editorial Challenges in the Early Songs of Gabriel Fauré", *Notes* 68:2 (December 2011), pp. 239–83
— "Gabriel Fauré's Middle-Period Songs, Editorial Quandaries, and the Chimera of the 'Original Key'",
    Journal of the Royal Musical Association 139:2 (autumn 2014), pp. 303–37

Hunter, David. *Understanding French Verse: A Guide for Singers.* New York: Oxford UP, 2005

Jankélévitch, Vladimir. *Gabriel Fauré et ses mélodies.* Paris: Plon, 1938

Johnson, Graham. *Gabriel Fauré: The Songs and their Poets.* Aldershot: Ashgate, 2009
— and Richard Stokes. *A French Song Companion.* New York: Oxford UP, 2002.

Jones, J. Barrie (ed. and trans.): *Gabriel Fauré: A Life in Letters.* London: Batsford, 1988

Jourdan-Morhange, Hélène. *Mes amis musiciens.* Paris: Les Éditeurs français réunis, 1955

Kilpatrick, Emily. "Moot Point: Editing Poetry and Punctuation in Fauré's Early Songs".
    Nineteenth-Century Music Review 9:2 (December 2012), pp. 213–235

Le Roux, François and Romain Reynaldy. *Le Chant intime: de l'interprétation de la mélodie française.* Paris: Fayard, 2004

Nectoux, Jean-Michel. *Gabriel Fauré: les voix du clair-obscur.* Paris: Fayard, 2008 (revised edition)
    English edition: *Gabriel Fauré: A Musical Life*, transl. Roger Nichols. Cambridge: Cambridge UP, 1991

— (ed.) *Gabriel Fauré: Correspondance*, présentée et annotée par Jean-Michel Nectoux. Paris: Flammarion, 1980.
    English edition: *Gabriel Fauré: His Life through his Letters*, trans. J. A. Underwood.
    London and New York: Marion Boyars, 1984

— and Daitz, Mimi S. *Gabriel Fauré: Mélodies et Duos* (Volume 1: *Premières mélodies, 1861–1875* [critical edition]).
    Paris: Hamelle-Leduc, 2010 (HA 9729)

Phillips, Edward. *Gabriel Fauré: A Research and Information Guide.* 2nd edn. New York & London: Routledge, 2010

Strobel, Klaus. *Das Liedschaffen Gabriel Faurés.* Hamburg: Verlag Dr Kovač, 2000

On questions of pronunciation, see *inter alia* the guidelines and observations by Roger Nichols in the Peters Editions
The Art of French Song (EP 7519–7120) and collected songs of Duparc (EP 7778), in addition to
Bernac, *The Interpretation of French Song* and Grubb, *Singing in French.*
Internet resources are ever-changing, but presently (2014) include the Centre international de la mélodie française,
under the direction of François Le Roux (www.melodiefrancaise.com).

Les ressources Internet sont en constante évolution, mais comprennent actuellement (2014) le Centre international de la mélodie française,
sous la direction de François Le Roux (www.melodiefrancaise.com).

Richtlinien und Betrachtungen zur Aussprache finden sich u. a. bei Roger Nichols in den bei Edition Peters erschienenen Ausgaben
The Art of French Song (EP 7519–7120) und den sämtlichen Liedern Duparcs (EP 7778) sowie bei Pierre Bernac,
The Interpretation of French Song und Thomas Grubb, *Singing in French.*
Internetquellen wechseln ständig; eine aktuelle Quelle (2014) ist das Centre international de la mélodie française
unter der Leitung von François Le Roux (www.melodiefrancaise.com).

SONGS / MÉLODIES / LIEDER

À Madame Miolan-Carvalho

1. Le Papillon et la fleur

(Victor Hugo)

Gabriel Fauré (1845–1924)[1]

Original keys: D♭ (C/D)

(Op. 1 no. 1)

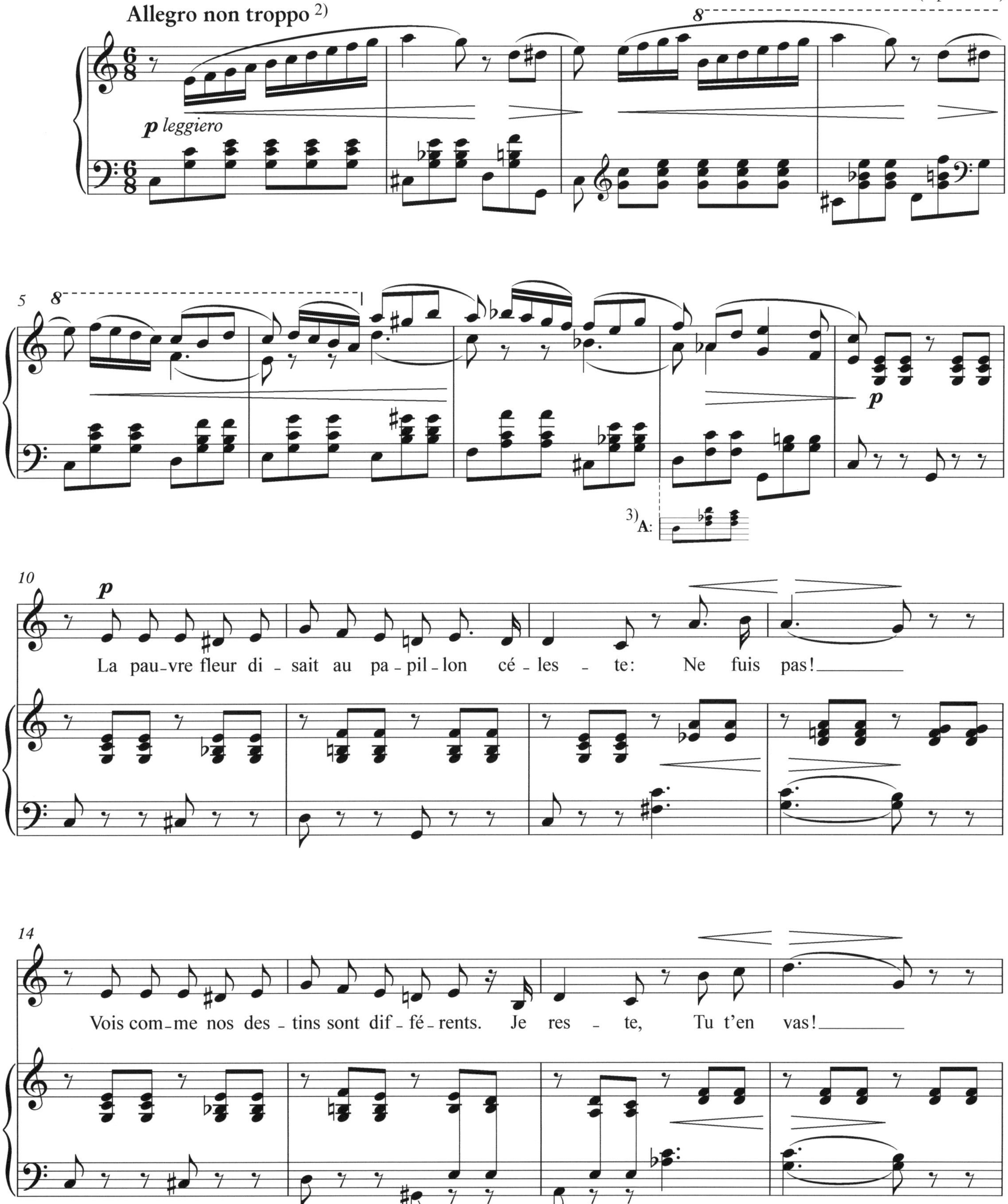

Allegro non troppo 2)
p leggiero
8
p
3) A:
p
La pauvre fleur disait au papillon céleste: Ne fuis pas!
Vois comme nos destins sont différents. Je reste, Tu t'en vas!

1) Regarding opus numbers 1-8 see Preface / À propos des numéros d'opus 1 à 8 voir Préface / Zu den Opusnummern 1 bis 8 vgl. Vorwort
2) *Allegretto* in some sources / *Allegretto* selon quelques sources / *Allegretto* nach einigen Quellen
3) Likewise for bars 28, 48 and 68 / De même aux mesures 28, 48 et 68 / Ebenso in Takt 28, 48 und 68

1) *Ossia:*  , likewise for bars 41 and 61 / de même aux mesures 41 et 61 / ebenso für Takt 41 und 61

2. Puisque j'ai mis ma lèvre

(Victor Hugo)

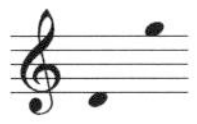

Original keys: C/B♭

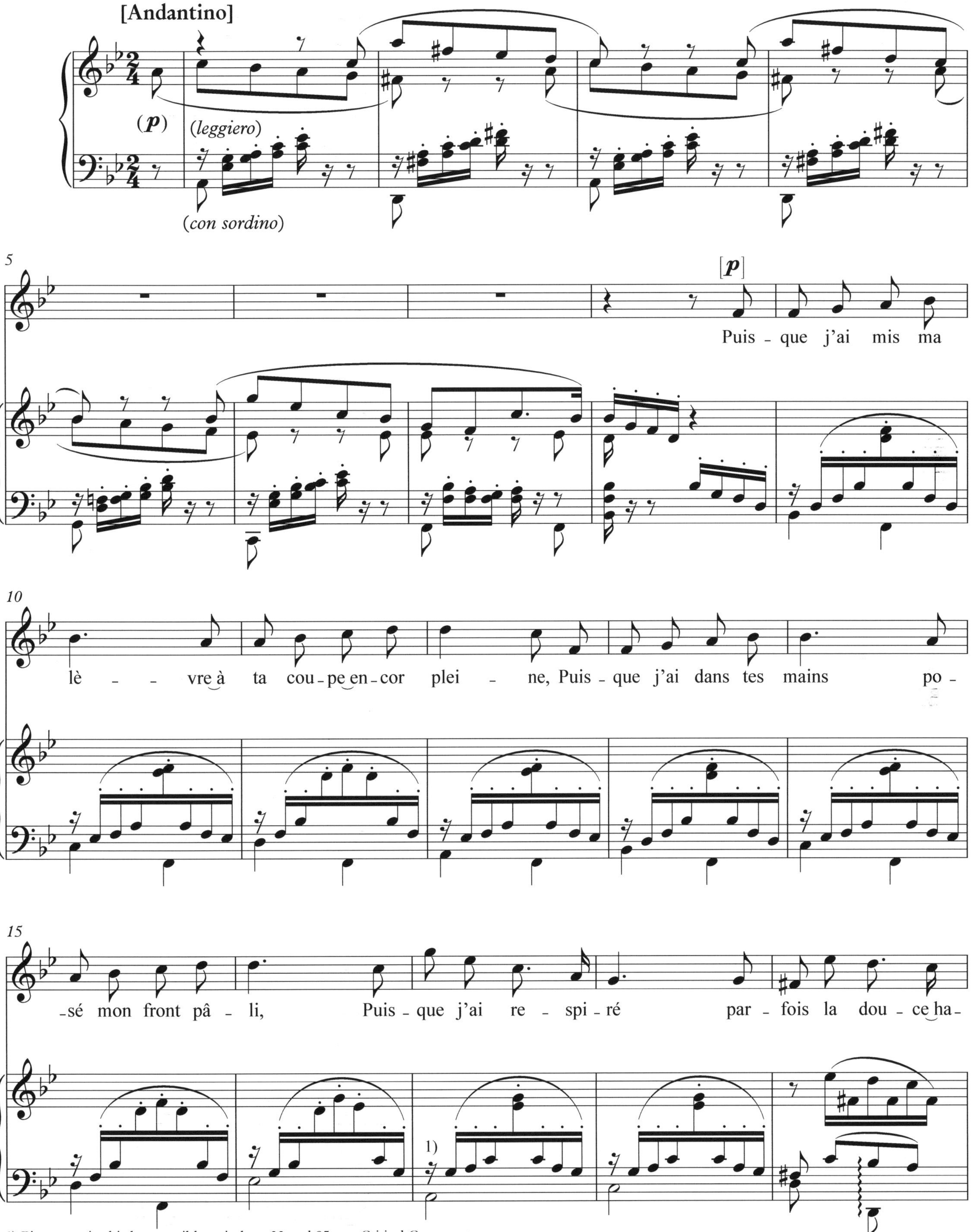
[Andantino]
(p)
(leggiero)
(con sordino)
5
[p]
Puis - que j'ai mis ma
10
lè - - vre à ta cou - pe en - cor plei - ne, Puis - que j'ai dans tes mains po -
15
- sé mon front pâ - li, Puis - que j'ai re - spi - ré par - fois la dou - ce ha -
1)

1) Piano part in this bar possibly as in bars 33 and 85; see Critical Commentary
Partie de piano peut-être comme aux mesures 33 et 85 ; voir commentaire critique
Lesart möglicherweise wie in Takt 33 und 85; vgl. Kritischen Bericht

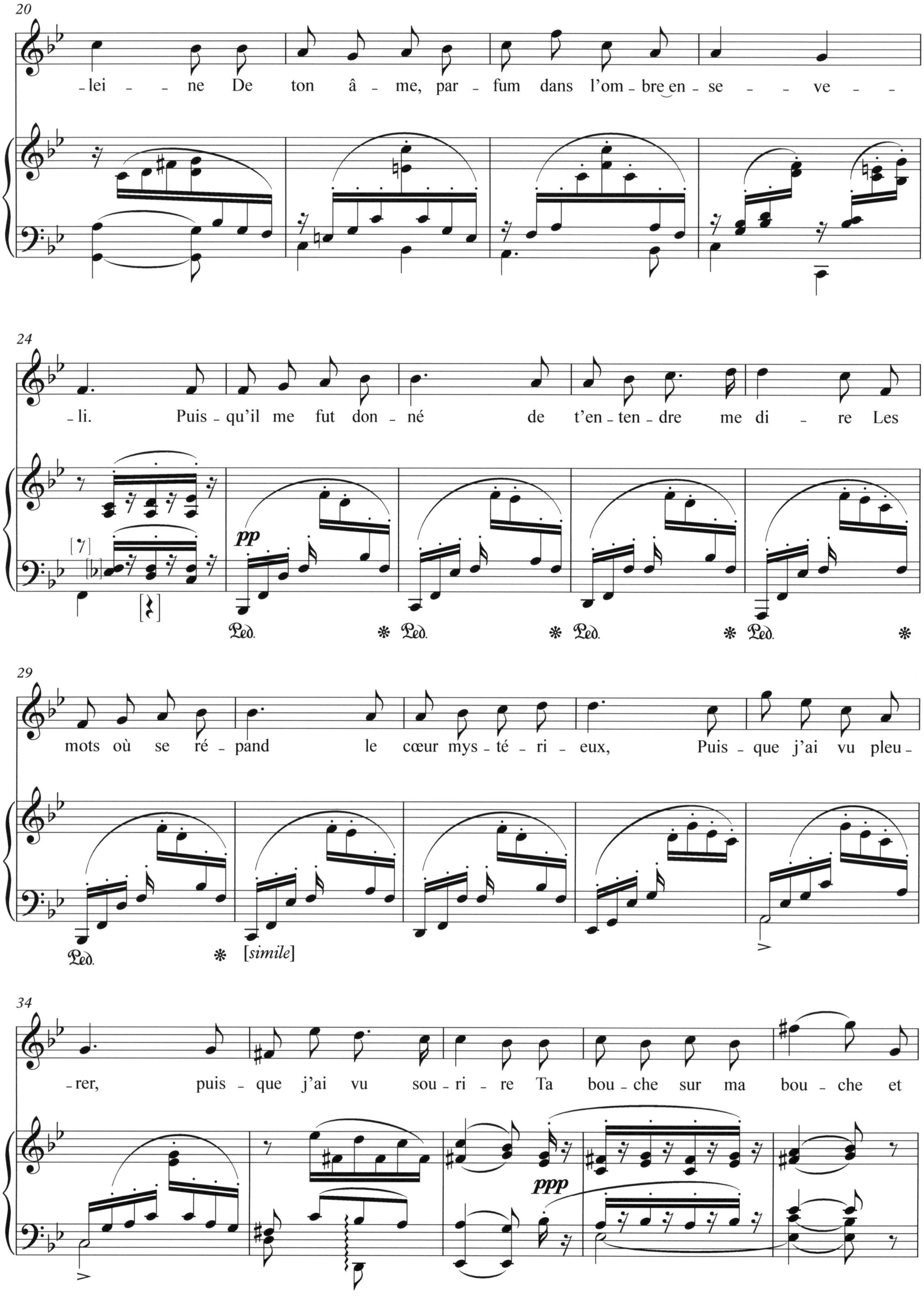
-lei - - ne De ton â - me, par - fum dans l'om - bre en - se - - ve - -
- li. Puis - qu'il me fut don - né de t'en - ten - dre me di - re Les
mots où se ré - pand le cœur mys - té - ri - eux, Puis - que j'ai vu pleu -
- rer, puis - que j'ai vu sou - ri - re Ta bou - che sur ma bou - che et
pp
Ped.
[simile]
ppp

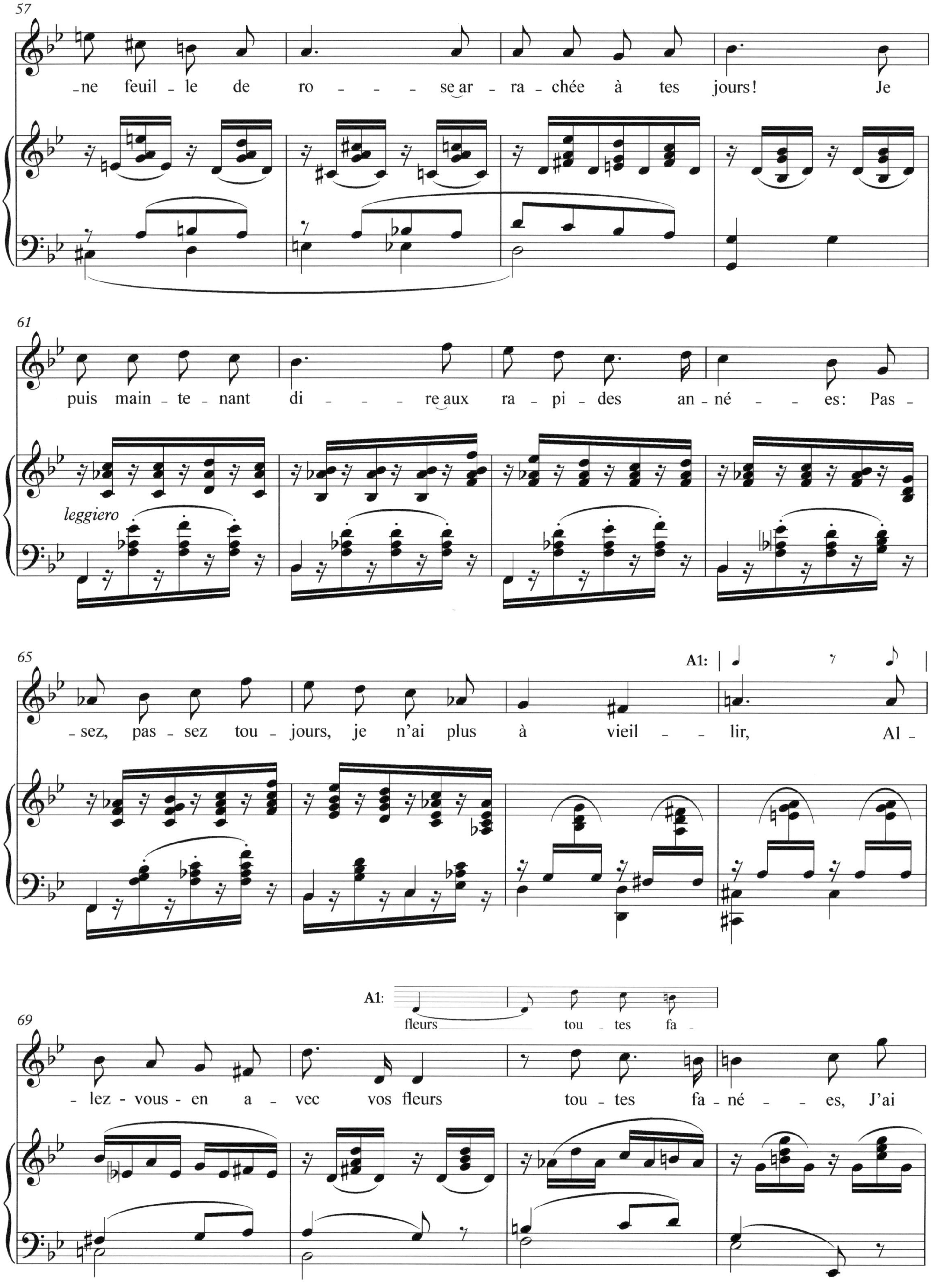
57
‿ne feuil ‿ le de ro ‿ ‿ ‿ se‿ar ‿ ra ‿ chée à tes jours! Je
61
puis main ‿ te ‿ nant di ‿ ‿ ‿ re‿aux ra ‿ pi ‿ des an ‿ né ‿ ‿ es: Pas ‿
leggiero
65
A1:
‿ sez, pas ‿ sez tou ‿ jours, je n'ai plus à vieil ‿ ‿ lir, Al ‿
A1:
fleurs tou ‿ tes fa ‿
69
‿ lez ‿ vous ‿ en a ‿ vec vos fleurs tou ‿ tes fa ‿ né ‿ ‿ es, J'ai

1) See Critical Commentary / Voir commentaire critique / Vgl. Kritischen Bericht

À Madame Henri Garnier

3. Mai

(Victor Hugo)

Original keys: A♭ (G)

(Op. 1 no. 2)

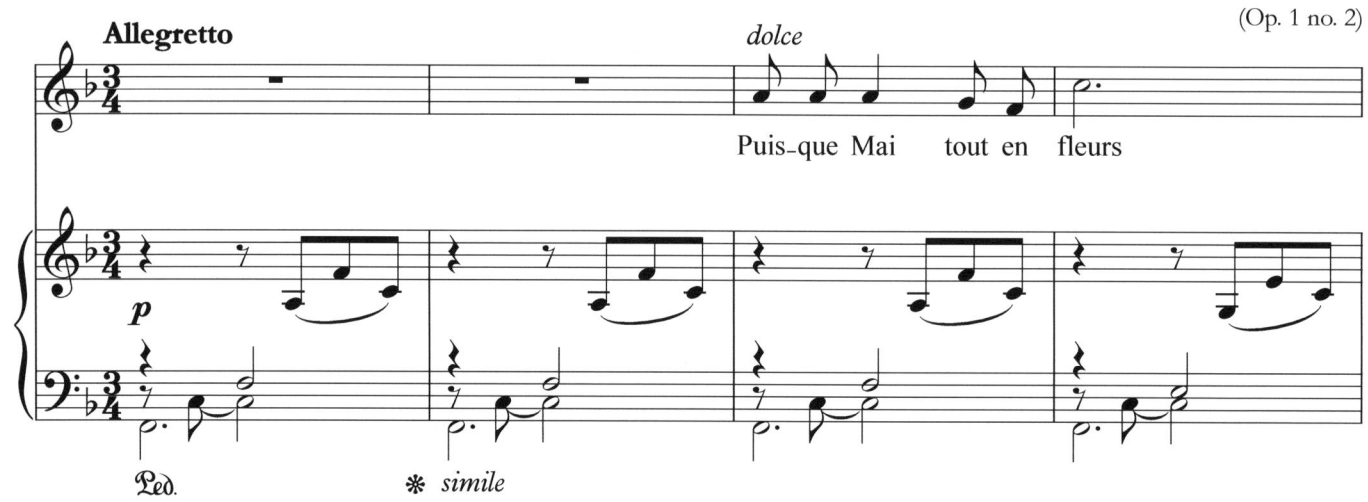

Edition Peters

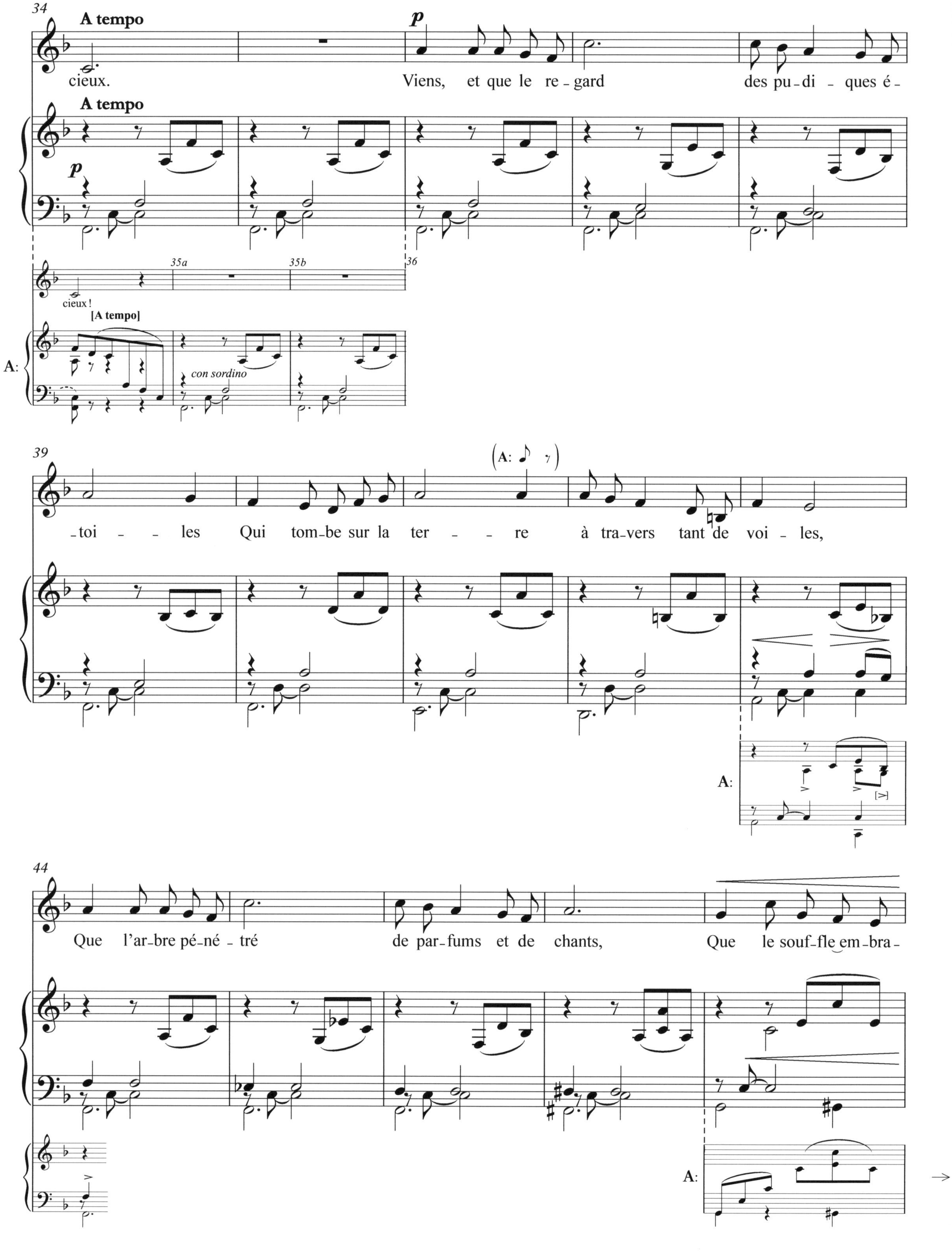
34
A tempo
p
cieux. Viens, et que le re-gard des pu-di-ques é-
A tempo
p
cieux!
35a
35b
36
[A tempo]
A:
con sordino
39
(A:)
-toi - - les Qui tom-be sur la ter - - - re à tra-vers tant de voi - les,
A:
44
Que l'ar-bre pé-né-tré de par-fums et de chants, Que le souf-fle em-bra-
A:

14 À Madame Claire de Gomicourt

4a. S'il est un charmant gazon
Version I, 1864
(Victor Hugo)

Original key: F

1) *Ossia* readings from Version II; see Critical Commentary
   Les *ossia* selon Version II ; voir commentaire critique
   Ossia-Fassungen nach Version II; siehe Kritischen Bericht

Edition Peters 33575

4b. S'il est un charmant gazon
(Rêve d'amour)
Version II

À Madame Claire de Gomiecourt

(Victor Hugo)

(Op. 5 no. 2)

Original keys: (E♭/F)

1) See Version I and Critical Commentary / Voir Version I et commentaire critique / Vgl. Version I und Kritischen Bericht

22

À mon ami Adam Laussel

5. Tristesse d'Olympio
(Victor Hugo)

Original key: e

Grave

Les champs n'é-taient point noirs, les cieux n'é-taient pas mor-nes,
Non, le jour ray-on-nait dans un a-zur sans bor-nes Sur la ter-re é-ten-du.
L'air é-tait plein d'en-cens et les prés de ver-du-res Quand il re-vit ces lieux où par tant de bles-su-res Son cœur s'est ré-pan-du! Hé-las! se rap-pe-

Edition Peters

33575

1) Editorial suggestion: see Critical commentary / Proposition éditoriale: voir commentaire critique / Vorschlag der Herausgeber: vgl. Kritischen Bericht

À Madame Henriette Escalier

6. Dans les ruines d'une abbaye

(Victor Hugo)

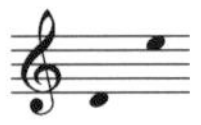

Original key: (A)

(Op. 2 no. 1)

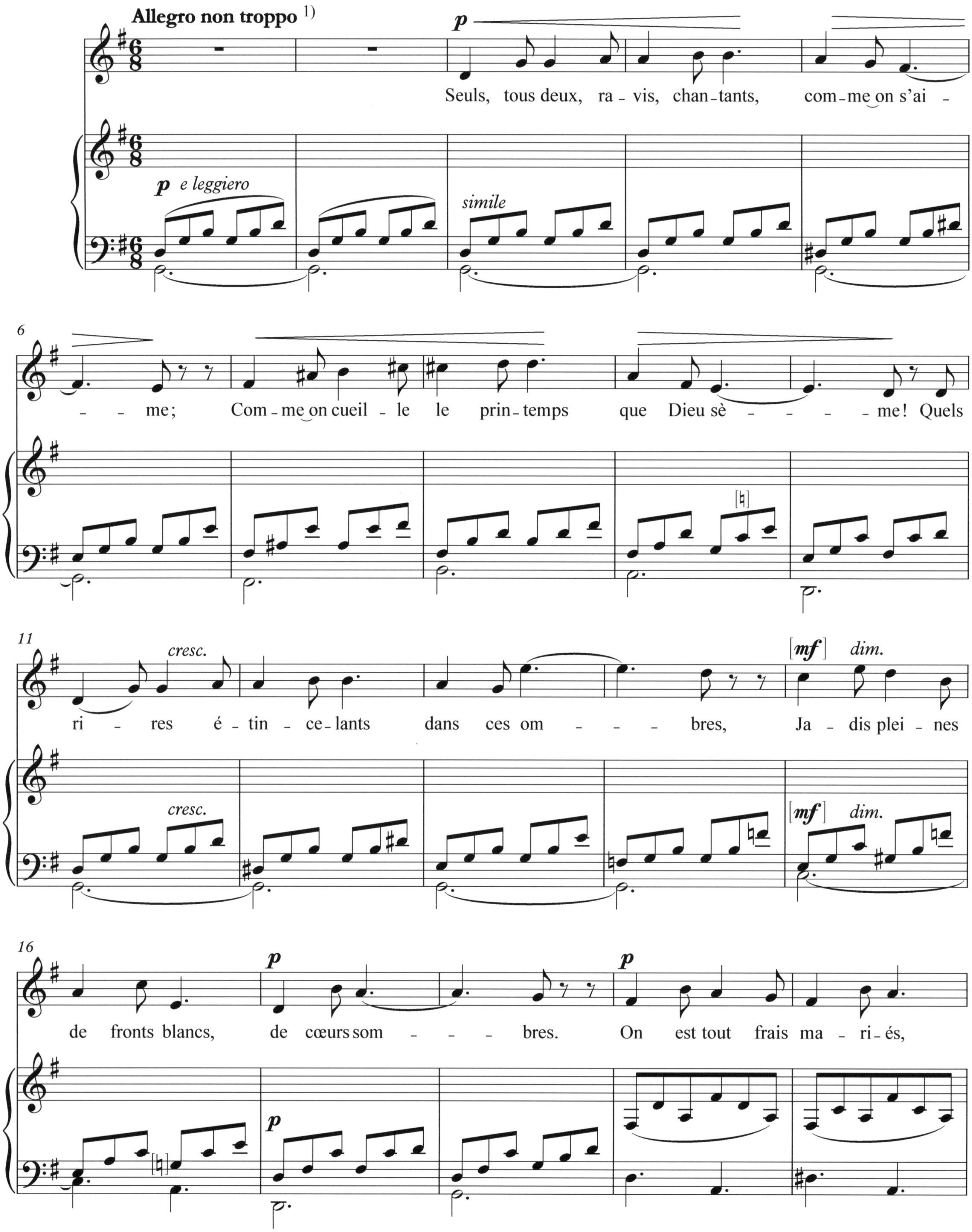
Allegro non troppo 1)
p
p e leggiero
simile
Seuls, tous deux, ra - vis, chan - tants, com - me on s'ai - - - me; Com - me on cueil - le le prin - temps que Dieu sè - - - - - me! Quels
cresc.
ri - res é - tin - ce - lants dans ces om - - - - bres, Ja - dis plei - nes
[mf] dim.
de fronts blancs, de cœurs som - - - - bres. On est tout frais ma - ri - és,

1) *Allegretto* in high-voice sources / *Allegretto* selon les sources pour voix élevées / *Allegretto* nach den Quellen für hohe Stimme

À Mademoiselle Anna Dufresne

7. L'Aurore

(Victor Hugo)

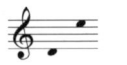

Original key: A♭

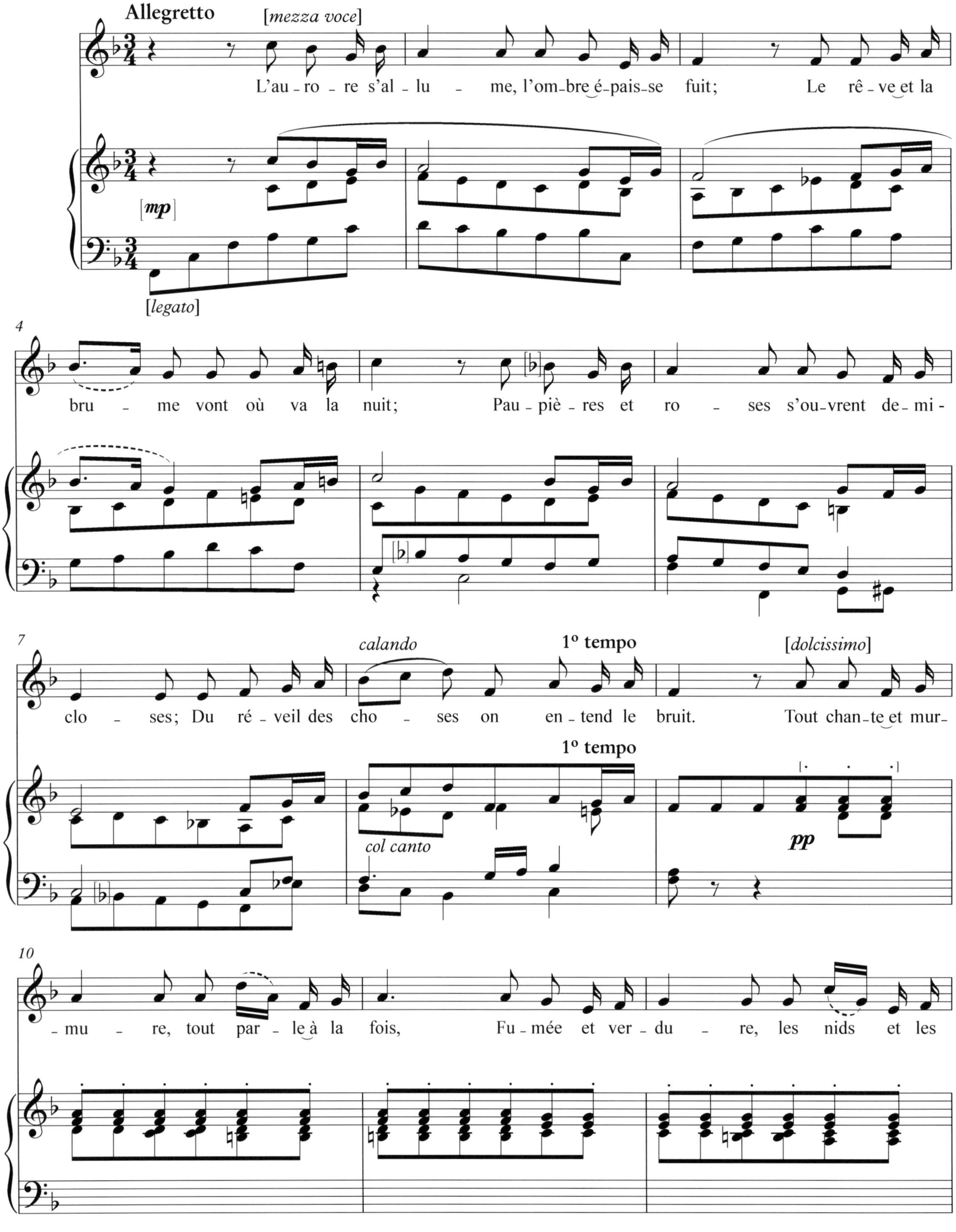
Allegretto
[mezza voce]
L'au - ro - re s'al - lu - me, l'om-bre é-pais-se fuit; Le rê - ve et la
[mp]
[legato]
bru - me vont où va la nuit; Pau - piè - res et ro - ses s'ou-vrent de - mi -
calando
1º tempo
[dolcissimo]
clo - ses; Du ré - veil des cho - ses on en - tend le bruit. Tout chan - te et mur -
col canto
pp
- mu - re, tout par - le à la fois, Fu - mée et ver - du - re, les nids et les

1) See Critical Commentary / Voir commentaire critique / Vgl. Kritischen Bericht

À Monsieur Romain Bussine

8. L'Absent
(Victor Hugo)

Original key: a

(Op. 5 no. 3)

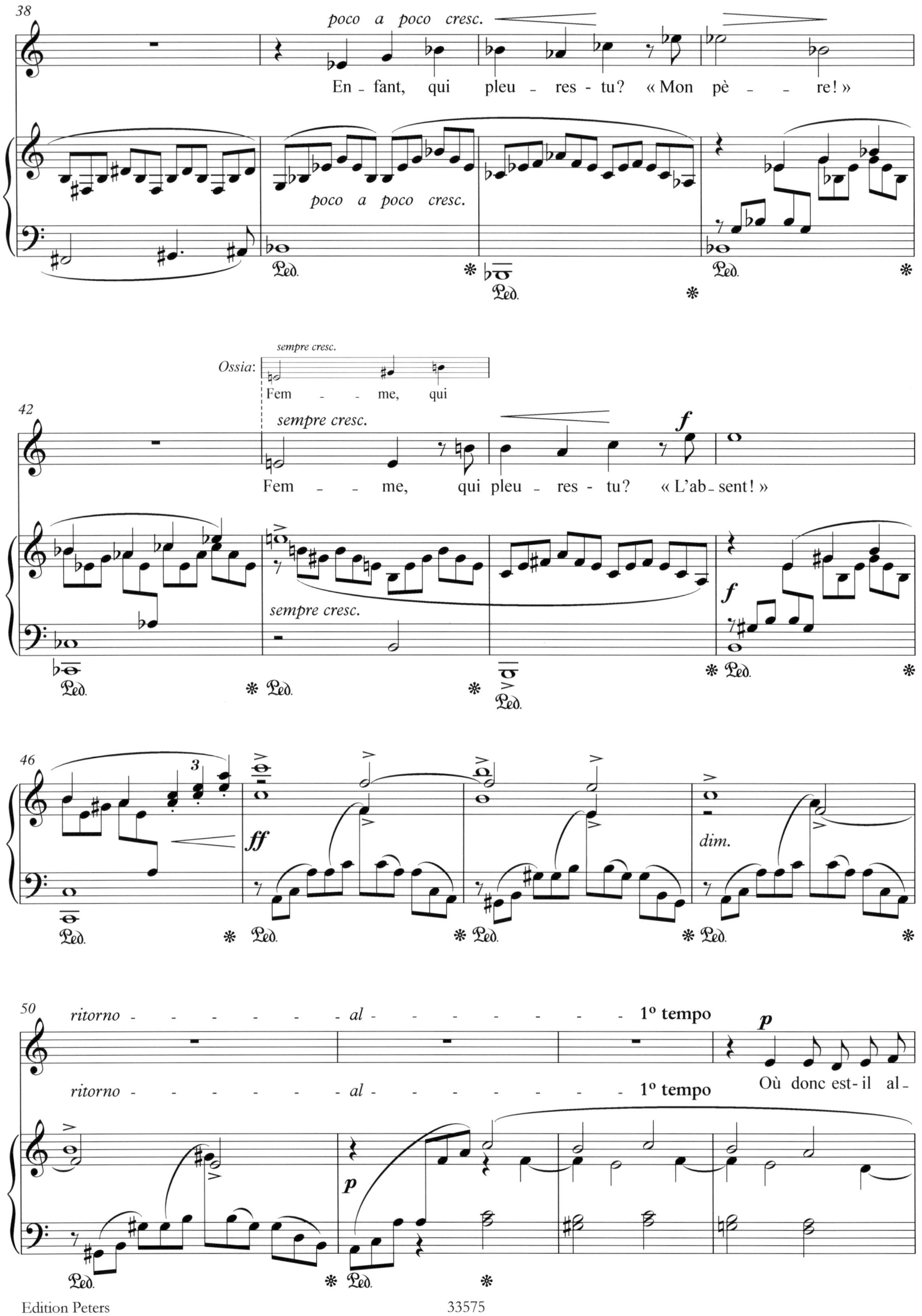
38
poco a poco cresc.
En - fant, qui pleu - res - tu? « Mon pè - re! »
poco a poco cresc.
sempre cresc.
Ossia:
Fem - me, qui
42
sempre cresc.
f
Fem - me, qui pleu - res - tu? « L'ab - sent! »
sempre cresc.
f
46
3
ff
dim.
50
ritorno - al - 1º tempo
p
Où donc est-il al -
ritorno - al - 1º tempo
p

1) Regarding dynamics see Critical Commentary / À propos des dynamiques voir commentaire critique / Zur Dynamik vgl. Kritischen Bericht

À Madame Marie Trélat

9. Lydia

(Leconte de Lisle)

(Op. 4 no. 2)

Original key: (F)

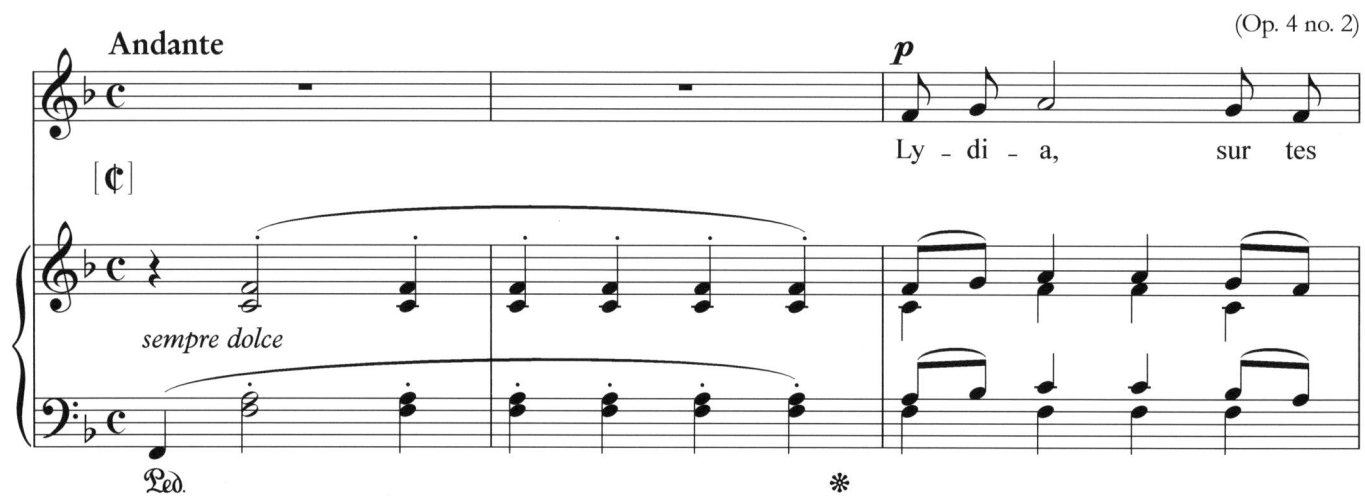

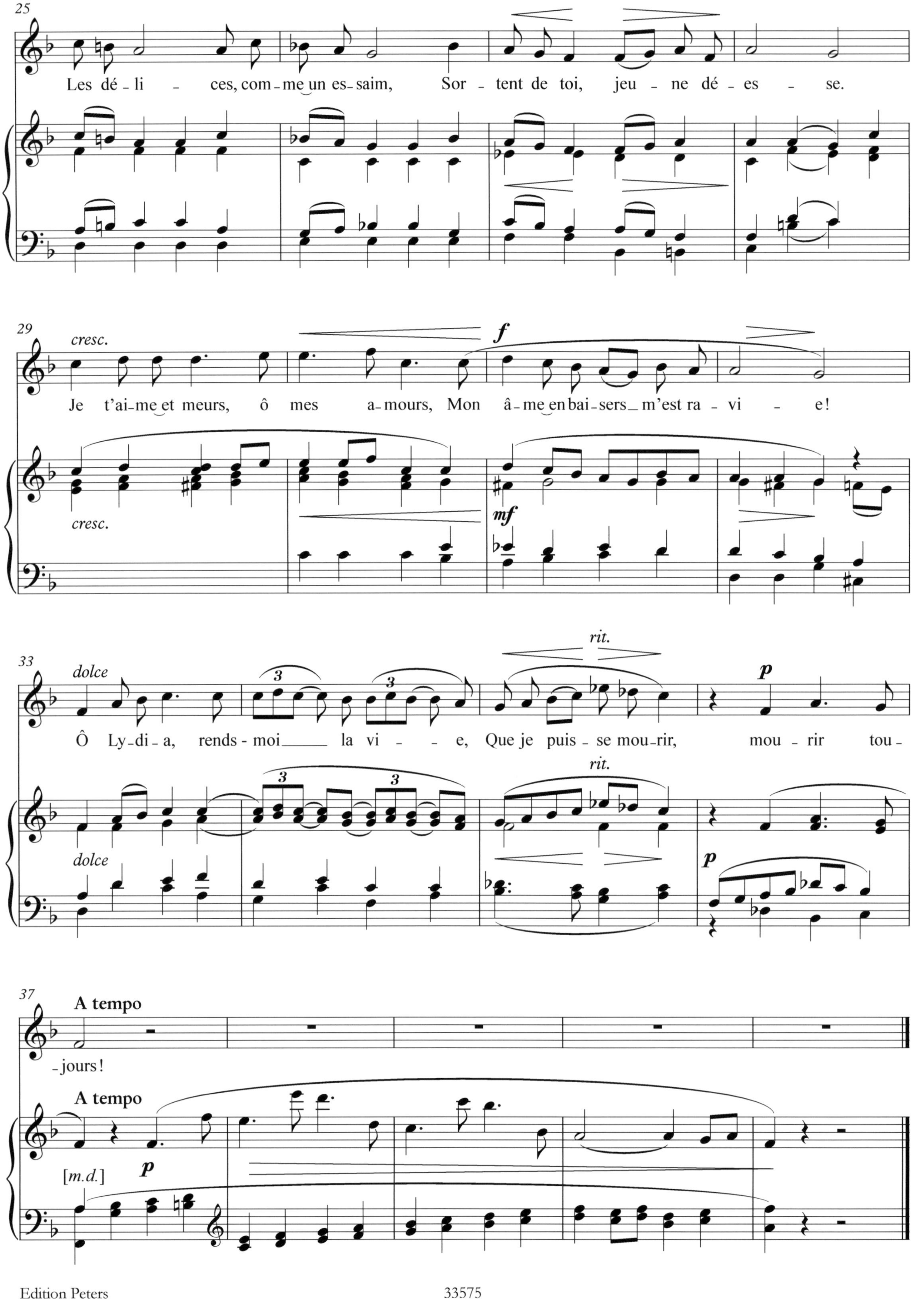
25
Les dé-li - ces, com-me un es-saim, Sor - tent de toi, jeu - ne dé - es - se.
29
cresc.
f
Je t'ai-me et meurs, ô mes a-mours, Mon â-me en bai-sers m'est ra - vi - e!
cresc.
mf
33
dolce
Ô Ly-di-a, rends-moi la vi - e, Que je puis-se mou-rir, mou-rir tou-
rit.
p
dolce
37
A tempo
-jours!
A tempo
[m.d.]
p

À Monsieur Félix Lévy

10. Hymne
(Charles Baudelaire)

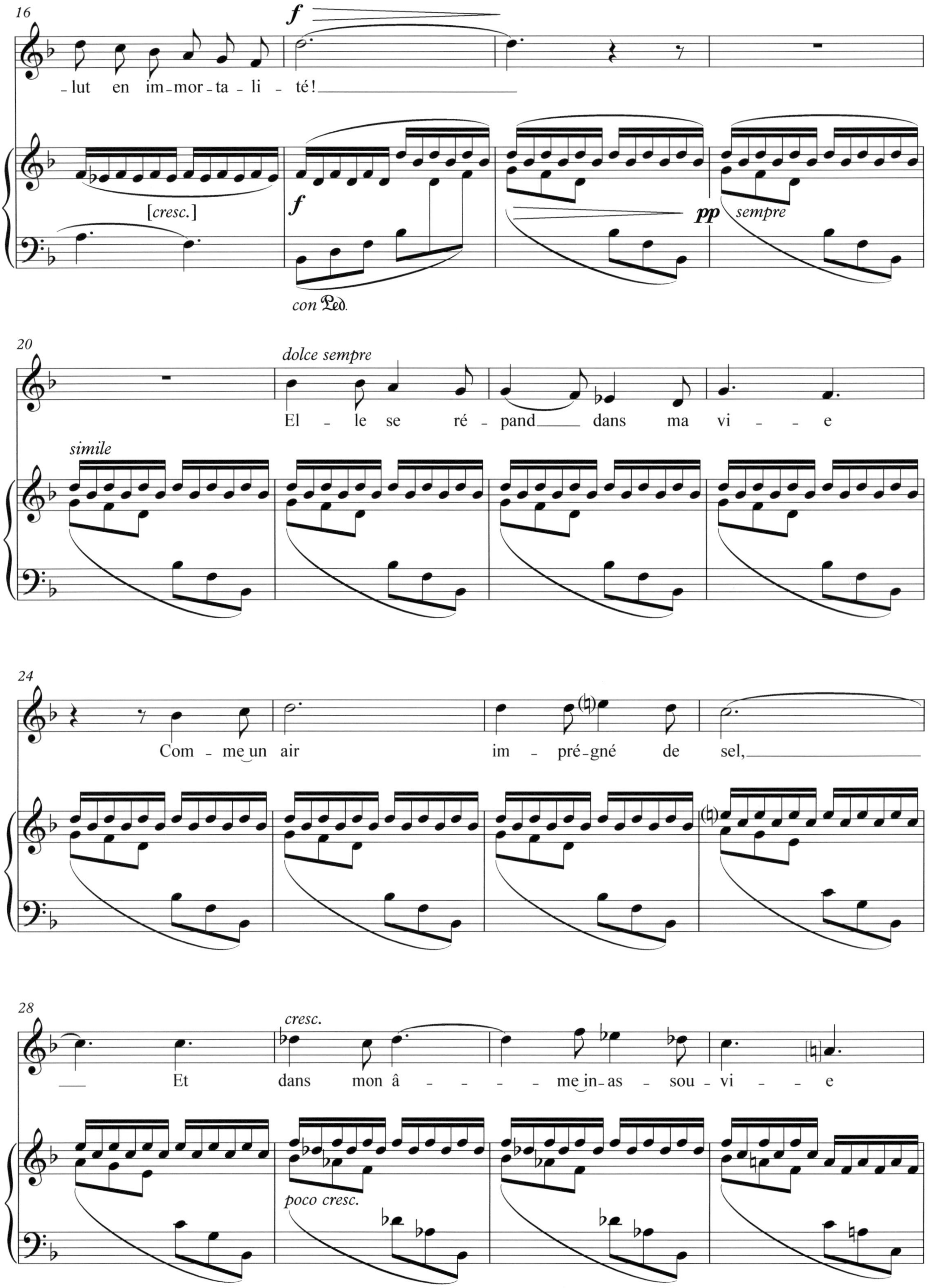
16
f
-lut en im-mor-ta-li-té!
[cresc.]
f
pp sempre
con Ped.
20
dolce sempre
El-le se ré-pand dans ma vi-e
simile
24
Com-me un air im-pré-gné de sel,
28
cresc.
Et dans mon â-me in-as-sou-vi-e
poco cresc.

À Monsieur Henri Duparc

11. La Rançon

(Charles Baudelaire)

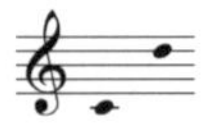

Original keys: b (c)

(Op. 8 no. 2)

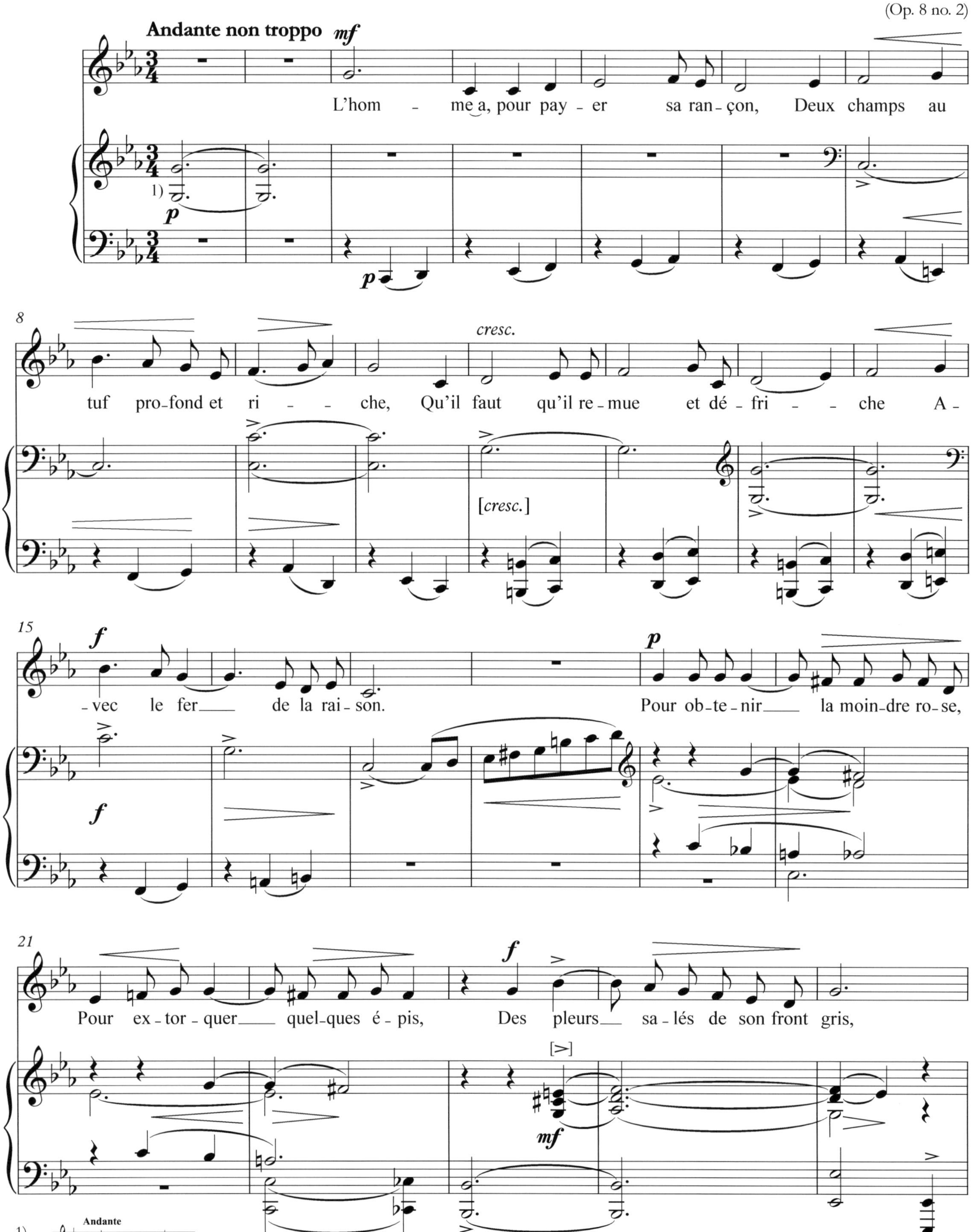
Andante non troppo
mf
L'hom - me a, pour pay - er sa ran - çon, Deux champs au
1)
p
8
tuf pro-fond et ri - - che, Qu'il faut qu'il re-mue et dé-fri - - che A -
cresc.
[cresc.]
15
f
-vec le fer de la rai - son.
p
Pour ob-te-nir la moin-dre ro-se,
21
f
Pour ex-tor-quer quel-ques é-pis, Des pleurs sa-lés de son front gris,
[>]
mf

1) C: 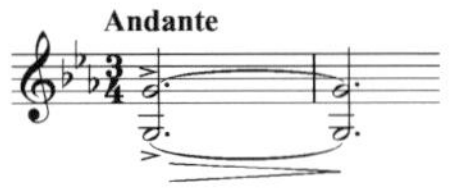
Andante

À Madame M[arie] Camille Clerc

12. Chant d'automne

(Charles Baudelaire)

Original keys: (a/c♯)

(Op. 5 no. 1)

Andante [animato] [1)]

1) Cf. tempo equivalence across bars 56–57 / Voir relation de tempo entre mes. 56 et 57 / Vgl. Temporelation zwischen Takt 56 und 57

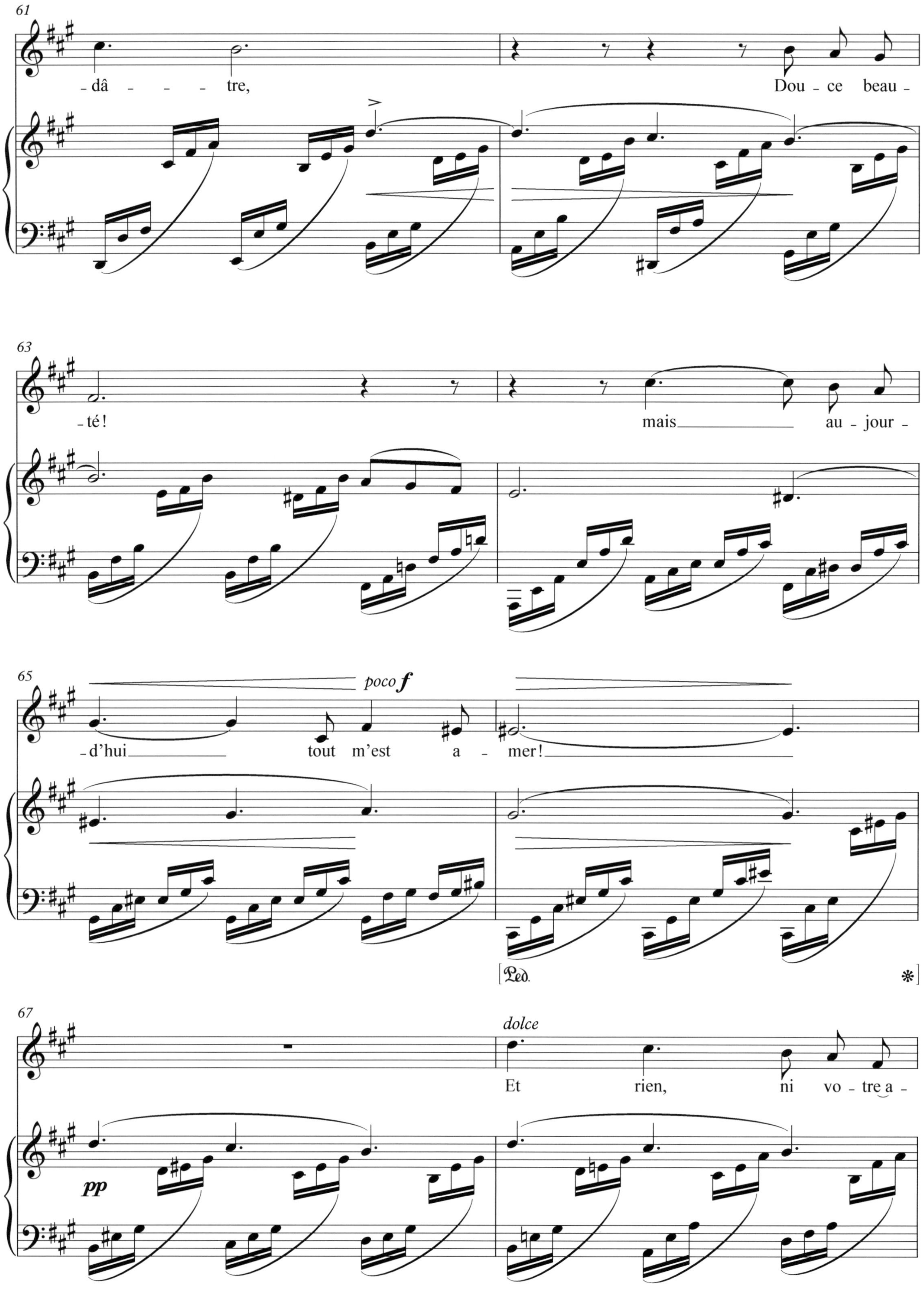
61
-dâ - - - tre,
Dou - ce beau -
63
-té!
mais au - jour -
65
poco f
-d'hui tout m'est a - mer!
Ped.
*
67
dolce
Et rien, ni vo - tre a -
pp

À Madame Édouard Lalo

13. Les Matelots

(Théophile Gautier)

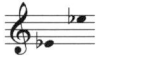

Original key: (E♭)

(Op. 2 no. 2)

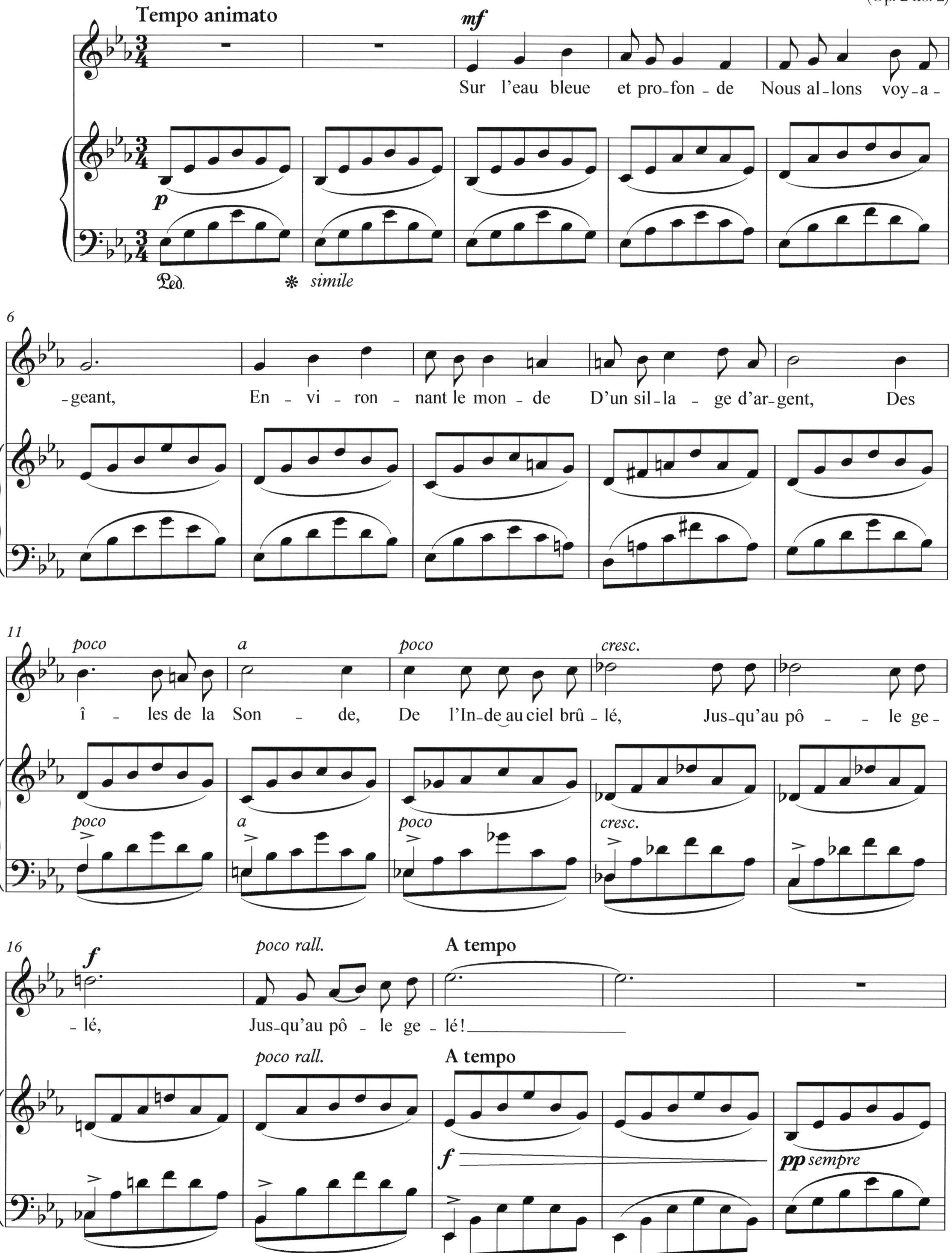
Tempo animato
mf
Sur l'eau bleue et pro-fon-de Nous al-lons voy-a-
p
Ped.
✻ simile
6
-geant, En-vi-ron-nant le mon-de D'un sil-la-ge d'ar-gent, Des
11
poco a poco cresc.
î-les de la Son-de, De l'In-de au ciel brû-lé, Jus-qu'au pô-le ge-
poco a poco cresc.
16
f
poco rall.
A tempo
-lé, Jus-qu'au pô-le ge-lé!
poco rall.
A tempo
f
pp sempre

À Monsieur E. Fernier

14. Seule!
(Théophile Gautier)

Original key: e

(Op. 3 no. 1)

1) *Ossia*: also at bars 32 and 50 / également aux mesures 32 et 50 / ebenso in Takt 32 und 50

1) Pre-1890 sources / Sources avant 1890 / Nach den Quellen vor 1890

15. Chanson du pêcheur (Lamento)

À Madame Pauline Viardot

(Théophile Gautier)

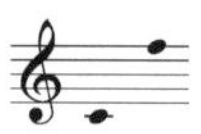

Original key: f

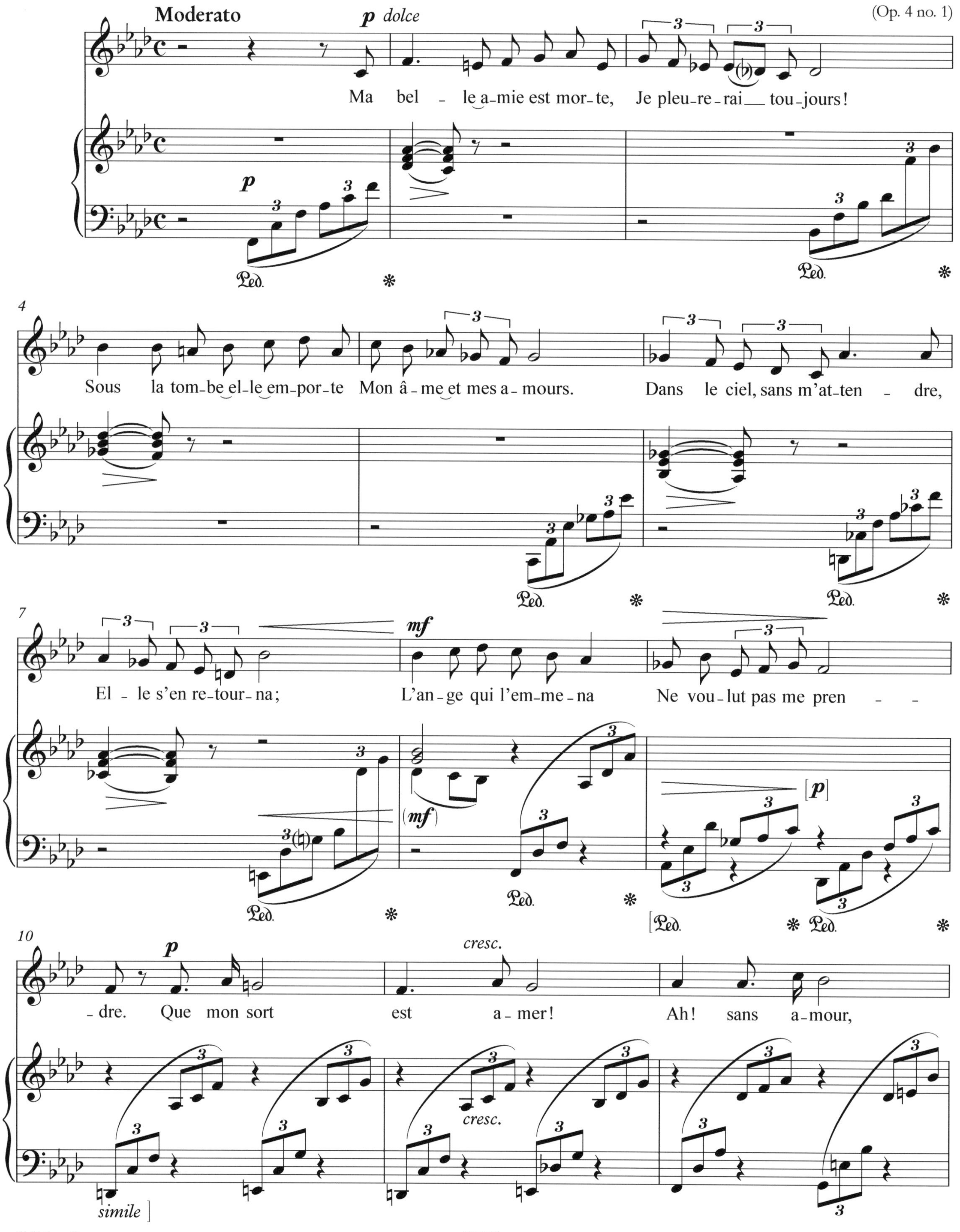

(Op. 4 no. 1)

Ma belle amie est morte, Je pleurerai toujours!
Sous la tombe elle emporte Mon âme et mes amours.
Dans le ciel, sans m'attendre, Elle s'en retourna;
L'ange qui l'emmena Ne voulut pas me prendre.
Que mon sort est amer! Ah! sans amour,

66

À Madame Édouard Lalo

16. Tristesse
(Théophile Gautier)

Original keys: (c/d)

(Op. 6 no.2)

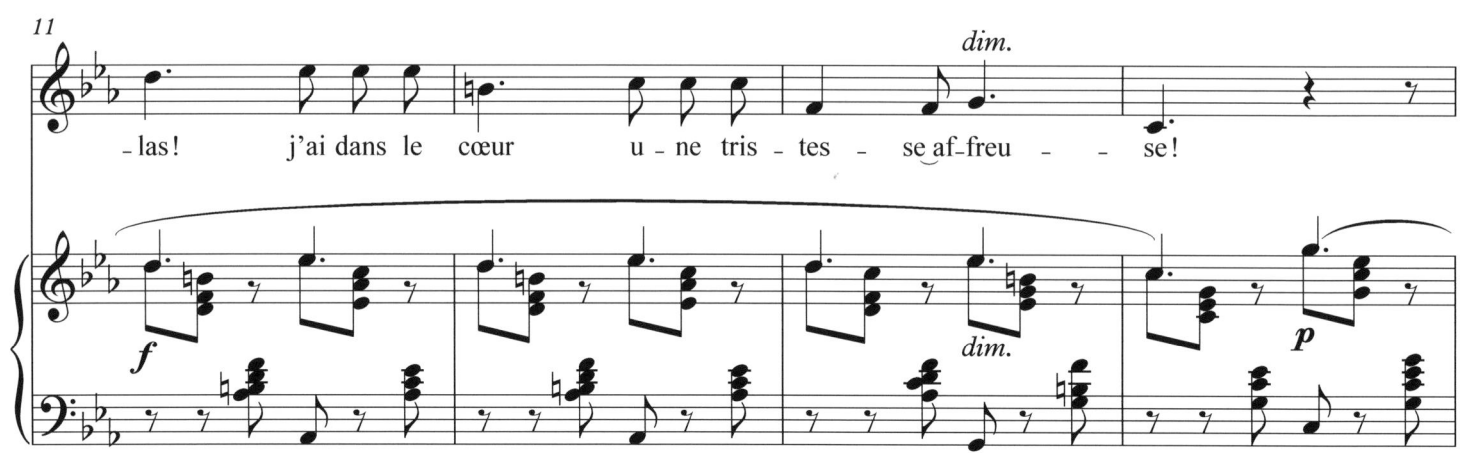

Av-ril est de re-tour, La pre-miè-re des ro— —ses, De ses lè-vres mi-clo— —ses, Rit au pre-mier beau jour; La ter-re bien-heu— —reu— —se S'ou-vre et s'é-pa-nou—it, Tout ai—me, tout jou—it, Hé— —las! j'ai dans le cœur u-ne tris-tes— —se af-freu— —se!

Edition Peters 33575

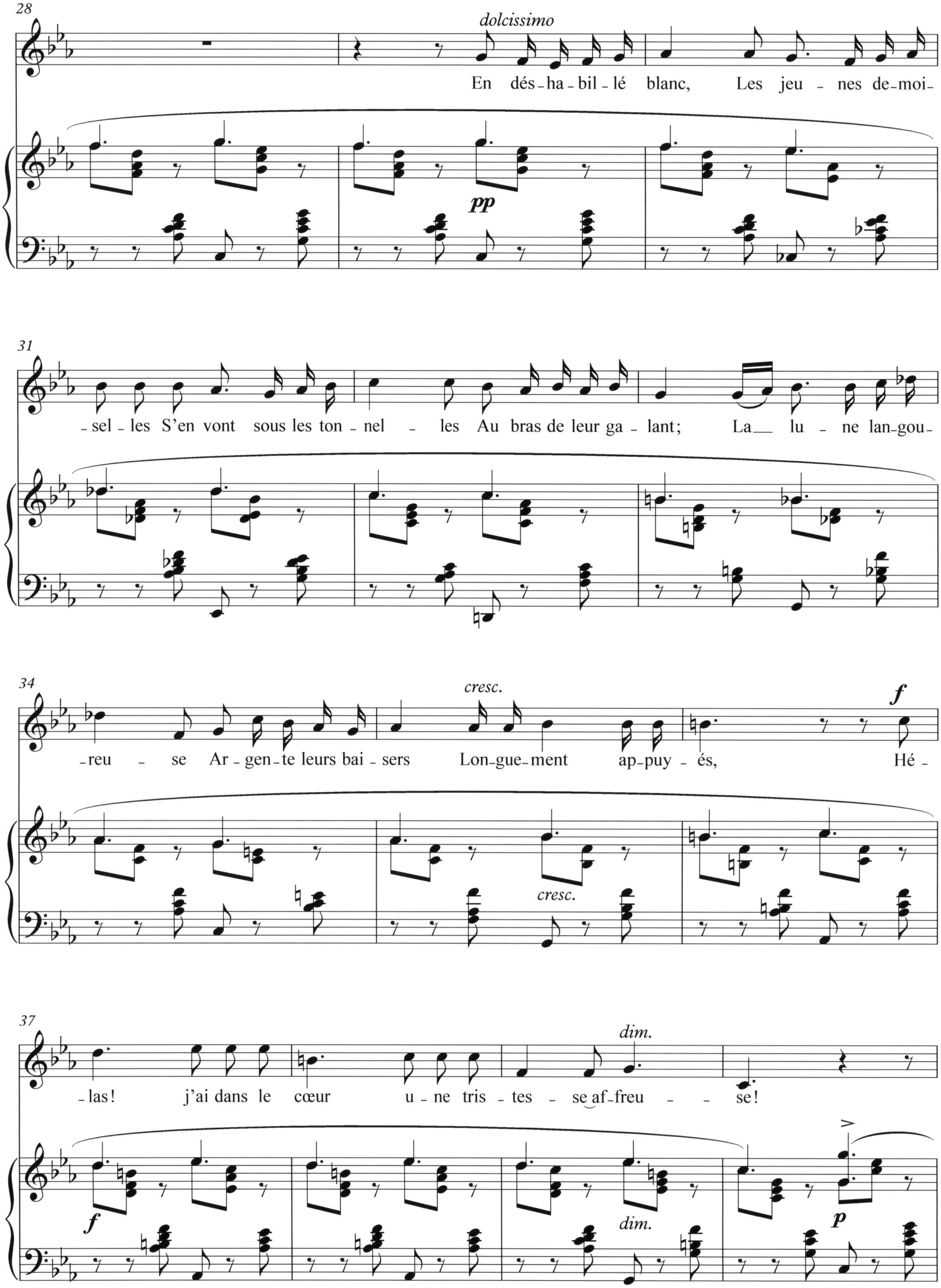
28
dolcissimo
En dés-ha-bil-lé blanc, Les jeu-nes de-moi-
pp
31
-sel-les S'en vont sous les ton-nel-les Au bras de leur ga-lant; La lu-ne lan-gou-
34
cresc.
f
-reu-se Ar-gen-te leurs bai-sers Lon-gue-ment ap-puy-és, Hé-
cresc.
37
dim.
-las! j'ai dans le cœur u-ne tris-tes-se af-freu-se!
f
dim.
p

70

À Madame Amélie Duez

17. Aubade
(Louis Pomey)

Original keys: (F/A)

(Op. 6 no. 1)

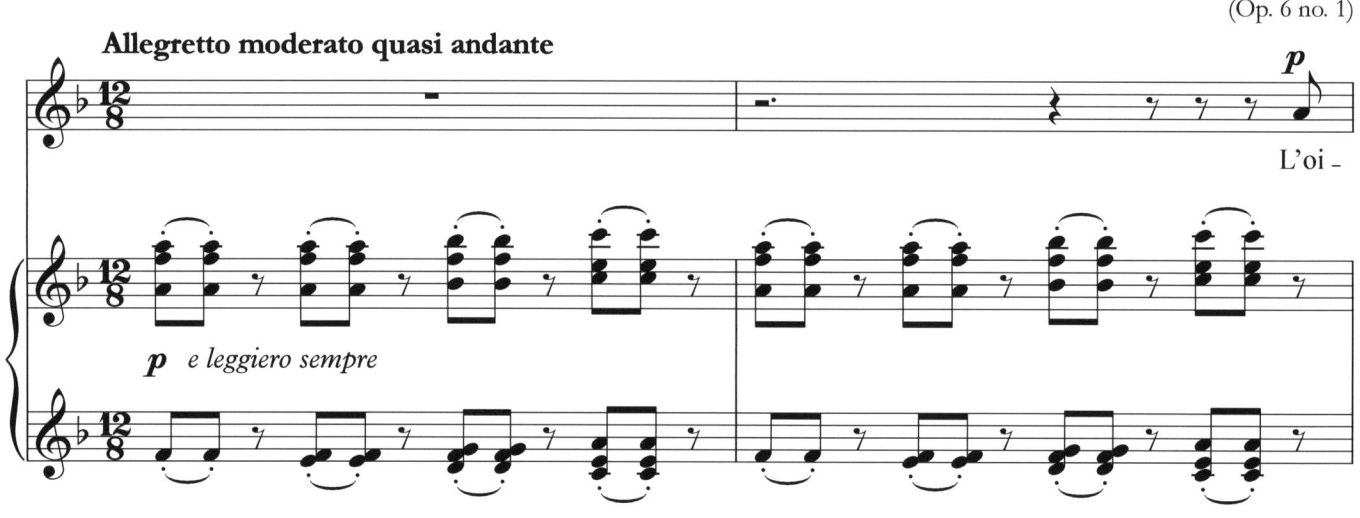

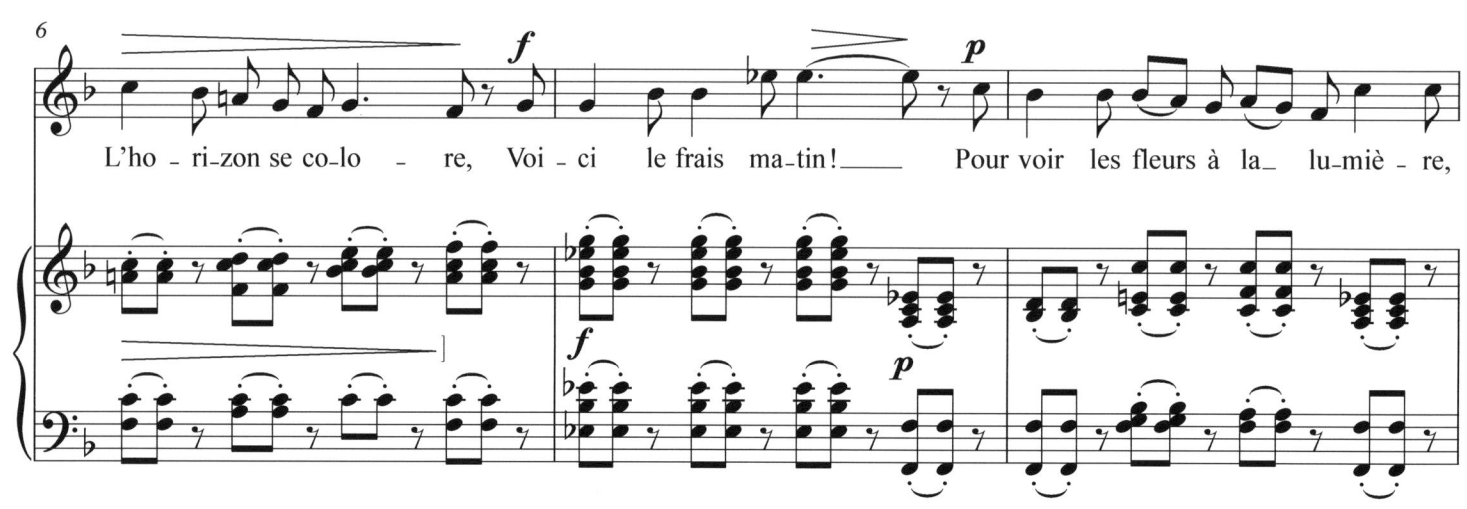

Edition Peters   33575

1) See Critical Commentary / Voir commentaire critique / Vgl. Kritischen Bericht

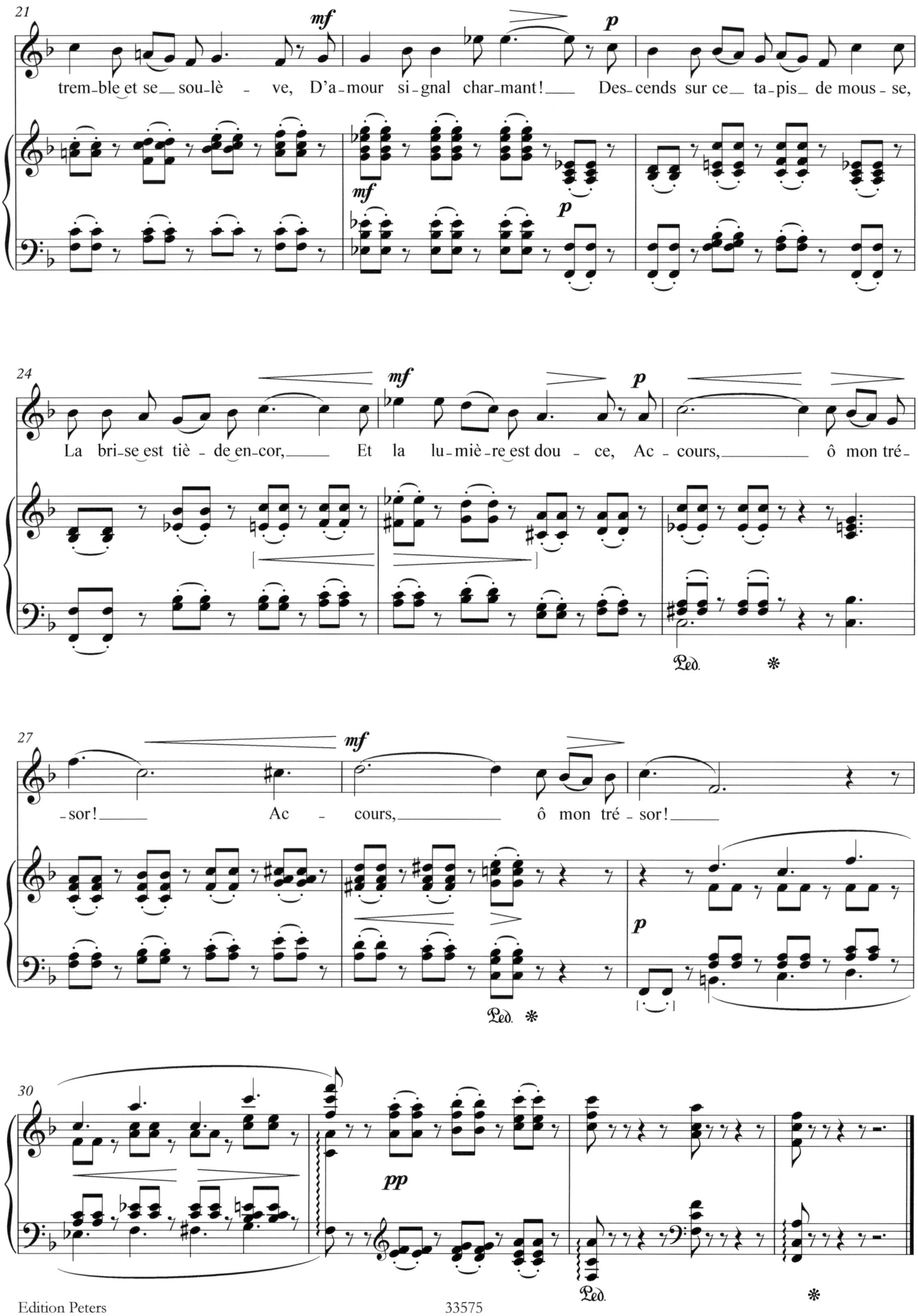
21
mf
p
trem-ble et se-soulè-ve, D'a-mour si-gnal char-mant! Des-cends sur ce-ta-pis-de mous-se,
24
mf
p
La bri-se est tiè-de en-cor, Et la lu-miè-re est dou-ce, Ac-cours, ô mon tré-
Ped.
27
mf
-sor! Ac-cours, ô mon tré-sor!
p
Ped.
30
pp
Ped.

À Madame Pauline Viardot

18. Barcarolle
(Marc Monnier)

Original key: g

(Op. 7 no. 3)

Andante con moto (♩. = 60)

74

19. Ici-bas !

À Madame Georges Lecoq, née MacBrid[e]

(Sully Prudhomme)

Original key: f♯

(Op. 8 no. 3)

1) **Rc-m:**  (and equivalently at bars 10 and 18)
(et pareillement aux mesures 10 et 18)
(ebenso in Takt 10 und 18)

78

À Madame Claudie Chamerot

20. Au bord de l'eau
(Sully Prudhomme)

Original keys: d [fragment] / c (c♯)

1) ♩. ♩. also feasible; see Critical Commentary
également possible; voir commentaire critique
ebenso möglich; vgl. Kritischen Bericht

2) See Preface: Tempo, metre and rhythm
Voir Préface: Tempo, mètre et rythme
Vgl. Vorwort: Tempo, Metrum und Rhythmus

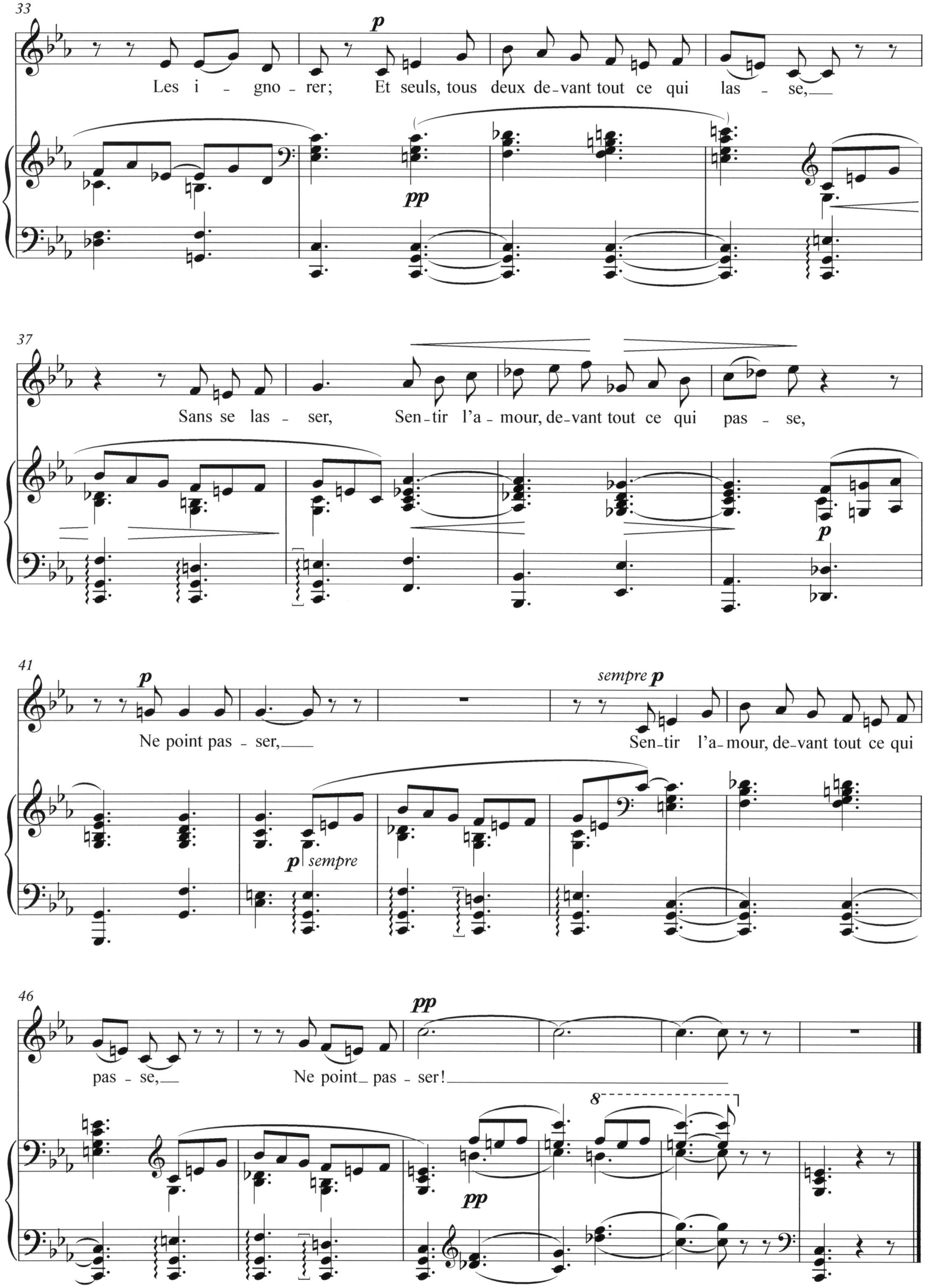
33
p
Les i - gno - rer; Et seuls, tous deux de-vant tout ce qui las - se,
pp
37
Sans se las - ser, Sen-tir l'a - mour, de-vant tout ce qui pas - se,
p
41
p
Ne point pas - ser,
sempre p
Sen-tir l'a-mour, de-vant tout ce qui
p sempre
46
pas - se,
pp
Ne point pas - ser!
8
pp

À Madame Marguerite Baugnies

21. Après un rêve

(Romain Bussine / traditional Tuscan)

Original key: c

(Op. 7 no. 1)

Andantino

dolce

Dans un som-meil__ que char-mait ton i-ma-ge
Le - va - ti, sol,__ che la lu - na è le - va - ta;

Je rê-vais le bon-heur, ar-dent mi - ra - - - - ge,
Le - va da - gli oc - chi miei tan - to dor - mi - - - - re.

Tes yeux é-taient plus doux,__ ta voix pu-re et so - no - - re, Tu ray-on-
Il tra - di - tor del son - no m'ha in - gan - na - ta; Il bel lo - a -

-nais com-me un ciel__ é-clai-ré par l'au-ro - - re;
- man - te m'ha fat - - to spa - ri - - re.

À Madame la Baronne de Montagnac, née de Rosalès

22. Sérénade toscane

(Romain Bussine / traditional Tuscan)

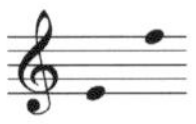

Original key: (c)

(Op. 3 no. 2)

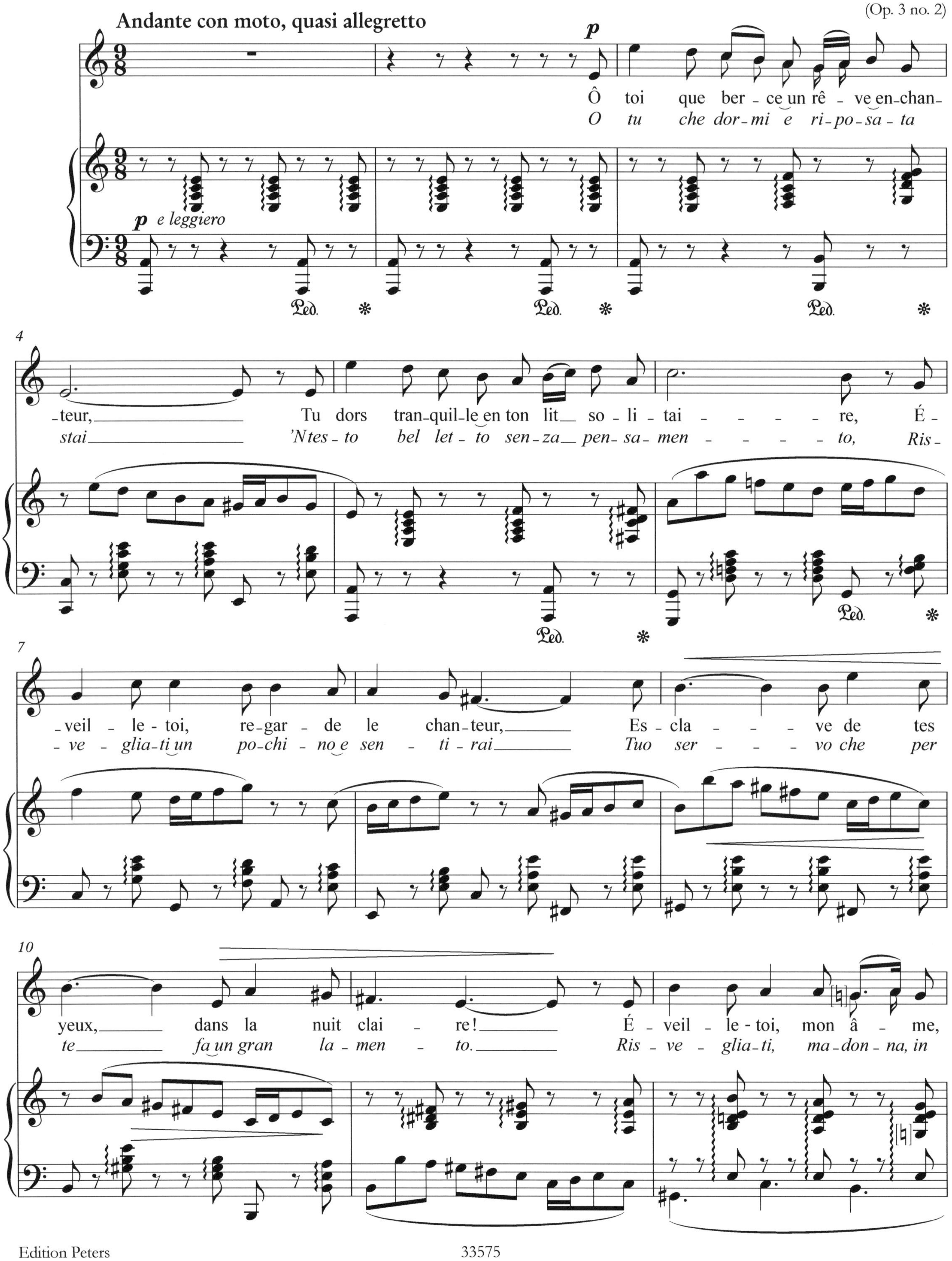
Andante con moto, quasi allegretto
p
Ô toi que ber - ce un rê - ve en-chan-
O tu che dor-mi e ri-po-sa-ta
p e leggiero
-teur, Tu dors tran-quil-le en ton lit so-li-tai - - - - re, É-
stai 'Ntes-to bel let-to sen-za pen-sa-men - - - - to, Ris-
-veil - le-toi, re-gar - de le chan-teur, Es-cla - - - ve de tes
-ve - glia-ti un po-chi - no e sen - ti-rai Tuo ser - - - vo che per
yeux, dans la nuit clai - re! É - veil - le-toi, mon â - me,
te fa un gran la - men - to. Ris - ve - glia-ti, ma-don - na, in

88

À Madame la Vicomtesse de Gironde

23. Sylvie
(Paul de Choudens)

Original keys: A♭ (A♭/F)

(Op. 6 no. 3)

Allegretto moderato

1) *Ossia* , also in bars 8, 28, 30 and 50 / de même aux mesures 8, 28, 30 et 50 / ebenso in Takt 8, 28, 30 und 50

Edition Peters

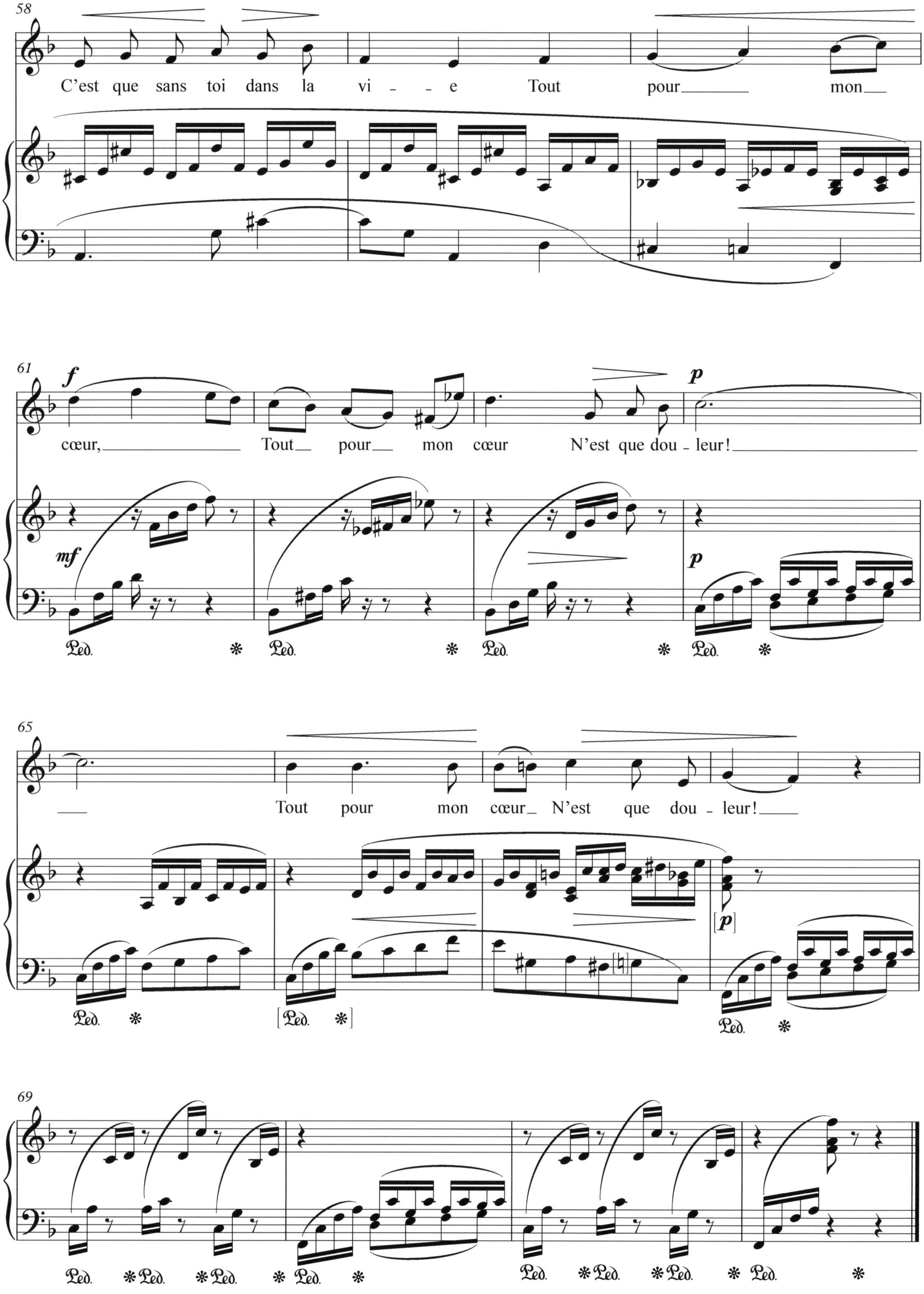

58
C'est que sans toi dans la vi - - e Tout pour mon
61
cœur, Tout pour mon cœur N'est que dou - leur!
65
Tout pour mon cœur N'est que dou - leur!
69

À Madame la Comtesse de Cauville

24–26. Poème d'un jour

(Charles Grandmougin)

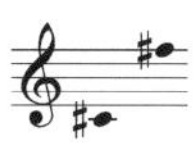

Original keys: D♭ (B)

I. Rencontre

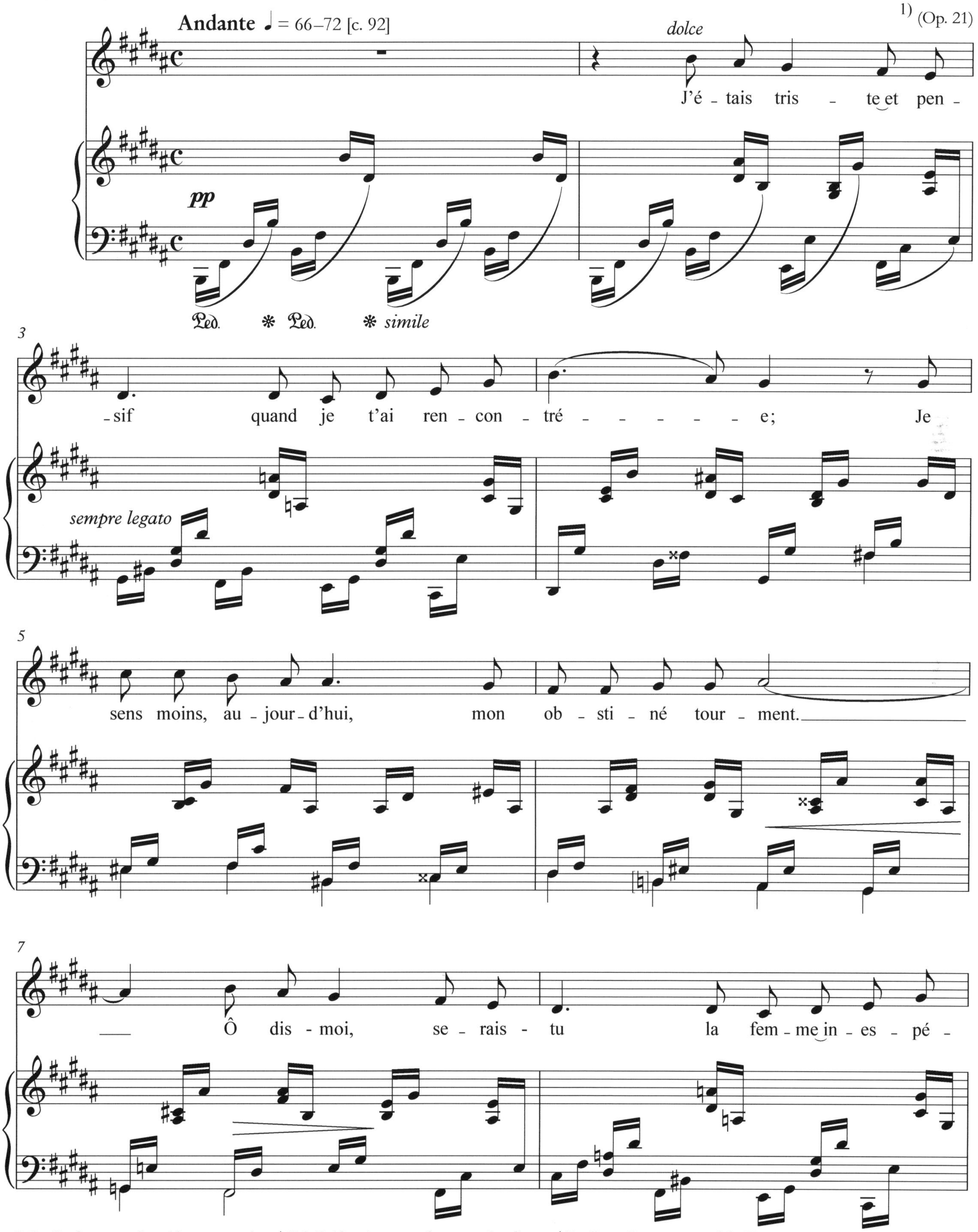
1) (Op. 21)
Andante ♩ = 66–72 [c. 92]
dolce
J'é - tais tris - te et pen - sif quand je t'ai ren - con - tré - - - - - - e; Je sens moins, au - jour - d'hui, mon ob - sti - né tour - ment. Ô dis - moi, se - rais - tu la fem - me in - es - pé -
pp
Ped. * Ped. * simile
sempre legato
3
5
7

1) See Preface regarding this opus number / Voir Préface à propos de ce numéro d'opus / Zu dieser Opusnummer siehe Vorwort

1) See Critical Commentary / Voir commentaire critique / Vgl. Kritischen Bericht

(Poème d'un jour)

Original keys: f♯ (e)

II. Toujours

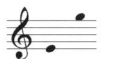

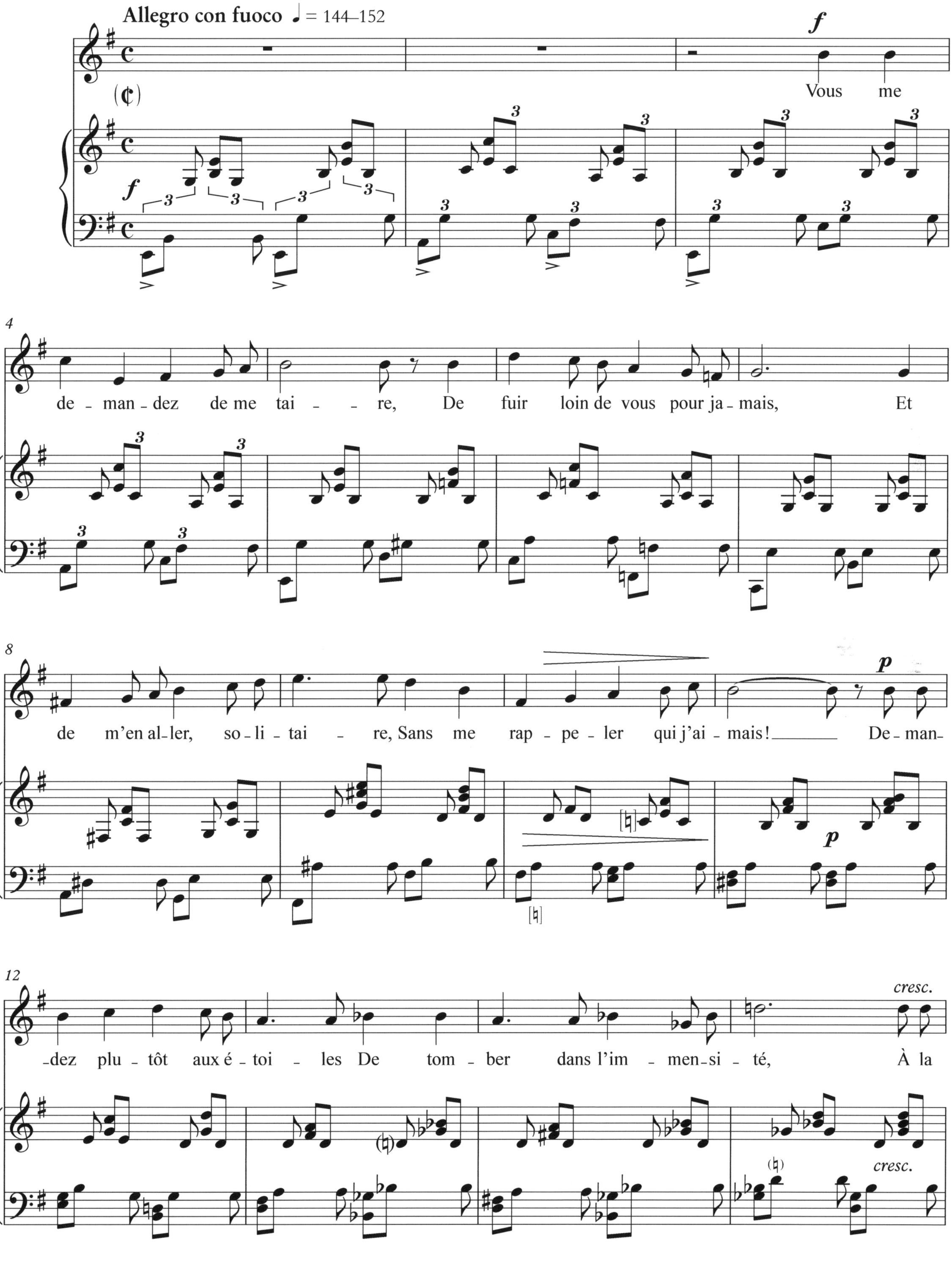
Allegro con fuoco ♩ = 144–152
f
Vous me
(¢)
f
4
de - man - dez de me tai - - re, De fuir loin de vous pour ja - mais, Et
8
de m'en al - ler, so - li - tai - re, Sans me rap - pe - ler qui j'ai - mais! De - man-
p
p
12
-dez plu - tôt aux é - toi - les De tom - ber dans l'im - men - si - té, À la
cresc.
cresc.

(Poème d'un jour)
III. Adieu

Original keys: G♭ (E)

1) See Critical Commentary / Voir commentaire critique / Vgl. Kritischen Bericht

À Madame Camille Saint-Saëns

27. Nell
(Leconte de Lisle)

Original keys: (E♭/G♭)

Op. 18 no. 1

Andante, quasi allegretto ♩ = 66 [96] [1)]

Ta ro- se de pour- pre, à ton clair so- leil, Ô Juin, é- tin- cel- le en- i- vré- e; Pen- che aus- si vers moi ta cou- pe do- ré- e: Mon cœur à ta ro- se est pa- reil.

Sous le mol a- bri de la feuil- le om- breu- se Mon- te un sou- pir de vo- lup-

pp sempre e sempre legato

espressivo

1) See Preface: Tempo, metre and rhythm / Voir Préface: Tempo, mètre et rythme / Vgl. Vorwort: Tempo, Metrum und Rhythmus

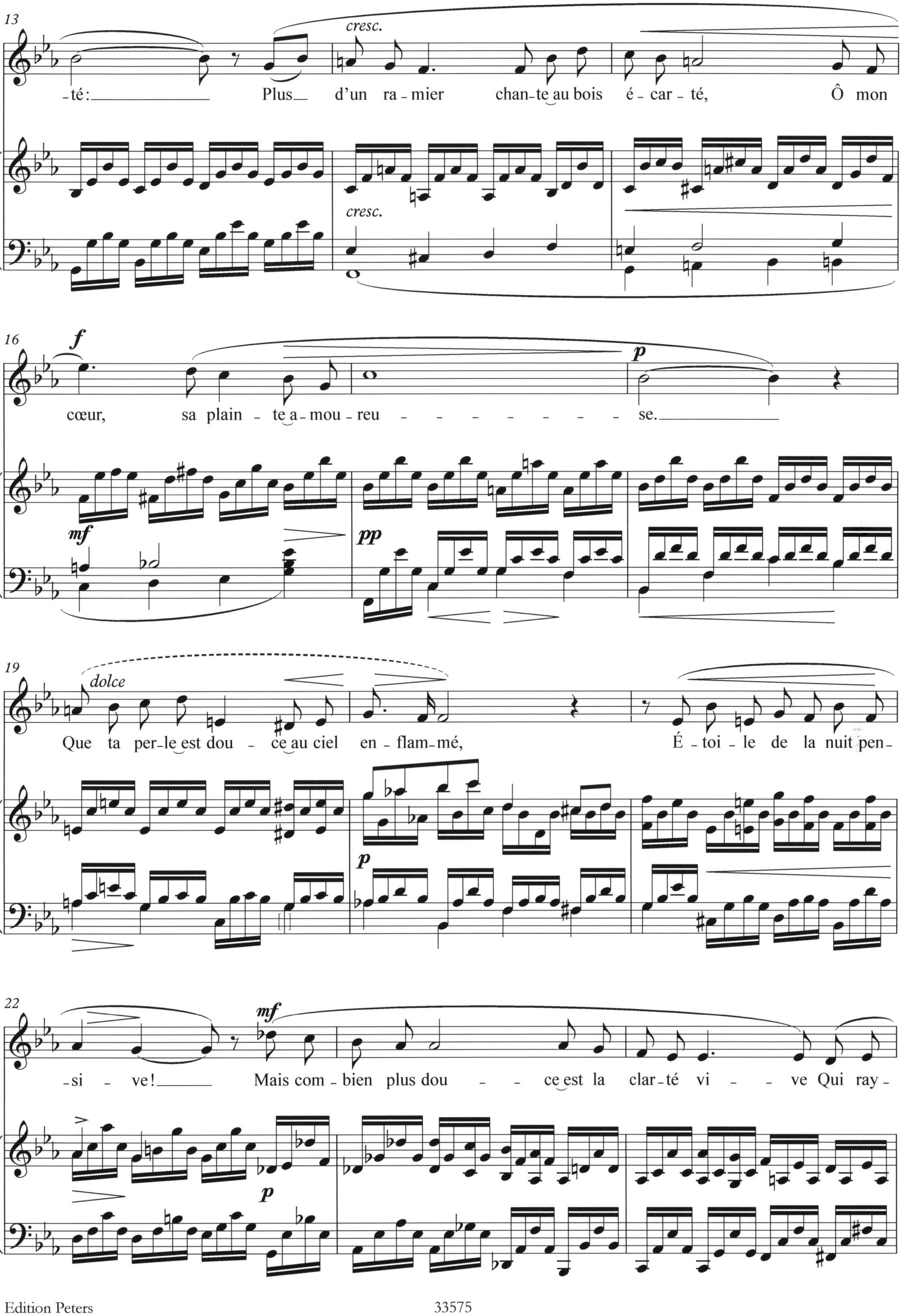
13
cresc.
-té: Plus d'un ra-mier chan-te au bois é-car-té, Ô mon
cresc.
16
f
cœur, sa plain-te a-mou-reu - - - - - - - - se.
mf
pp
p
19
dolce
Que ta per-le est dou-ce au ciel en-flam-mé, É-toi-le de la nuit pen-
p
22
mf
-si - ve! Mais com-bien plus dou - - - ce est la clar-té vi - - - ve Qui ray-
p

À Emmanuel Jadin

28. Le Voyageur

(Armand Silvestre)

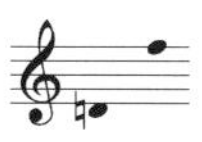

Original keys: (f/**a**)

Op. 18 no. 2

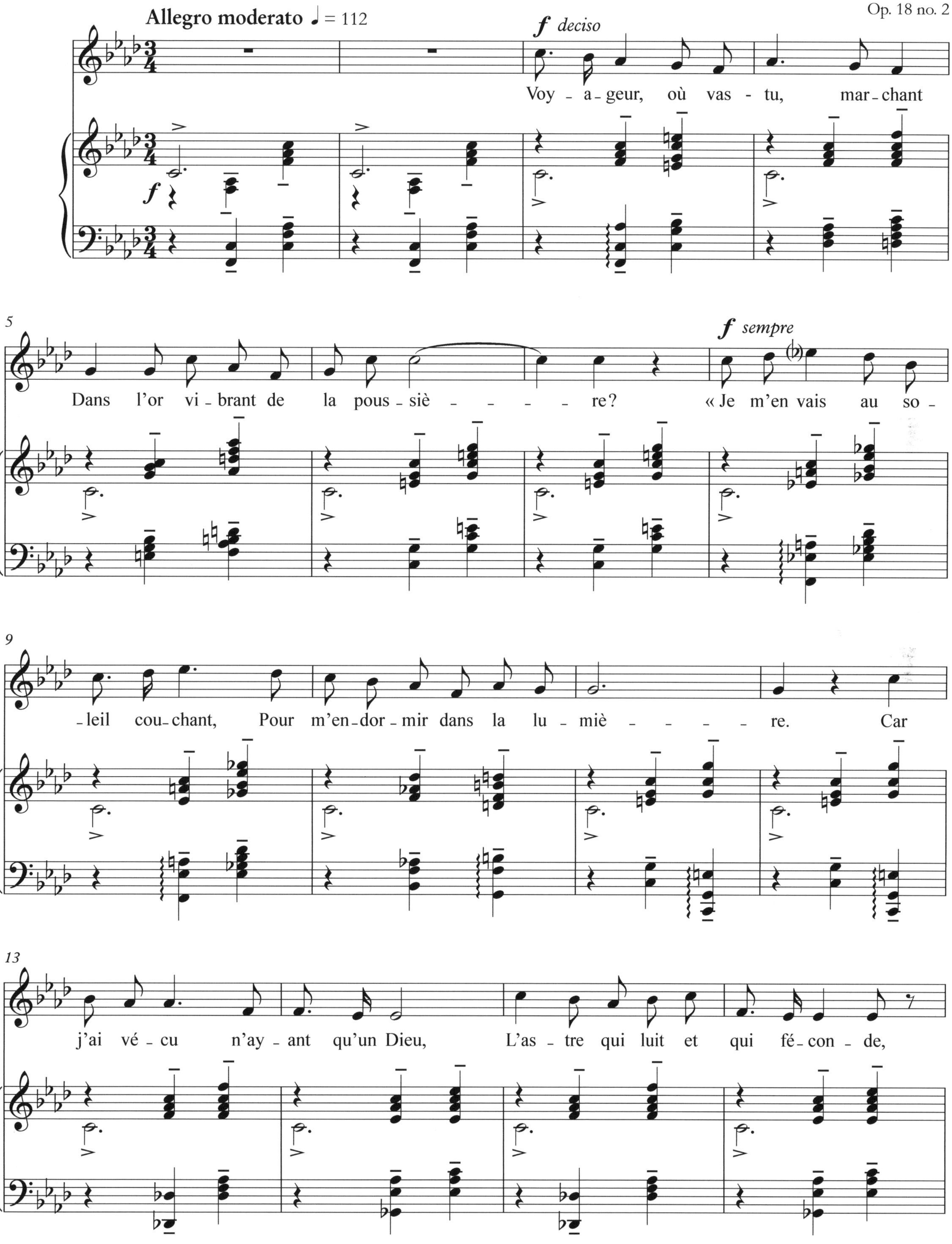
Allegro moderato ♩ = 112
f deciso
Voy - a - geur, où vas - tu, mar - chant
Dans l'or vi - brant de la pous - siè - - - - - re?
f sempre
« Je m'en vais au so - leil cou - chant, Pour m'en - dor - mir dans la lu - miè - - - - - re.
Car j'ai vé - cu n'ay - ant qu'un Dieu, L'as - tre qui luit et qui fé - con - de,

108

À Mademoiselle Alice Boissonnet

29. Automne

(Armand Silvestre)

Original keys: (b/c♯)

Op. 18 no. 3

Edition Peters   33575

À Mademoiselle Alice Boissonnet

30. Les Berceaux
(Sully Prudhomme)

Original keys: (b♭/c)

Op. 23 no. 1

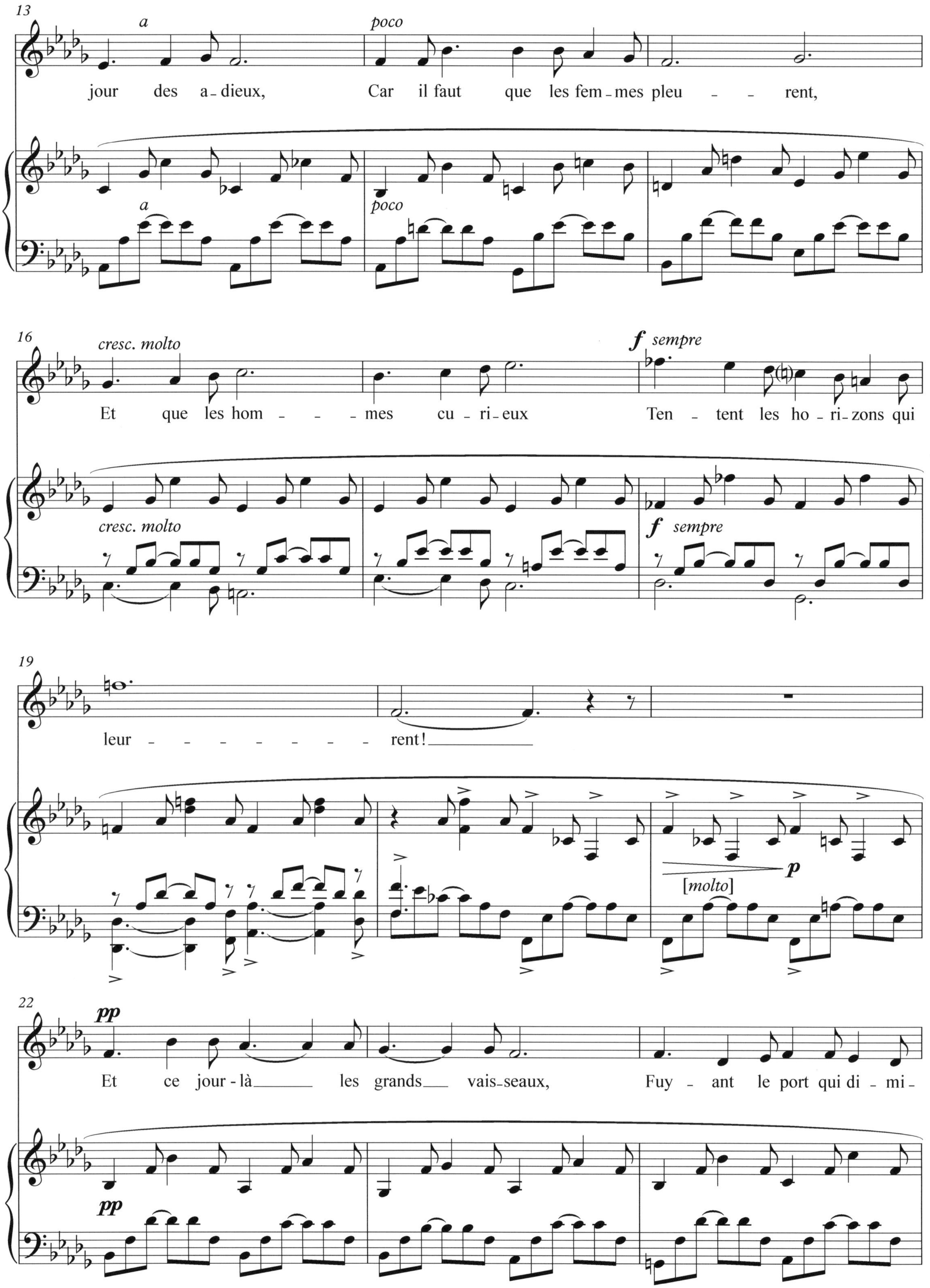
13
a
poco
jour des a-dieux, Car il faut que les fem-mes pleu - - - rent,
16
cresc. molto
f sempre
Et que les hom - - - - mes cu-ri-eux Ten - tent les ho-ri-zons qui
19
leur - - - - - - - - - rent!
[molto]
p
22
pp
Et ce jour-là les grands vais-seaux, Fuy - ant le port qui di-mi-

1) See Critical Commentary / Voir commentaire critique / Vgl. Kritischen Bericht

À Madame A. Castillon

31. Notre amour

(Armand Silvestre)

Original keys: (D/E)

Op. 23 no. 2

Allegretto ♪ = 126 [c. 160]

leggieramente

p

p leggiero e legato

No-tre a-mour est cho _ se lé _ gè _ re, Com-me les par-fums que le vent Prend aux ci _ mes de la fou-gè _ re, Pour qu'on les res - pi - re en rê - vant; No-tre a--mour est cho _ se lé - gè _ _ _ _ re!

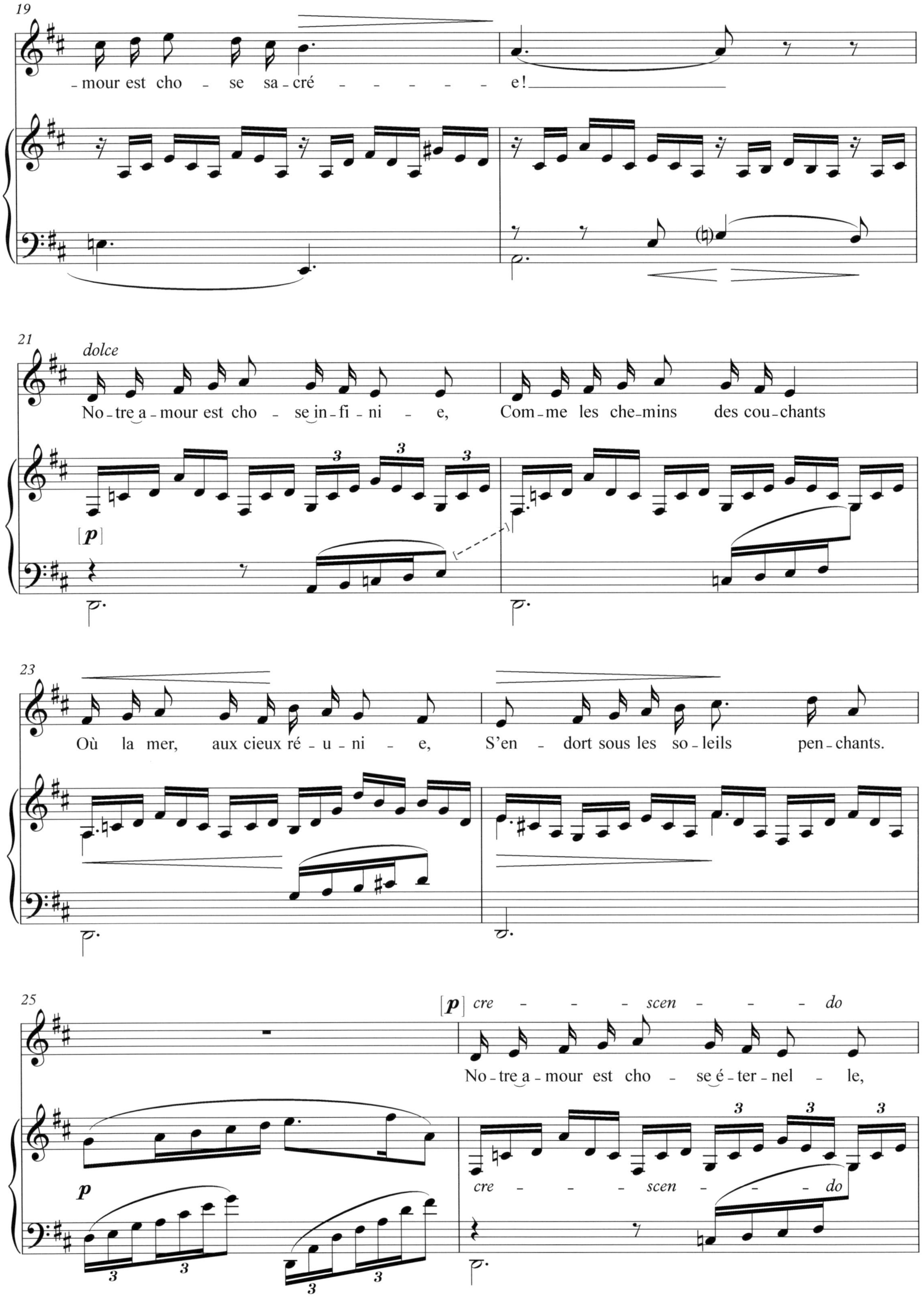
19
-mour est cho - se sa-cré - - - - - - e!
21
dolce
No-tre a-mour est cho - se in-fi-ni - e, Com-me les che-mins des cou-chants
[p]
23
Où la mer, aux cieux ré - u - ni - e, S'en - dort sous les so-leils pen-chants.
25
[p] cre - - - scen - - - do
No-tre a-mour est cho - se é-ter-nel - le,
p
cre - - - scen - - - do

À Mademoiselle Alice Boissonnet

32. Le Secret

(Armand Silvestre)

Original keys: (**D♭**/F)

Op. 23 no. 3

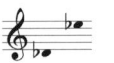

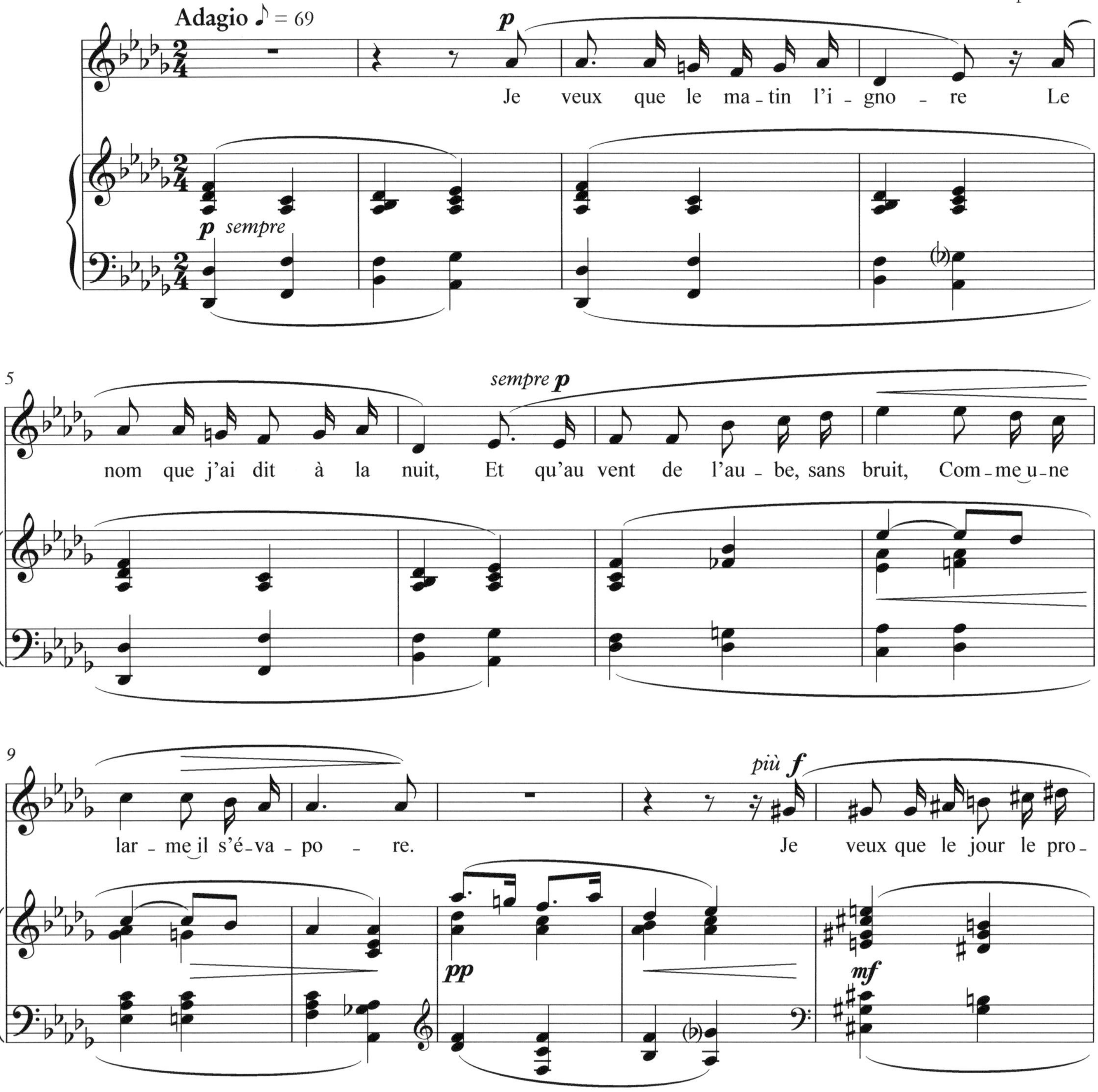
Adagio ♪ = 69
p
Je veux que le ma - tin l'i - gno - re Le
p sempre
sempre p
nom que j'ai dit à la nuit, Et qu'au vent de l'au - be, sans bruit, Com - me u - ne
più f
lar - me il s'é - va - po - re. Je veux que le jour le pro -
pp
mf
p
- cla - me L'a - mour qu'au ma - tin j'ai ca - ché, Et sur mon
p

À Mademoiselle Jane Huré

33. Chanson d'amour

(Armand Silvestre)

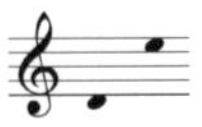

Original keys: (**F**/G)

Op. 27 no. 1

Allegro moderato ♩ = 116 [c. 152]

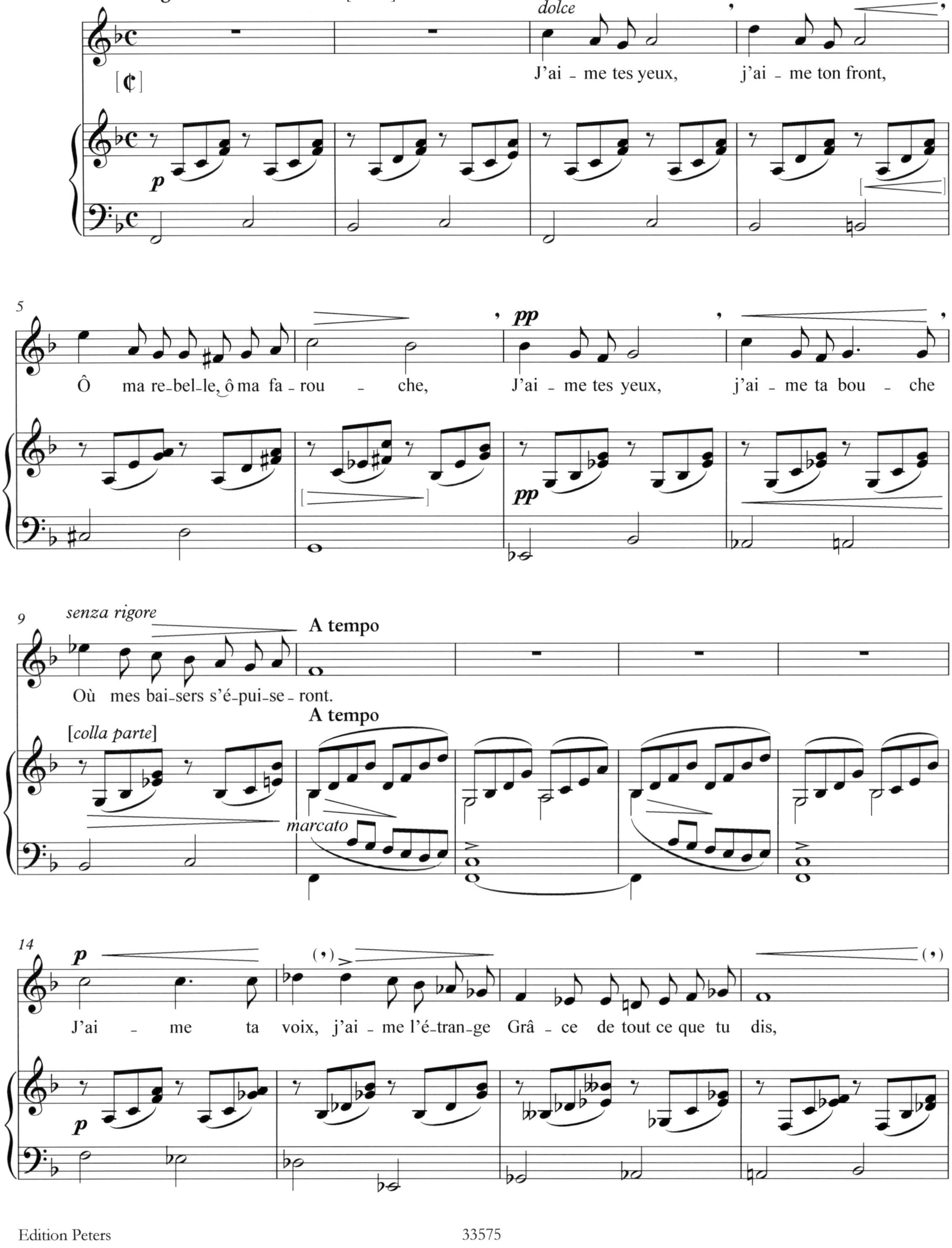
dolce
[¢]
J'ai - me tes yeux, j'ai - me ton front,
p
5
Ô ma re-bel-le, ô ma fa-rou - che,
pp
J'ai - me tes yeux, j'ai - me ta bou - che
9
senza rigore
A tempo
Où mes bai-sers s'é-pui-se-ront.
[colla parte]
marcato
14
p
(,)
J'ai - me ta voix, j'ai - me l'é-tran-ge Grâ - ce de tout ce que tu dis,

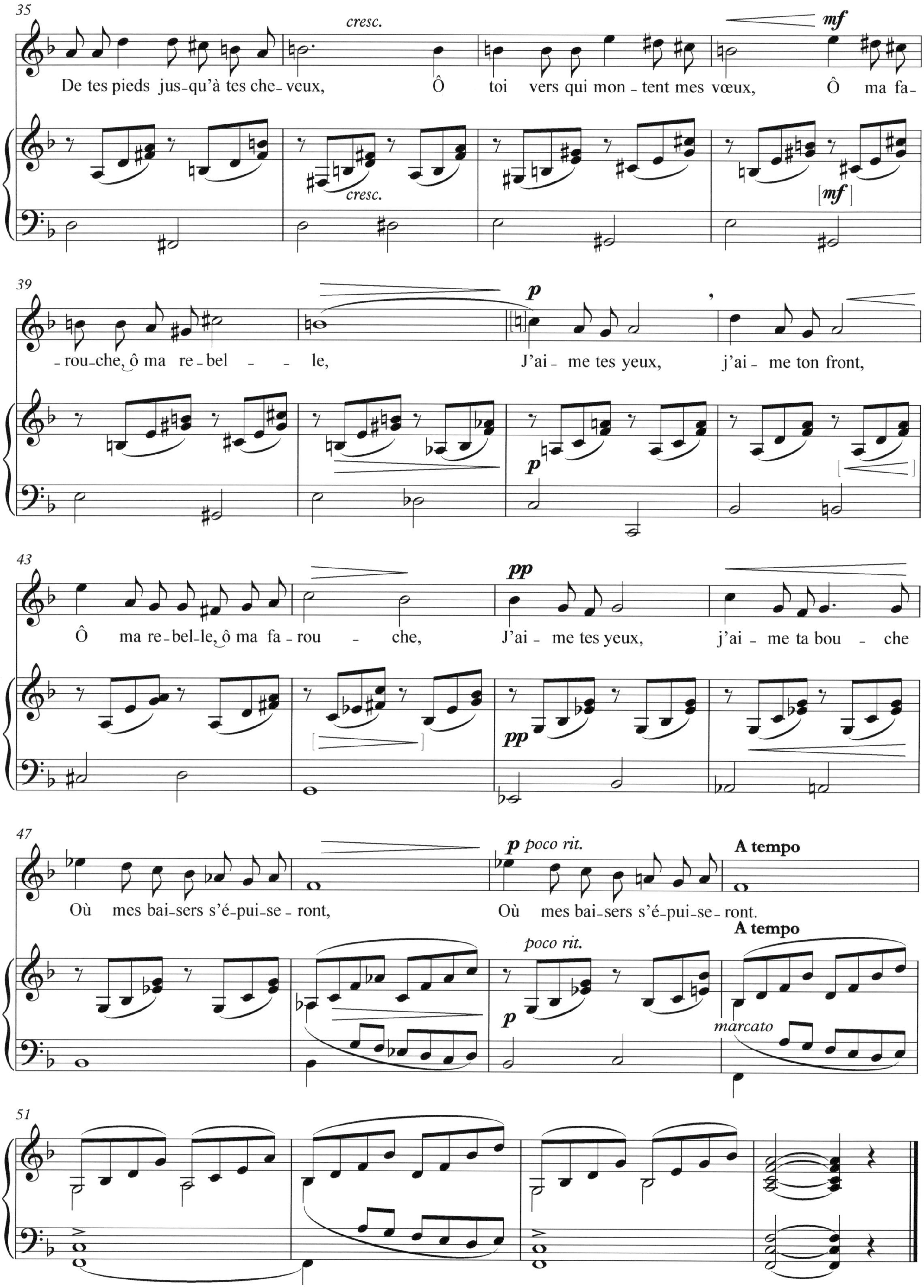
35
cresc.
mf
De tes pieds jus-qu'à tes che-veux, Ô toi vers qui mon-tent mes vœux, Ô ma fa-
cresc.
[mf]
39
p
-rou-che, ô ma re-bel - - le, J'ai-me tes yeux, j'ai-me ton front,
p
43
pp
Ô ma re-bel-le, ô ma fa-rou - che, J'ai-me tes yeux, j'ai-me ta bou - che
pp
47
p poco rit.
A tempo
Où mes bai-sers s'é-pui-se-ront, Où mes bai-sers s'é-pui-se-ront.
poco rit.
A tempo
p
marcato
51

À Madame Henriette Fuchs

34. La Fée aux chansons
(Armand Silvestre)

Original keys: E (D/F)

Op. 27 no. 2

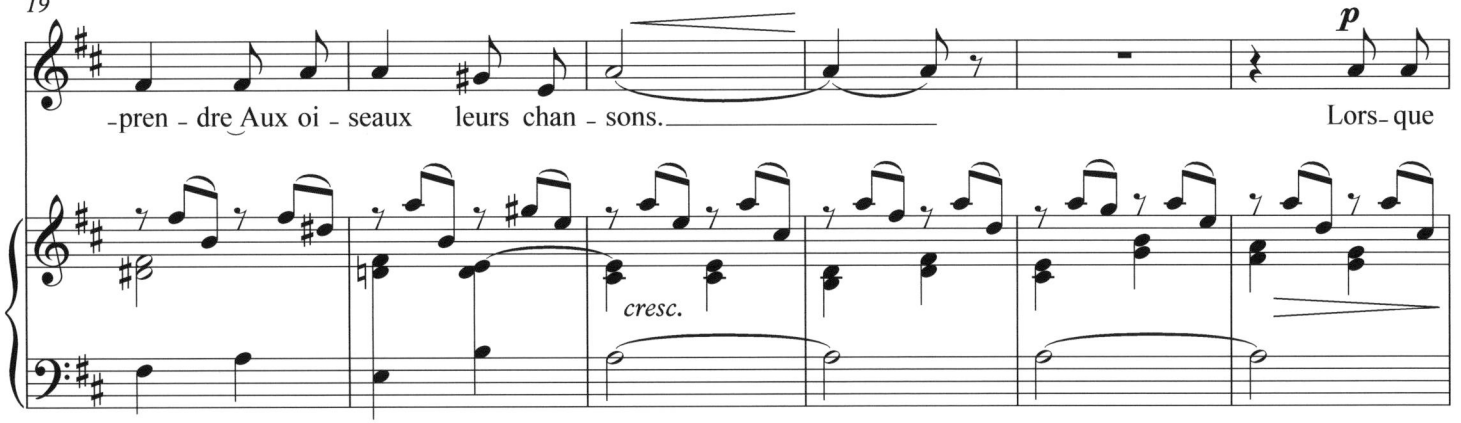

1) **A:** *Allegro*

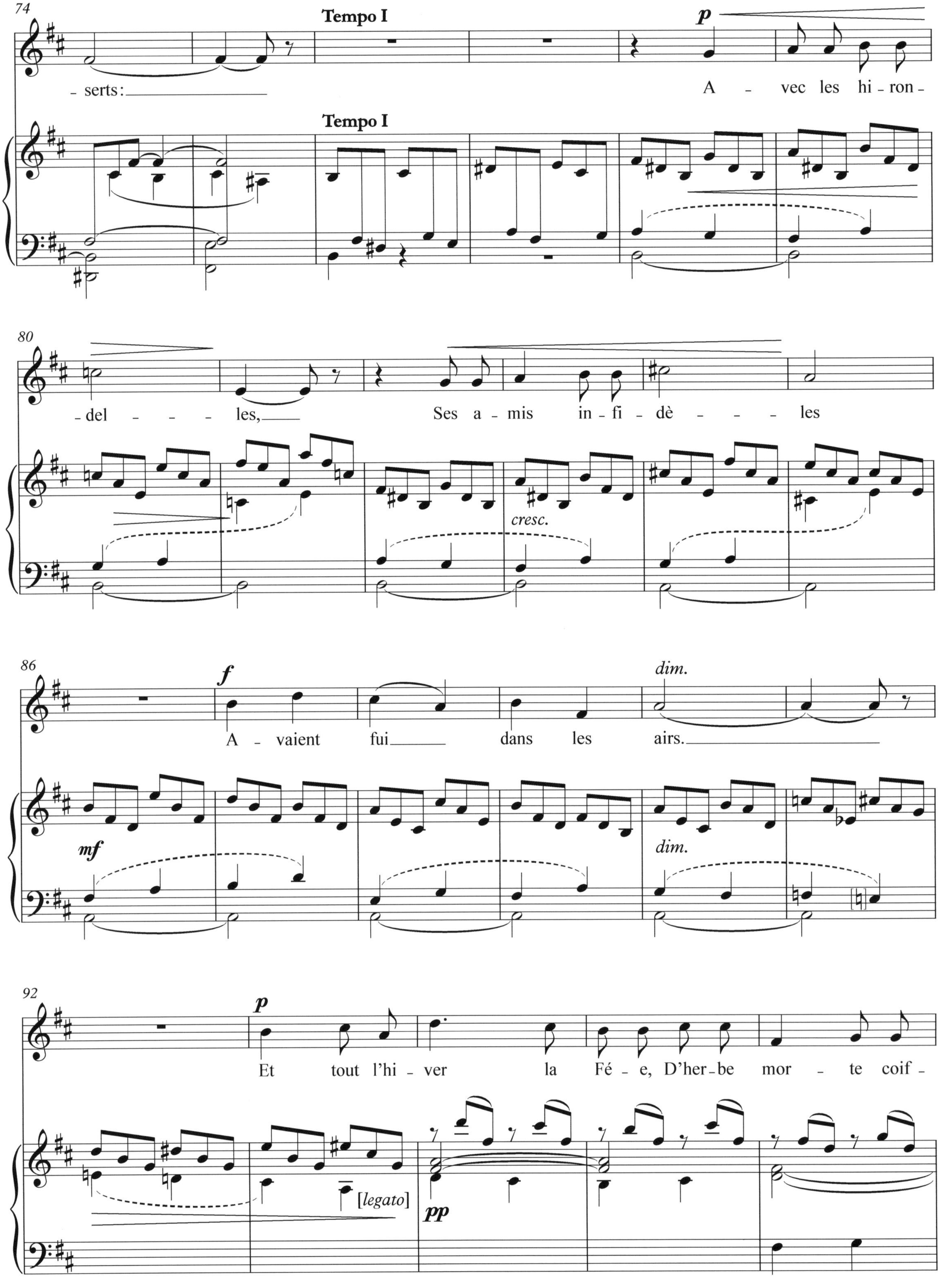
74
Tempo I
p
- serts:
A - vec les hi - ron -
Tempo I
80
- del - - - les,
Ses a - mis in - fi - dè - - - les
cresc.
86
f
A - vaient fui dans les airs.
mf
dim.
dim.
92
p
Et tout l'hi - ver la Fé - e, D'her - be mor - te coif -
[legato]
pp

Table of known chronology and dedicatees /
Tableau chronologique ; dédicataires /
Chronologie und Widmungsträger

SNM = Société nationale de musique
(a) = contralto (b) = baritone (s) = soprano (t) = tenor

Title	Composed	First public performance (pianist almost certainly Fauré in each case)	Dedicatee
Le Papillon et la fleur	1861	Caroline Miolan-Carvalho (s), Casino de St-Malo, 13 August 1868	**Caroline Miolan-Carvalho**: a well-known soprano (married to Léon Carvalho, director of the Théâtre Lyrique in Paris), she created the role of Marguerite in Gounod's *Faust*. Fauré accompanied her (standing in for Saint-Saëns) in a recital at Saint-Malo; amidst opera arias she sang this song to thank her accompanist, and he accordingly dedicated it to her
Puisque j'ai mis ma lèvre	1862	[not known]	[none]
Mai	c. 1862 – early 1864	Felix Lévy (t), SNM, 22 March 1873	**Mme Henri Garnier**: nothing known (possibly the wife of the photographer and lithographer Henri Garnier?)
S'il est un charmant gazon (Rêve d'amour)	c. 1863 – early 1864	Marguerite Baron, SNM, 12 December 1874	**Claire de Gomiecourt**: nothing known
Tristesse d'Olympio	?1865	[not known]	**Adam Laussel**: École Niedermeyer classmate
Dans les ruines d'une abbaye	1866–68	Léonce Valdec, SNM, 12 February 1876	**Henriette Escalier**: friend of Fauré, good amateur singer, later married to Alexandre Dumas *fils*
L'Aurore	c. 1868–70	[not known]	**Anna Dufresne**: nothing known
L'Absent	1871	[not known]	**Romain Bussine**: singing teacher at the Conservatoire, a co-founder of the SNM and close friend of Fauré
Lydia	1868–70	Marie Trélat (a), SNM, 10 February 1872	**Marie Trélat**: singer, singing teacher and hostess of a popular musical salon
Hymne	1870	Félix Lévy (t), SNM, 22 March 1873	**Félix Lévy**: fine amateur tenor and host of a musical salon
La Rançon	?1871	[not known]	**Henri Duparc**: composer and friend of Fauré
Chant d'automne	?1871	André Quirot (b), SNM, 6 January 1883	**Marie Clerc**: wife of the industrialist Camille Clerc; the family were amongst Fauré's closest friends and staunchest supporters
Les Matelots	1870–72	Julie Lalo (a), SNM, 8 February 1873	**Mme Édouard Lalo [Julie Besnier de Maligny]**: wife of the composer, a fine contralto and hostess of a musical salon
Seule!	1871	Marie Trélat (a), SNM, 10 February 1872	**Émile Ferrier**: nothing known
Chanson du pêcheur (Lamento)	1872	Julie Lalo (a), SNM, 8 February 1873	**Pauline Viardot**: renowned contralto and salon hostess
Tristesse	c. 1872–74	[not known]	**Mme Édouard Lalo**: see above

Aubade	c. 1873	[not known]	**Amélie Duez**: amateur singer married to the painter Ernest Duez; they hosted a salon
Barcarolle	1873	[unknown singer], SNM, 27 December 1873; then Marie-Clémence de Reiset, vicomtesse de Grandval, SNM, 20 March 1875	**Pauline Viardot**: see above
Ici-bas!	1874	Marguerite Baron, SNM, 12 December 1874	**Mme Georges Lecoq (née MacBrid[e])**: nothing known
Au bord de l'eau	1875	Louise de Miramont-Tréogate, SNM, 19 January 1878	**Claudie Chamerot**: daughter of Pauline Viardot, also an excellent singer
Après un rêve (Levati sol che la luna è levata)	1877	Henriette Fuchs (s), SNM, 11 January 1879	**Marguerite Baugnies [later de Saint-Marceaux]**: salon hostess and lifelong champion of Fauré
Sérénade toscane (O tu che dormie riposata stai)	1877–78	[not known]	**Mme la Baronne de Montagnac, neé [Henriette] de Rosalès**: close friend of Marguerite Baugnies (see above)
Sylvie	1878	Henriette Fuchs (s), SNM, 11 January 1879	**Mme la Vicomtesse de Gironde [née Lucy Denière]**: cousin of Marguerite Baugnies (see above)
Poème d'un jour	1878	M. Mazalbert (t), SNM, 22 January 1881	**Mme la Comtesse de Gauville**: salon hostess
Nell	1878	Henriette Fuchs (s), SNM, 29 January 1881	**Mme Camille Saint-Saëns [Marie Laure Émile Truffot]**: wife of the composer, who was Fauré's lifelong friend
Le Voyageur	?1878	[not known]	**Emmanuel Jadin**: painter and friend of Fauré; one of the Baugnies/Saint-Marceaux circle
Automne	1878	Henriette Fuchs (s), SNM, 29 January 1881	**Alice Boissonnet**: probably a pupil in Fauré's harmony class at the church of the Madeleine, with whom he may have had a romance in summer 1878
Les Berceaux	1879	Jane Huré, SNM, 9 December 1882	**Alice Boissonnet**
Notre amour	?1879	possibly Jane Huré,[1] SNM, 9 December 1882	**Mme C. Castillon**: singer, wife of the composer Alexis de Castillon
Le Secret	1881	André Quirot (b), SNM, 6 January 1883	**Alice Boissonnet**
Chanson d'amour	1882	possibly Jane Huré,[1] SNM, 9 December 1882	**Jane Huré**: singer, aged 17 in December 1882
La Fée aux chansons	1882	Maurice Bagès de Trigny (t), SNM, 12 May 1888	**Henriette Fuchs**: singer and the founder of the choral society La Concordia (which counted Widor and Debussy among its accompanists)

[1] The SNM programme for 9 December 1882 lists two unidentified Fauré songs; Georges Servières (*Gabriel Fauré*, Paris: Henri Laurens, 1930, p. 22) names them as *Les Berceaux* and *Notre amour* and recalls hearing Huré perform them *chez* Saint-Saëns the same month. Nectoux (*Gabriel Fauré: A Musical Life*, p. 537) lists the second song instead as *Chanson d'amour*, perhaps on the basis of its date and dedication.

Critical Commentary

Abbreviations

BnF mus. = Bibliothèque nationale de France, Paris, music department

v. = voice   pf. = piano   LH = left hand   RH = right hand

General editorial procedure is described in the prefatory **Notes on the edition and performance**. The present edition follows the named priority source for each song except as noted in the list of variants. Enharmonic spelling in transpositions follows sources in the same key. Omissions of nuances, phrasing, articulation or obvious accidentals and prolongation dots in early sources are passed over in silence, unless the omission suggests a viable variant. Useful cautionary accidentals are tacitly incorporated from any source that supplies them, including parallel passages; redundant accidentals are tacitly removed. Missing portions of ties (starts or completions across system breaks) are tacitly completed or incorporated from any source when the context allows no ambiguity. Dynamics that sources place above or below the system (usually because of restricted space) are relocated between the staves, as printed sources often do relative to manuscripts, except when musical logic suggests they were intended for just one hand or line. Orthographic variants (*mezzo **p**, **m.p.***; *dimin.*) are tacitly standardized (***mp***; *dim.*); instructions like *Pédale à chaque mesure* are renotated more explicitly (with *simile* for subsequent bars). Sequential duplications such as $<$ *cresc.* are retained, as the $<$ can sometimes be read as an independent gesture or an intensification. Fauré's ambiguous use of 8 under bass notes for either *8a bassa* or *coll'8^a* is clarified according to context, as noted below. Layout across piano staves is occasionally tacitly modified for clarity, provided it does not obscure polyphonic sense or implied hand layout. Secondary source variants are listed only when of special interest or if they impinge on a problem. Manuscripts are often revealing for the exact placing of nuances; where no autograph survives the earliest print is paid corresponding attention as the closest-to-manuscript source. Useful but non-essential nuances or other performing indications from secondary sources are shown in editorially added parentheses. Minor variants to vocal lines for the purpose of accommodating English texts (mostly in Metzler editions) are ignored. The present edition tacitly standardises the textual underlay, which can be haphazard in printed sources (Fauré's manuscripts are often more meticulous in that regard), and adds liaison symbols where appropriate. Music examples below are shown in their source key; any that quote multiple sources in different keys are given in the present edition's medium-voice key.

Manuscript collections now in BnF mus. include those of Fauré's family (donated by his daughter-in-law Blanche Fauré-Fremiet), plus the Hamard bequest (from an in-law of Fauré's son Emmanuel), Fauré's friends Camille and Marie Clerc (donated by their granddaughters Mmes Ceillier & Maspéro), Émilie Girette-Risler (donated by her family), and the Paris Conservatoire, including three manuscripts bequeathed in 1911 by the collector Charles Malherbe.

Publication history

Of the present volume's songs, nos. 3, 9, 10 and 14 were first published together in 1871 by Georges Hartmann (see below), and nos. 24–26 (*Poème d'un jour*) by Durand & Schœnewerk in 1880. Between 1869 and 1879 Antoine Choudens (who bought out the rights for Hartmann's slim volume in 1876) issued the present nos. 1, 3–4, 6 and 8–23 singly; in 1879 he combined them in a first 20-song collection of Fauré songs (*Vingt mélodies*), nearly all in medium-voice keys. After Julien Hamelle became Fauré's main publisher in 1880, he bought out all of these and reprinted individual songs (*éditions séparées*) from the existing plates;[1]

he also reprinted the *Vingt mélodies* (traditionally known as the First Collection) around 1887. In 1890 he reissued the volume with *Hymne* transposed down a tone to F, and published a corresponding high-voice volume that reprinted *Hymne* in its original key of G; in 1908 he then reissued each of these with slightly amended contents (see below). All these reissues incorporated minor musical retouches.

Choudens had originally published nine songs in both medium- and high-voice *éditions séparées* (the present nos. 1, 3, 4, 9, 12, 14, 16, 17 and 23), and the remaining eleven songs in single keys (some high, some medium). Hamelle later added both medium- and low-voice editions of nos. 6 and 20 together with low-voice ones of nos. 15 and 21; between 1890 and the 1920s he issued more *éditions séparées* as unamended offprints from the high- and medium-voice *recueils*.

The present nos. 27–34 were first published by Hamelle as *éditions séparées* (1880–1883) in either two or three keys, then incorporated in 1897 in a Second Collection (*Vingt Cinq Mélodies*, published in medium- and high-voice editions) originally comprising twenty-five songs from op. 18 through to *Prison* and *Soir* of 1894, including *Poème d'un jour* by arrangement with Durand. In 1908 Hamelle issued a Third Collection, comprising Fauré's songs up to op. 87. Wishing to present this with twenty songs, he transferred to it the last six songs from the Second Collection, reissuing the latter also with twenty songs (moving *Barcarolle* there from the First Collection to make up the total). The First Collection he simultaneously reissued, bringing in *Noël* (op. 43 no. 1, which had not appeared in the Second Collection) to fill the gap left by *Barcarolle* and maintain twenty songs there too. Fauré viewed all this redistribution with disgust but was unable to prevent it.[2] There is no doubt, however, that the musical retouches introduced in these successive reprints are authorial.

Meanwhile, the London publisher Metzler, with whom Fauré signed a contract in January 1896, had issued separate editions (with English and French texts) of each of nos. 15, 24–27 and 31–32. Selected songs were also issued by various publishers in New York and Boston between 1904 and 1915; wholly sourced from French editions, these are disregarded here. In addition, Hamelle issued several songs with obbligato violin or cello parts devised by others and printed separately; these leave the basic text unchanged and are again disregarded here except in the unusual case of *Sérénade toscane* (explained below).

Source sigla

A   Autograph manuscript (A1, A2 etc. as necessary). A is also used collectively for all autographs of any particular song.

C   Non-autograph manuscript copy

Nearly all the present manuscripts are notated in black ink, sometimes faded to sepia, using both sides of the paper. The present edition lists basic information of these along with any specially pertinent details; fuller details can generally be found in Phillips, *Gabriel Fauré: A Research and Information Guide*.

Hart Q̲UATRE̲ / *MÉLODIES* / *pour* CHANT *par* / *GABRIEL FAURÉ*: G. Hartmann, Paris [1871]: first edition of *Lydia*, *Hymne*, *Mai* and *Seule !* (in that order). Under the mention of Hartmann as publisher, the title page lists "J. McDowell, London" as his agent. This volume appeared at only one pitch, mixing what eventually became medium- and high-voice versions.

Es   Single prints (*éditions séparées*) issued by Choudens, Père et Fils, Paris and by J. Hamelle, Paris. High-, medium- and low-voice versions are distinguished as necessary by the suffixes -e, -m and -g (*voix élevées, voix moyennes, voix graves*).

---

[1] Choudens subsequently reused several of the plate numbers involved for publications by other composers; according to email correspondence of January 2010 the firm now has no record of its Fauré publications.

[2] Nectoux (ed.), *Gabriel Fauré: His Life through his Letters*, pp. 274–276, letter of August 1907 to Edgard Hamelle. Why *Noël* was not simply brought into the Second Collection, leaving *Barcarolle* undisturbed, is not clear; it may have involved pagination and paper economy.

Mz	Single prints issued by Metzler and Co. L^td, London, 1896–97. The title pages for *Chanson du pêcheur* and *Nell* list each as available in two keys, the others in just one key, sometimes high-voice. All traced exemplars, however, are medium-voice: Metzler, who also acted as Hamelle's agent, may simply have sold Hamelle high-voice exemplars.
F	Feuilleton (magazine or newspaper) publications
Rc	Collections (*recueils*) comprising:

(1) VINGT / MÉLODIES / POUR / CHANT ET PIANO / PAR / GABRIEL FAURÉ, Choudens [1879] (A.C. 4595); reprinted c. 1887 by Hamelle with a very few musical retouches (same plates and plate number, title page similar but re-engraved), then reissued by him in 1890 with a redesigned title page, more musical retouches and *Hymne* transposed a tone down (otherwise from the existing plates) as *Premier Recueil* / 20 / *Mélodies* / *Pour* / *Chant et Piano* / PAR / GABRIEL FAURÉ (J. 3149 H.),[3] along with a corresponding high-voice edition (J. 3150 H.) which reprints *Hymne* from the existing plates; both versions reprinted in 1908 from the same plates with a few retouches, but *Barcarolle* removed and *Noël* (op. 43 no. 1) inserted as no. 20

(2) 2e RECUEIL / VINGT CINQ MÉLODIES / *pour* UNE VOIX / *avec accompagnement de Piano* / *par* / GABRIEL FAURÉ. Hamelle [1897] (J. 4102 H. and J. 4103 H., medium- and high-voice editions); reprinted at least three times with minor amendments [c. 1899, 1902 and 1904], then reissued in 1908 (same plates and plate numbers) minus the last six songs, the word CINQ removed from the cover and title pages, *Barcarolle* brought in from (1) above as no. 20 (reprinted from its existing plates), and a few musical revisions. This source introduces metronome indications absent in the earlier single prints.

High- and medium-voice versions of **Rc** are distinguished as necessary by the suffixes **-e** and **-m**. Successive editions of these are distinguished as necessary by publication year in subscript ($_{79}$, $_{[87]}$, $_{90}$, $_{97}$, $_{[99]}$, $_{[02]}$, $_{[04]}$ or $_{08}$, estimated years in brackets), with arrows indicating chronological concurrence: thus **Rc-m**$_{\rightarrow[87]}$ indicates the 1879 and c. 1887 editions (First Collection), **Rc-m**$_{[02]\rightarrow}$ all (Second Collection) editions from the reprint of c. 1902 on.[4] Roman and Arabic numerals indicate the location of songs in these collections, designating respectively volume and song numbers.

VM/VE	Respectively all medium-voice or high-voice (*voix moyennes* or *voix élevées*) printed sources (not manuscripts)
O	Orchestral transcriptions
T	Text as in poems (see below and pp. XXVIII–XLI)

Any sources not traced or not consultable are listed below in italics. These are quoted from publishers' work lists and title pages, or from Nectoux and Daitz (*Gabriel Fauré: Mélodies et Duos*), including a few documented by them through plate numbers in the *livres de cotages* of Choudens and Hamelle; it is possible that some of these were never issued. Many early *éditions séparées* issued in small print runs are now very rare or untraceable, a situation exacerbated by Hamelle's (and sometimes Choudens's) negligence over making requisite legal deposits to the Paris Conservatoire or Bibliothèque nationale. First editions listed below refer to earliest traced exemplars, a few of which may in fact be early reprints (a probable case is noted below involving text variants in *Les Berceaux*).

---

[3] As on the title page; the front cover reads *1er Recueil* / VINGT / *Mélodies* / *Chant et Piano* / GABRIEL FAURÉ. The cover of the Second Collection is worded equivalently.

[4] Dates of reprinting may not have coincided across high- and medium-voice editions, though some amendments appear in each around the same time.

Poem sources

Fauré's chosen poems are listed below in their first publication along with the edition Fauré most probably used (if other than the first):

Victor Hugo

Les Chants du crépuscule (Paris: Renduel, 1835): XXVII, "La pauvre fleur disait…" [**Le Papillon et la fleur**]; XXV, **Puisque j'ai mis ma lèvre**; XXXI, "Puisque mai tout en fleurs…" [**Mai**]; XXII, "Nouvelle chanson sur un vieil air" [**S'il est un charmant gazon**]; XX, "L'aurore s'allume…" [**L'Aurore**]. The last of these has 17 stanzas, of which Fauré sets just nos. 1–3.

Les Rayons et les ombres (Paris, 1840): XXXIV, **Tristesse d'Olympio**. 38 stanzas (divided 8+30), of which Fauré sets nos. 1, 8, 9–10 and 31–32

Les Chansons des rues et des bois (Paris and Brussels: Lacroix, Verboeckhoven et Cie, 1865): part VI no. XV, **Dans les ruines d'une abbaye**. 9 stanzas, of which Fauré omits no. 6

Les Châtiments (Brussels: Samuel; and Geneva, New York: Imprimerie universelle, 1853): part III (*La famille est restaurée*) no. XI, "Sentiers où l'herbe se balance…" [**L'Absent**]

> Hugo's poetry appeared in innumerable editions and re-editions between 1835 and 1880; defining which was used by Fauré (or his house editors) is often impossible, especially given the discrepancies in punctuation across musical and poetic sources. For the five poems from *Les Chants du crépuscule*, as well as *Tristesse d'Olympio* (*Les Rayons et les ombres*), Fauré's source was probably an edition of the late 1850s or early 1860s; present edition follows 1858 Hachette, tacitly correcting a few obvious misprints therein by reference to other editions. The 1870 Hetzel edition of *Les Châtiments* is a likely source for *L'Absent*. *Les Chansons des rues et des bois* appeared only four years before Fauré's *Dans les ruines d'une abbaye* was published, and its text is consistent in all early editions.

Leconte de Lisle

Poèmes antiques (Paris: Ducloux, 1852): **Lydia** (*Études latines*, no. XVII, captioned "imité de Gallus"); **Nell** (captioned "imité de Burns"). Fauré's likely source was *Poésies complètes* (Paris: Poulet-Malassis et de Broise, 1858).

Charles Baudelaire

Hymne (8 May 1854, letter to Mme Sabatier) and **La Rançon** (between September 1851 and January 1852): both published in *Le Présent* (15 November 1857) and *La Petite Revue* (16 December 1865); included in *Les Épaves* (February 1866) as nos. X and XIX; also in *Le Parnasse contemporain* (31 March 1866), then the posthumous 1868 edition of *Les Fleurs du mal*, as nos. XCIV and XCVIII. Fauré omits the third of the 5 stanzas of *Hymne*. **Chant d'automne**: probably September or October 1859; first published in *La Revue contemporaine* (November 1859), incorporated into *Les Fleurs du mal* (1861 edition) as no. LVI, then renumbered as LVII in the 1868 edition. 7 stanzas (divided 4+3), of which Fauré omits nos. 2, 6 and 7

> Slight punctuation variants across sources suggest that Fauré may have seen *Hymne* in *Le Parnasse contemporain* and *La Rançon* in *La Petite Revue*, but circumstantial evidence points to the 1868 edition of *Les Fleurs du mal* (Paris: Lévy) as his likely source for all three settings.

Théophile Gautier

La Comédie de la mort (Brussels: Laurent, and Paris: Desessart, 1838): **Lamento** (**Chanson du pêcheur**) and **Tristesse**

Poésies complètes (Paris: Charpentier, 1845): **Les Matelots** (1841) and [**Seule!**] (1845), in the section *Poésies nouvelles*. The collection also ncluded *Tristesse* and *Lamento*, in the section *Poésies diverses*. First published in *La Presse*, 28 April 1845, as "Guzla", [*Seule!*] is untitled in *Poésies complètes*. *Les Matelots* has 5 stanzas, of which Fauré omits nos. 2 and 4.

Poésies complètes went through many reprints before Gautier's death in 1872, as did its component parts (as *Premières poésies*, *Poésies nouvelles* etc.). Fauré's likely source was an 1866 or 1870 edition.

Louis Pomey

Aubade, c. 1873, unpublished

Marc Monnier

Poésies de Marc-Monnier (Paris: Lemerre, 1872): **Barcarolle** (in the section *Musiques*, subtitled "(Musique de F. Grast)"). 5 stanzas, the last one (omitted by Fauré) reprising the first

Sully Prudhomme

Stances et poèmes (Paris: Achille Faure, 1865): **Ici-bas, tous les lilas meurent** (in the section *La Vie intérieure*); "Le long du quai" [**Les Berceaux**]. Fauré or his house editors probably also consulted the 1872 Lemerre re-edition, which retitles the former *Ici-bas*.

Les Vaines Tendresses (Paris: Lemerre, 1875): **Au bord de l'eau**. 24 lines, of which Fauré omits lines 9–12

Romain Bussine

Freely adapted and translated from anonymous Tuscan texts collected by Niccolò Tommaseo in *Canti popolari toscani, corsi, illirici, greci* (Venice, 1841): [**Après un rêve**], no. 11 of the third set of *Serenate*; [**Sérénade toscane**], Tuscan text comprising no. 12 of the second set of *Serenate* (lines 1–4 of *Sérénade toscane*) along with a flexible combination of nos. 2–3 of the third set. French publication untraced except for publication year, 1879, noted by Nectoux (*Gabriel Fauré: His Life through his Letters*, p. 76 n2).

Paul de Choudens

Sylvie, c. 1878, unpublished

Armand Silvestre

Les Ailes d'or: Poésies nouvelles, 1878–1880 (Paris: Charpentier, 1880): **Le Voyageur**, "Chanson d'automn" [*sic*] [**Automne**], **Notre amour** and **La Fée aux chansons**, all in the section *Vers pour être chantés*

Le Pays des roses: Poésies nouvelles, 1880–1882 (Paris: Charpentier, 1882): "Mystère" [**Le Secret**] and **Chanson d'amour**, both in the section *Vers pour être chantés*

> As some of Fauré's settings predate the poems' publication in collected form, it is likely that he obtained his texts directly from the poet (see Preface), or from periodical publications now untraced.

Charles Grandmougin

Poème d'un jour: no publication traced

Musical sources and variants

1. Le Papillon et la fleur

Keys: C and D

A Autograph, BnF mus., Ms. 17754 (ex Fauré family library), undated; in D♭. A title page (see facsimile, p. IV) shows a variant autograph title, under a drawing reportedly by Saint-Saëns.[5] The piano part ends with bar 25, which reprises bar 1 (and shows the only dynamic, ***p***); the remainder (starting a new page) is notated for voice only, with 8-bar rests between strophes; the final ritornello is absent. Some pencilled interpretative annotations, in an unidentified hand and out of character with Fauré's normal markings, are ignored here as inauthentic.

Es First publication: Choudens [1869], in C (A.C. 1753(1)) and D *(A.C. 1753(2))*; reissued by Hamelle (J. 2692 H. and J. 2692bis H.). Additional *éditions séparées* were issued by *Choudens (A.C. 3317), in D, with Italian text (*Il Fiore e la Farfalla*); and by Hamelle (J. 2692ter H.), in E♭ {dates untraced}*

Rc I/1, in C and D

Priority source: **Rc-m**, with added revisions from **Rc-e**

Variants

Text. Bar 15: musical sources: *différents, je*. Bars 23, 63: musical sources omit comma. Bar 56: *Toute* as in **T** and **A**, other sources have *Tout*. Bar 58: **T** and **A** have *Oh!* (not *Ah!*). Bars 64–65: *Comme toi* as in **Rc-m**, *Comme à toi* as in **T** and other musical sources

Tempo heading as in **Rc-m**; **Es**, **Rc-e**: *Allegretto* (no tempo heading in **A**)

Bars 1, 3, pf. **Es** starts ⟨ at ♪ 4

Bars 2, 4, pf. **A**: RH ♪♪ not ♪ 𝄾 across the half-bar

Bars 5–9, 26–29, 46–49, pf. Dynamics in **Rc-m** only

Bars 7–12, 14–16. **A**: continuous top slur bar 7 beat 2 to bar 9 (omits lower slur), bass ♪ 𝄾 not ♪ 𝄾 𝄾 from bar 9

Bar 10, v. **Rc-m**₇₉: [music example] La pau- vre fleur di - ; all other sources (including **A**) as present edition, the **Rc-m** plates evidently amended thus for **Rc-m**₍₈₇₁₎→ (cf. **Preface** under **Tempo, metre and rhythm**)

Bar 13, v. **A**: beat 2 ♩ 𝄾

Bars 15, 16, 36, 40, v. **A**: last 2 notes ♪. ♪ (omits dot in bar 36)

Bar 15, pf. **A**: RH chord 2 repeats chord 1

Bars 18–23, pf. **A** omits lower note of each LH dyad

Bars 21, 41, 61, pf. *Ossia* as in **Es** and **Rc-e**, main reading as in **A** (bar 21) and **Rc-m**

Bars 24, 44, pf. ***p*** as in **Rc-e**; **Es** and **Rc-m** place it half a bar later (**Es-m** omits 1st occurrence)

Bars 24, 44, 64, both. *Rall.* as placed for pf. in all printed sources except **Rc-m** which starts it between ♪s 1 and 2; printed sources start it for v. from ♪ 1 (**A** omits it). Bar 24 v. ⌢ in **Es** only

Bars 26–29, see note to bars 5–9 etc.

Bar 30, v. *Dolce* in **Rc-m** only

Bar 31, v. **Rc-m**, beat 2 ♪. ♪♪

Bar 36, see note to bars 15 etc.

Bar 38, v. **Rc-m**: last ♪ a tone lower

Bar 41, see note to bars 21 etc.

Bar 44, pf. **Rc-e** omits LH slur and tie. See also notes to bars 24 etc.

Bars 44, 64, v. **A** gives pitches as in bar 24

Bars 45, 65, pf. All printed sources give LH ♪ 1 a 3rd higher in bar 45, as do **VE** sources in bar 65; in bar 45 **Rc-e** also gives LH ♪ 4 a 3rd higher (cf. bars 5, 25)

Bars 46–49, see note to bars 5–9 etc.

Bar 50, v. **A**, beat 1: 𝄾 ♪♪

Bar 50, both. **Rc-e** and **Es**: ***p*** *animato*, above v. staff only, doubtless an unintended conflation of ***p*** and *più*; **Rc-m** shows *più animato* for both v. and pf. but omits v. ***p***. Cf. notes concerning Tempo heading and to bars 5–9 etc.

---

[5] The drawing is attributed to Saint-Saëns in Norman Suckling, *Fauré* (London: Dent, 1946), p. 61 and James Harding, *Saint-Saëns and his circle* (London: Chapman and Hall, 1965), p. 87. The manuscript itself, which Fauré had lost, was found and returned to him in 1922 by Marcel Proust (Fauré-Fremiet (ed.), *Gabriel Fauré: lettres intimes*, p. 282).

Bar 60, v. A: last 2 notes ♪ ♪

Bar 61, see note to bars 21 etc.

Bars 62–69, both. Main reading as in **Rc-m**, footnote reading as in **Rc-e** (except see above re bars 45, 65). The latter's textural variants, along with <, are new to **Rc-e** (the pf. LH variant in bar 67 possibly a misprint, the bar 65 *f* overprinting the barline, probably added at proof); bar 64 v. *f* and *Comme à* are shared with **Es** (which omits other dynamics in this passage). All printed sources share the preceding *cresc.* from bar 58 (except **Es** prints it for v. only). Cf. also notes to bars 24 etc. and 44 etc.

2. Puisque j'ai mis ma lèvre

Keys: B♭ and C

C Copy by Julien Koszul (headed "Puisque j'ai mis..! / Romance / Par / Gabriel Fauré"): BnF mus., Rés. Vmb. Ms. 107 (donated by Henri Dutilleux);[6] dated at the end "8 x^bre [décembre] 1862"; in C. The music fills an oblong folio plus the 1st recto of a similar bifolio that continues with *Mai*; at bar 9 the annotation *con sordino* is in Fauré's hand. Some dynamics, nuances and articulation are present, but no pedalling. Bars 52–59 are absent, doubtless through inadvertent elision (via the shared syllable -*jours*).

A1 Complete autograph, no title page but the music headed "Poésie de Victor Hugo / mise en musique par [signed] Gabriel Fauré", the end again signed and dated "30 septembre 1863": collection of Thierry Bodin, Paris; in C. Its pages, curiously, are numbered 207–210 in Fauré's hand, forming a bifolio once evidently sewn into a larger volume now untraced. **A1** shows more detailed performing indications than **C** (some of them uncharacteristically fussy and absent again in **A2**).

A2 Complete autograph, the end signed and dated "Gabriel Bébé Py-Fauré / 26 octobre 1863": Beinecke Rare Books and Manuscripts Library, Yale University (Koch collection), FRKF 679.4; in B♭. The autograph title recto features an unidentified 9-bar Haydn-minuet-like melodic sketch in F (ending "etc. etc. etc.") over Fauré's annotation "Poésie de Victor Hugo / mise en musique par Gabriel Fauré" (again no other title). Relative to **C** and **A1**, **A2** presents revised textures and syllabification, omits tempo fluctuations and shows different (sparser) dynamics, perhaps by occasional oversight but arguably to avoid fussiness.

Priority source: **A2**, with opening nuances from **C** and **A1** shown in parentheses

Variants

Text. Capitalisation haphazard in musical sources; tacitly adjusted to match **T**. **A1–2** omit punctuation in bars 50–51, as do all musical sources in bar 64. At bars 51–52 **C** has *vio-lé* [sic] *toujours!* (eliding at this point to bar 60). Bar 84: **A1–2** have a comma (no punctuation in **C**)

Nuances and tempo fluctuations in **A1** and **C** only: Tempo: *rallen-tan-do* at bar 39 (**C** starts it from ♪ 2), 𝄐 in middle of bar 40 (v. and pf.), *animato* from bar 60 ♪ 4 (**A1** only), *rallen-tan-do* from bar 74 (starting at ♪ 4 in **C**), *a tempo* from bar 76 ♪ 3 (starting a ♪ later in **C**), *ral-len-tan-do* from bar 89 in **A1**, from bar 91 ♪ 2 in **C**. Dynamics and nuances (**A1** unless otherwise specified): opening anacrusis and bar 1 *p* and *con sordino* (also in **C**, which adds *leggiero* above bar 1 LH); bar 8 *p* (mid-bar, between pf. RH staff and v.); bar 9 **C** repeats pf. *con sordino* (autograph) and *p*, bars 15–16 pf. < *p* > along with v. *pp* at *Puis*-; bar 24 pf. *pp* (also in **C**, no dynamic in either source at bar 25, though **C** has *con sordine*); bar 33 v. *pp* (**C** has *dolce* instead a ♪ earlier); bars 34–35 v. < > centred at *Puis*- (cf. also note to bars 17 etc.); bar 36 v. *dolcissimo* at *Ta* (also in **C**); bar 38 v. *ppp* (**C** has *pp*, then pf. < across bar 64 and > across bar 66, absent in **A1**); v. < across bar 69 to bar 70 ♪ 2 (**C** has it just across bar 69), *pp* at bar 71 ♪ 2, *dolce* at bar 72 ♩ 2 (**C** instead has > across bar 71); bar 84 v. *pp* at *Mon* (**C** has *dolce* instead a ♪ later); bar 88 pf. *pp* at *Mon* (also in **C**, plus *dolcissimo* for v. in place of **A1**'s *rallentando*); bar 90 v. *pp* (also in **C**). See also note immediately following

Bars 1–7, pf. **A2** omits initial ⁊ in bars 2–7. Bar 4 lower-voice slur completion as in **C**, omitted in **A** (new system); phrasing as in **A1** from bar 4 ♪ 4 (**A2** omits new slur from there and subsequent ones), except that **A1** ends last slur above barline ending bar 7 (**C** ends it a barline earlier and ends each of the preceding upper slurs a note or more early). **C** and **A1** give beat 1 bass note as ♩ in bars 1–7 (with pedal in **A1** across ♪s 1–4 in bars 1–2) and an 8ve lower in bars 1 and 3; **C** doubles it at the lower 8ve in bars 5 and 7.

C, A1: bar 5 LH dyads 1–4 𝄢

Bar 8, pf. **A1** gives RH dyad 1 upper voice as ♪, lower-voice ♩ non-staccato and beamed to following 3 ♪s (downstemmed); **C** stems this beat as **A2**

Bar 10, 82, v. **C, A1:** ♩ ♪ c″–b′ for *lè-vre* and *breu-ve*; in **A1** the latter syllable (but not the ♪) is deleted in blue pencil and rewritten immediately before *à* and *et*

Bars 17, 19, 27, 35, 63, v. **C, A1:** beat 2 rhythm ♪ ♪

Bars 17–24, pf. **A1:**

C likewise except gives bar 19 beat 2 bass an 8ve lower (with linking *arpa* slur to tenor note), omits bar 20 bass tie, supplies RH staccato dots across bars 20–22, and attaches bar 20 beat 2 c′ to ♪ 6 not 7. **A2** omits accidentals in bars 21 and 23. The footnote query to bar 17 is prompted by analogy with **C**/**A1** and bars 33 and 85, suggesting a possible slip of the pen in **A2** (confusion with bar 18), albeit a viable one

Bars 25–32, 77–84, pf. ♪s 1–4 beamed as in **C** and **A1** at bars 25–31; **A2** beams ♪s 4–8 together in bars 27 and 31 and elsewhere beams ♪s 1–4 together downwards. (Cf. note to bars 72–87.) **C** repeats *con sordino* at bar 25 and adds a ♩ downstem to LH ♪ 1 in bars 25–32 (cf. also note to bars 32–40); **A1** omits pedalling from bar 28

Bars 32–40, pf. **A1:**

C likewise except that bars 32–34 omit slurs and show an added ♩ downstem to LH ♪ 1, bar 35 beat 2 omits bass

---

[6] Koszul, an École Niedermeyer classmate of Fauré's, was Dutilleux's grandfather. His own settings of *Puisque j'ai mis ma lèvre*, *Mai* and *S'il est un charmant gazon*, published in 1875–1879, show some marked affinities with Fauré's.

upper 8ve, nuances differ as noted above, and bar 40 omits prolongation dots. **A2** starts new RH and LH slurs from bar 37 chord 1 (new page, bar 36 ending as present edition, continuity corroborated by **C** and **A1** as above)

Bars 41–60, pf. **C**, **A1**: bass ♩ not ♪ in bars 41–44, 𝄾 in place of last ♪ in bar 44, RH 𝄾 ♪ in each beat of bars 46 and 54 (the latter in **A1** only), bar 49 beat 2 LH ♪ 𝄾 not ♩. **A1**: bars 48 and 56 RH beat 1 as beat 2, bar 52 LH beat 2 𝄾 ♪ (just the upper note). **A1**:

bars 50–51

bars 59–60

C reads similarly in bars 50–51 and 60 (having omitted bars 52–59), except for an added LH slur across bar 51 and an added LH *c′* above *a* in bar 60 beat 2. Bar 50 LH slur in **C** and **A1** only (lack of space in **A2**)

Bar 58, pf. **A2** omits beat 2 RH slur and LH upper accidental (**A1** in turn omits LH slurs)

Bars 58–60, v. **A1**: bar 58 rhythm ♩ ♪♪ with *ro-se* on notes 1–2, then *ar-ra-chée* (starting at note 3) amended to *dé-ta-chée*, bar 60 rhythm ♩ 𝄾 ♪ (*animato* from last note); **C** has neither the bar 60 prolongation dot nor 𝄾, doubtless the result of its elision there from bar 52

Bars 59–69, pf. **A1**:

(bracketed accidentals absent, *sic* tenor slur start in bar 59); **C** likewise (from bar 60) but supplies missing accidentals, renders each ♪ (except bass notes) from bar 61 as ♪ 𝄾, adds *leggiero* at bar 61, gives bar 64 bass an 8ve lower and adds *c′* to bar 66 last chord, plus variant dynamics as listed above. **A2** omits RH accidental in bar 68, and phrasing from bar 68 beat 2. Present medium-voice edition gives bar 62 last RH chord as in **A2** (*f′/a♭/b♭ /f″*); high-voice edition gives it as in **C** and **A1** (see above) to avoid physical awkwardness

Bar 62, v. **A1**: ♩ ♪ for *di-re* (cf. bar 50 *ossia*); **C** concurs with **A2**

Bars 68–71, v. *Ossia*s (**C**, **A1**) relate directly to text punctuation; Fauré's aim in the main reading (**A2**) was probably to avoid a snatched breath after *fanées*. See also above regarding variant dynamics in **C** and **A1**

Bars 72–87, pf. **C**, **A1**: bars 72–77

bars 78–84 as bars 10–16 (without dynamics), bars 85–87 as bars 17–19 in **A1** (see above) except bar 87 beat 2 bass an 8ve lower than in bar 19. **A2** omits bar 72 beat 2 slur and starts new slur from bar 73 note 1, also omits bar 87 pf. RH slur. See also note to bars 25–32 etc.

Bars 88–92, both. **A1**:

(*sic* slurs in bar 89); **C** likewise except omits bar 88 final pf. LH ♪ 𝄾, omits bar 92 prolongation dots (giving final rest as 𝄼 under 𝄐 for v. and pf. RH), final pf. LH note ♪ 𝄾 not ♪, plus variant nuances listed above. The present bar 92 *ossia* is editorially derived from this. **A2** starts pf. LH slur from bar 89 ♪ 1 (over the beams) instead of a note earlier (possibly through lack of space; cf. note to bar 37); **A2** then carries RH slur past bar 89 ending a system, LH slur to barline (bar 90 as present edition; cf. **A1** above), and omits final v. 𝄼 (supplied by **C**)

3. Mai (Puisque Mai tout en fleurs)

Keys: F and A♭

A   Complete autograph, Beinecke Rare Books and Manuscripts Library, Yale University (Koch collection), FRKF 679.2; in A♭. The single loose folio (no title page) is unsigned and undated, the music headed by Fauré "N° 4 / Mai ! / à Madame H. Garnier" (what constituted nos. 1–3 can now only be guessed), then "Soprano" to the left of the first vocal staff. Evidently a presentation copy, **A** indicates some dynamics and the most detailed pedalling of any source, with a variant central ritornello and ending.

Hart   First publication: Hartmann [1871], in G (G.H.584)

Es   Choudens [1877], in F (A.C. 3602) and G (*A.C. 3757*); reissued by Hamelle (*J. 2698 H.* and *J. 2698*^bis *H.*)

Rc   I/2, in F and G

Secondary source

CA   Incomplete copy mostly by Julien Koszul, part-autograph, unsigned, undated: BnF mus., Rés. Vmb. Ms. 107; in A♭. The song, on the inside pages of an oblong bifolio, follows *Puisque j'ai mis ma lèvre* (see above), the musical text mostly as in **A** (including the longer central ritornello) but without tempo heading, fingering, dynamics or pedalling; in two places a clean reading matches a revised reading in **A**. Up to bar 24 the piano part is in Koszul's hand, as is the vocal musical line up to bar 34 and text underlay up to bar 26; the remainder is in Fauré's hand. After repeat marks at the end of bar 34, the second strophe is notated in part, the piano indicated just by "etc." from under the voice re-entry, with vocal text underlay for 8 bars, then 8 bars without underlay, ending with bar 52 (= printed bar 51).

Priority source: **Rc-m**, with details from **Rc-e**. Bar number references below are always to the bars as numbered in the present edition, regardless of source.

Variants

Text. Bars 51–52, **A** : *champs, que*

Tempo. **A**: *Moderato*

Bar 1, pf. **A**: ***pp***

Bars 1–5, 27–33, 60–66, pf. Pedalling as in **A**, which repeats bar 1 pedalling up to bar 5 beat 1 (editorially rephrased at bar 2).

No pedalling in **Hart**; remaining sources have only 𝒫ed/ *Pédale à chaque mesure* at bar 1

Bars 3, 9, 13, 19, 38, 42, 46, v. **CA**: ♩ ♪♪♪♪, **A** and **Hart** likewise in bars 9, 13, 38, 42 and 46, **Es** in bars 9 and 42, **Rc-m** in bar 42. The inconsistently-applied revision of these to the present rhythm (matching all sources at bars 11 and 27) prompts the present editorial suggestion at bar 5

Bars 7, 40, pf. **A**: 1st LH ♪ originally a tone lower, bar 7 but not bar 40 amended to present reading (appearing in **CA** as an unamended reading, bar 7 only)

Bars 10, 43, pf. **Es-e**, **Rc**: prolongation dot after bass ♩, also **Es-m** in bar 43. **CA** (bar 10 only): as **A** but omits 1st >. **Rc-e** omits bar 10 <

Bars 15, 48, v. **A**: *dolce* (no v. dynamics before bar 15)

Bar 16, both. V. < as in **A**; **Hart**, **Es** and **Rc-e** end it at ♩ 2, **Rc-m** just before ♩ 3. Pf. < as in **Hart** and **VM** sources (absent in **A**); **VE** sources start it a ♪ later

Bars 17, 50, 66, pf. Printed sources end > a note earlier

Bar 18, pf. **Es** and **Rc-e** omit LH ♩·

Bar 19, both. **p** and *dolce* in **Rc-m** only

Bars 20–21, v. Syllabification as in **Rc-e**; all other sources give it as in music example below

Bars 20–25, 53–58, both. **A**:

(words as present edition), except that in bar 55 **A** omits *sf* and pf. > and starts < 2 ♪s later, with v. < overwritten by *crescendo* from ♪ 2. In bars 25 and 58 **A** shows middle note at ♪ 2 originally a tone lower, then amended as above. **CA** as **A** except bar 22 syllabification as in printed sources (but without the comma), bar 25 pf. chord 1 as above (matching the amended reading of **A**), and no dynamics

Bars 22, 55, pf. **Es-e**: ♮ not ♭ to penultimate RH ♪, likewise **Rc-e** in bar 22

Bars 25–27, 58–60, both. Tempo indications placed as in **A** (which indicates just *rallentando* for both v. and pf., starting it a ♪ later for v. in bar 58). All printed sources start *a tempo* a beat later, placing *rall.* at the start of bar 25 and just after the start of bar 58; *poco* in **Rc-m** only, above last ♪ of bar 24, probably added at proof. **CA** (bars 25–27 only): *rallentando* as in **A**, *a tempo* from the barline starting bar 27 (in Fauré's hand). Cf. Fauré's analogous manuscript placing of *a tempo* indications in *L'Aurore*

Bars 26, 59, pf. Printed sources single-stem LH using ties instead of prolongation dots; restemmed following the layout of **CA** and **A** at bar 26 (at bar 59 **A** leads middle voice upwards at beat 3 to coincide with 2nd top note)

Bar 28–30, 61–64, both. **A** starts *cresc.* from bars 30 and 63 (for v. only: cf. examples below)

Bars 31–33, both. **A**:

(then a page break); **CA** likewise except no dynamics, breaks bar 33 RH pf. phrasing between beats 1 and 2, and a few other minor notational variants. In bar 33 **Rc-m** omits pf. RH ♩

Bars 34–35 *ossia*, pf. **CA**: bar 34 beat 1 lowest 3 notes ♩ not ♪ 𝄾, bar 35 bass prolongation dot (as repeated in next bar) absent in **A**, present in **CA** (autograph)

Bars 38, 42, 46, see note to bars 3, 9 etc.

Bar 40, v. **Rc-m**→[1871]: last 2 ♪s a note lower

Bars 44–49, v. **A**: < across bar 44, > across bars 46–47, *dolce* at bar 48, < across bar 49 (not 48). Cf. note to bar 16

Bars 49–50, pf. **Rc-m** omits tie; **Es** and **Rc-e** omit bar 49 RH upper voice slur

Bars 53–60, see notes to bars 20–25 etc. and 25–27 etc.

Bars 56–57, both. **mf** and v. < in **Rc-m** only

Bars 61–65, pf. **Hart** dynamics: bar 61 no indication, bar 64 *cresc.*, < across bar 65 (v. dynamics as present edition); regarding **A** see below and note to bars 28–30 etc.

Bars 64–66, both. **A**:

Bar 67, pf. **Hart** gives LH beat 2 ♩ and 1st ensuing RH ♪ a 3rd lower, **Es-m** likewise for just RH; **Rc-e** prints the beat 2 ♩ on upper staff (as a lower voice). **pp** in **Hart** only, perhaps lost during amendment for **Es** (though cf. note to bars 61–65). Regarding tempo cf. bar 34 and the final cadences of *S'il est un charmant gazon*, *Lydia*, *Hymne*, *Les Matelots* and *Chanson du pêcheur*

4. S'il est un charmant gazon (Rêve d'amour)

Keys: E♭ and F

Version I

A Complete autograph, the end signed and dated "5 mai 1864": Beinecke Rare Books and Manuscripts Library, Yale University (Koch collection), FRKF 679.3; in F. Two small holes on the central fold of the single bifolio suggest it was once sewn into a folder or volume. After an autograph title recto the music is headed "dédiée à Madame Claire de Gomiecourt". The second strophe is indicated just by its text written under that of the first strophe.

Present text follows **A** except as below, notating the second strophe in full via a reprise of bars 1–8 (the reprise point unspecified in **A**). Vocal *ossia* readings come from version II below (added for performer convenience).

Variants

Text. Capitalisation haphazard in **A**; adjusted to match **T** and Version II below. Bars 12, 20, 58, 64, 66, 68: no punctuation in **A**

Bars 65, 67, v. **A** slurs together last 4 notes of bar 65 and first 4 of bar 67

Version II

Es First publication: Choudens [1875], in E♭ (A.C. 2012 (1)) and F (A.C. 2012 (2)); reissued by Hamelle (*J. 2695 H.* and *J. 2695*bis *H.*)

Rc I/10, in E♭ and F

Secondary source: **A** (see Version I above)

Priority source: **Rc-e**. Some details imported from **A** are editorially parenthesised; **A** otherwise is mentioned below only if it bears on a problem

Variants

Bars 3, 27, 51, pf. **Rc-e** omits RH slur

Bars 5, 53, 77, pf. **Rc-m**₉₀→ ties RH notes 1–2 (*sic*), as do all **VM** sources in bar 53 and **Rc-e** in bar 5 (no tie in any source in bar 29)

Bars 6–7, 30–31, 54–55, 78, pf. *dim.* as in **VE** sources at bars 54 and 78 and **Es-e** in bar 30 (where **Rc-e** omits it), editorially adjusted in bar 6 where **VE** sources start it a note earlier; **VM** sources place it at the start of bar 78, otherwise 2 notes later than present edition. RH top slur as in **VE** sources; **VM** sources (like **A**) break it across bars 6–7, 30–31 and 54–55. In bar 30 **Rc-e** gives bass as ♩·

Bars 8, 32, 56, pf. *p* placing as in **VM** sources; **VE** sources print it at or before note 1

Bars 13–14, v. Main reading as in **Rc-e**, *ossia* as in **Rc-m** and **A**. **Es**: ♩. ♪♪♪|♪♪♪

Bar 17, both. *Cresc.* placing as in **VM** sources; **VE** sources place it at start of bar (cf. bar 41)

Bars 17, 35, 37, v. **Es**, **Rc-m**→[87]: ♩. ♪♪♪; cf. notes to bars 41–44 and 59–61

Bar 20, both. **Rc-m** omits >

Bars 21–22, 45–46, v. **Es**, **Rc-m**→[87]: [music example] J'en veux fai-re le che-min cous-sin

Bar 23, pf. RH chord 1 as in **Es**; **Rc-m** omits middle note, **Rc-e** prints lowest note a 4th lower; cf. bar 47

Bars 23, 47, both. *Rall.* as in **VM** sources at bars 23 (pf.) and 47 (v. and pf.); **VE** sources start it from note 1, as do **VM** sources for v. in bar 23

Bars 24, 48, 72, pf. *A tempo / 1º tempo* placed as in **Es** (and **A**); **Rc** starts it at note 1

Bars 30–31, see note to bars 6–7 etc.

Bars 35, 37, see note to bars 17 etc.

Bars 37–39, pf. **VE** sources omit < >

Bars 41–44, v. Main reading as in **Rc-e**, *ossia* as in **Rc-m**₉₀→. **Es** and **Rc-m**→[87]: as *ossia* in bar 41, as main reading in bars 43–44 (**Es-m** and **Rc-m**→[87] place > across final ♩)

Bar 49, 51–52, pf. **Rc-m** omits *p*, *cresc.* and bar 51 ♩ downstems

Bar 56, pf. RH ♩ downstem in **Es** only

Bar 57, pf. **VE** sources omit *pp*, **VM** sources place it at note 1 (editorially nudged right)

Bar 59, pf. > in **VE** sources only

Bars 59–61, v. Main reading as in **Rc-e**, *ossia* as in other sources (except that **Es-e** notates bar 60 as ♩ ♩)

Bars 62–66, pf. **VM** sources: bar 62 LH ♩ a 3ʳᵈ lower. **Rc-m**: bar 64 lower note of last RH dyad a tone higher. **VE** sources end > just before bar 63 ♪ 6. Bass ties from bar 64 in **Rc-e** only

Bar 67, v. **Es**, **Rc-m**→[87]: Syllabification in beats 2–3 [music example] l'âme_ à l'â-

Bars 72, 76–78, see notes to bars 6–7 etc. and 24 etc.

Bars 75–76, pf. **VE** sources omit tie across barline; **Rc-m** omits tie start (system break) but prints completion

Bar 80, pf. **VM** sources give LH beat 1 on a single downstem

5. Tristesse d'Olympio

Keys: e and f♯

C   Scribal copy, unidentified hand, c. 1865: BnF mus., Vma ms. 919 (ex Fauré family library); in e. The music starts under the heading "à mon ami Adam Laussel. / Tristesse d'Olympio. / [left] Musique de Gabriel Fauré". The manuscript shows irregularly entered page numbers doubtless pencilled in later, plus pencilled pagination marks throughout that suggest preparation for another copy (now lost; no engraving is known). Some apparent slips of transcription in the *Allegro* section are shared across strophes, suggesting that the (lost) autograph notated the reprises in shorthand. The pf. RH slur in bar 38 and bass ties across bars 62–63 and 103–104 are in pencil but not visible on the BnF mus. microfilm, leaving the possibility that they were added after the microfilm was made.

Variants

Text. Capitalisation haphazard in **C** and much punctuation absent; both tacitly adjusted to match **T**. Bar 14: **C** omits final *s* of *verdures*. Bar 61: comma editorial (text repetition is Fauré's). Bar 93: **C** has *ronce*, otherwise as present main reading; *ossia* text as in **T** (music editorially adjusted to match)

Bar 10, pf. **C** places ♩ 1 on upper staff and stems (undotted) RH ♩ up on same stem as ♩.

Bar 16, 37, 39, pf. **C** extends slur past last note almost to barline, possibly intended to reach next bar

Bar 44, 85, 126, pf. **C** carries RH upper-voice slur to last ♩ of bar; editorially adjusted

6. Dans les ruines d'une abbaye

Keys: G and A

Es   **Es-e**: First publication: Choudens [1869], in A (A.C. 1865); reissued by Hamelle (J. 2693 H.). **Es-m**: Hamelle [c. 1890], in A♭ (J. 3109 H.). **Es-g**: Hamelle [c. 1911], in F (J. 6330 H.)

Rc   I/3, in A♭ and A

Priority source: **Rc-e**, with remedial input from **Rc-m**

Variants

Text. Capitalisation as in musical sources (except they have *frais* at bar 27). Bars 10, 34: musical sources have a comma. Bar 31: musical sources have *Gaîté*. Bar 38: musical sources have a comma (**T**: *!*); editorially amended to match bar 6. Bar 56: comma in **VM** sources only, presumably to mark the line-end. Bar 78: semicolon as in **VE** sources; **VM** sources and **Es-g** have a comma (**T**: full stop)

Bar 1, pf. **VE** sources omit *e leggiero*

Bar 1 onwards, pf. **VE** sources: RH slurs in just bars 19–34 and 51–66; other sources have RH single-bar slurs throughout. The present *simile* at bars 3, 37 and 69 is adopted as a shorthand replacement to mark the textural differentiation (as in **VE** sources) at bars 19 and 51

Bar 6, v. **VE** sources end > at note 1; other sources as in present edition

Bar 11–17, 43–49, pf. **VE** sources omit dynamics

Bars 21, 53, v. < as in **VE** sources at bar 21, as **Es-e** at bar 53; other sources continue it to the end of bar 21 and to either ♪ 4 or the end of bar 53

Bars 25–26, pf. < > in **Es-g** only, > ending just before ♪ 4 (editorially extended)

Bars 25–26, 57–58, v. < as in **Rc-m** and **Es-e** at bar 25, as in **VE** sources and **Es-g** at bar 57; other sources end it at barline or above pf ♪ 5, except that **Rc-e** omits bars 25–26 < > altogether. **Es-e** places bar 26 > half a bar earlier.

Bars 27–32, 59–64, both. **Rc-e**: dynamics as present edition except places v. < right across bars 29 and 61, places v. > just across bars 32 and 64 preceded by *dim.* halfway through bars 31 and 63, and omits pf. [<] at bar 29. Other sources give v. dynamics as just *crescendo* from last [♪] of bars 27 and 59 and *dim.* from halfway through bars 31 and 63, likewise for pf. at bars 59 and 63 in **VM** sources and **Es-g**, no pf. indications in either passage in **Es-e**. In the earlier passage **VM** sources print pf. [<] across bars 28–29, **Es-g** across just bar 28, [>] as in present edition across bars 31–32 (but ending in middle of bar 32 in **Es-g**). Present edition follows the basis of **Rc-e**, filling its pf. lacuna at bar 29 from bar 61, editorially trimming v. [<] to match bars 21 and 25 and simplifying the diminuendo notation to single [>] signs

Bars 32–33, pf. **Es-m**: last [♪] of bar 32 a semitone higher; ***p*** in **Rc-e** and **Es-g** only

Bar 51, v. ***p*** in **Es-m** and **Rc-e** only

Bars 53–58, see notes affecting bars 21–26

Bars 59–64, see note to bars 27–32 etc.

Bars 67–70, both. **VE** sources omit ***pp*** and instead print v. [<] across bars 67–68 then [>] across bars 69–70

Bar 71, v. **Rc-m**$_{79}$ gives note 3 a semitone lower

Bars 71–74, both. **VE** sources omit pf. dynamics and end v. [<] at last [♪] of bar 71

Bars 75–77, both. Dynamics as in **Rc-e**; other sources have *crescendo* from end of bar 75 (for v. only in **Es-e**) with no culminating indication

Bars 79–81, pf. *Dim.* as in **VM** sources and **Es-g**; **Rc-e**: [>] across bar 79, no indication in **Es-e**. ***p*** in **Rc-e** and **Es-g** only

Bars 81–83, both. **Es**, **Rc-m**: *rall.* from bar 82, *poco* added before it in **Rc-m** and **Es-g** (from bar 81 beat 2); **Rc-e**: *Poco rit.* from bar 81 note 1. Present edition combines final wording with original placing, the effect probably intended (characteristically) as a brief lingering (as suggested by editorial lines)

7. L'Aurore

Keys: F and A♭

C   Manuscript copy, unknown hand, with autograph annotations: BnF mus., Ms. 419c; in A♭. A title page shows the library stamps of Charles Malherbe and the Paris Conservatoire below the title (possibly autograph), surmounted by "G. Fauré" in blue pencil. The music starts under the heading "à Mademoiselle Anna Dufresne" / L'Aurore / Poësie de Victor Hugo [left]", the dedication probably autograph. Performing indications are mostly autograph, as are a few corrections. The 2 music pages are reproduced in facsimile on pp. 278–279 of Frits Noske (ed.), *La Mélodie française de Berlioz à Duparc* (Paris: Presses universitaires de France, 1954; English edition *French song from Berlioz to Duparc: The Origin and Development of the Mélodie*, transl. Rita Benton, New York: Dover, 1970/1988).

Variants

Text. Capitalisation sparse in **C**, **T** capitalises every new line; editorially adjusted to every 2nd line (cf. *Dans les ruines d'une abbaye*). Punctuation erratic in **C**; present edition follows **T**. Bar 23: **C** has *ce* not *le* (doubtless an error in the midst of *démence … immense … recommence, ce*)

Bar 5, pf. **C**: LH note 1 a 3rd lower; editorially amended (cf. bar 22)

Bar 8, pf. **C** aligns last bass [♩] under last RH [♪]; last tenor [♩] also originally aligned similarly, with preceding 2 tenor notes also a [♪] to the right, then rewritten by Fauré to line up correctly under RH. Voice-leading logic suggests correcting bass alignment similarly (rather than reading as [♩. ♪])

Bar 9, pf. **C**: LH dyad upper note on separate [♩] [*sic*] upstem (cf. bar 26); beat 3 lower staff [rest], editorially removed to match usage in bars 26–27; ***pp*** aligned between [♪]s 4 and 5

Bars 15–16, pf. **C** places RH slurs under bar 15 [♪]s 2–5 and over bar 16 [♪]s 2–6 (editorially adjusted)

Bar 18 v. **C**: note 1 [♪] not [♩], remainder of bar as present edition but alignment ambiguous (cf. bar 22)

Bar 19, pf. **C**: last [♪] a tone lower; cf. v. and bar 2

Bar 25, pf. Regarding *ossia* query, cf. note to bar 8

Bar 28, pf. **C** continues bass quaver beam to last note

8. L'Absent

Keys: a and c

A   Complete autograph, the end signed and dated "3 avril 1871": BnF mus., Ms. 419b (ex. coll. Malherbe); in a. The title page names it "Sentiers où l'herbe se balance / poésie de Victor Hugo / Extrait des Châtiments / Gabriel Fauré", probably autograph, in a mixture of ink and pencil. Bar 17 is repeated, the voice entering on the repetition. Dynamics are sparser for v. than for pf.; pedal is indicated only in the last three bars. An alternative text is pencilled in an unknown hand above the vocal staff over the present bars 3–44 (not always fitting exactly), comprising lines 1–4 and 6–8 from a poem by Louisa Siefert (1845–1877), *À ce qui n'est plus* (published in *Le Parnasse contemporain*, vol. II (1869–1871), p. 199):

> Pourquoi revenez-vous, creuser mon souvenir,
> Ô jours trop tôt perdus, ô trop chères pensées,
> Images que le temps doit avoir effacées,
> Mots que mon cœur jaloux ne peut contenir,
> […]
> J'avais promis l'oubli qui console et qui tue,
> L'oubli muet et calme, aux flots profonds et lourds.
> Les heures ont passé, je me souviens toujours […]

Although **A** did not serve for engraving, a few illogicalities in the printed sources can be related to calligraphic ambiguities in **A**, suggesting that it formed part of the source chain leading to publication.

Es   First publication: Choudens [1879], in a (A.C. 4321); reissued by *Hamelle* (J. 2707 H.)

Rc   I/11, in a and c. An offprint from the latter was later issued, retaining its plate number

Priority source: **Rc-m**, with some remedial input from **A**

Variants

Text. Bar 39: musical sources omit comma

Tempo and metre. **A**: *Andante*. ¢ as in **A** and **Es** (which omit tempo emendations at bars 29 and 50–52); other sources: C

Bar 4, v. **Rc-m**: notes 1–2 [♪ ♪] [*sic*], aligned as in present edition

Bars 5, 19, 65, v. **A**: single note for *-lance*, *-nêtre* ([♩]) and *sombre* (𝅝)

Bar 6, v. **Es** and **Rc-e** start *cresc.* at note 1. **A**, last 4 notes: [♪♪♪♪]

Bar 8, pf. **Es** misaligns LH dyad 2 under RH lower voice [♩], the dyad's upper note printed a 3rd lower and the [< >] centred around it. Doubtless in consequence, **Rc** centres [< >] just after the RH lower voice [♩]; **A** centres it as in present edition but starts [<] at [♩] 2

Bars 9–14, 23–27, pf. *Ossia* (bars 11–12, 23–24) as in **A**, which gives dynamics just as *cre - scen - do* from just before bar 9 [♩] 2 and start of bar 24, each inside a [<] from bar 9 [♪] 2 to bar 10 [♩] 2 and from bar 23 [♩] 2 to end of bar 24, with [>] from bar 12 [♩] 2 to bar 14 [♩] 1 and across bar 26 (omitting bar 14 [>]

and v. dynamics); cf. also note to bar 15. **Rc-e** omits each *dim.* and bar 25 𝆑 𝄾 at bars 12–13 beat 3 and bar 14 beat 1 in **A** only.

Bar 15, pf. **A**: RH chord lowest note downstemmed separately as ♩ (no pedal indication), ***p*** at LH ♩ 2

Bar 17, see source description for **A**

Bar 17, v. 𝄾♪ as in **Rc-m**; ♩ in other sources. **Rc-e** omits *dolce*

Bar 22, v. < in **Es** and **Rc-e** only

Bar 26, pf. **Rc-e**: ♭ not ♮ to LH ♩ 2 (no accidental in **A**)

Bar 28, pf. All printed sources: ***pp*** *sempre*, probably confusion with bar 29 (see below)

Bar 29, pf. RH beat 1 stemming and placing of ***pp*** as in **A** (which omits *sempre*); printed sources place ***pp*** at note 1 and beam notes 1–2 together. Printed sources start new slur from note 3; **A** starts it ambiguously between notes 2 and 3 (under the notes), but stemming supports the present reading. See also above regarding Tempo and metre

Bars 38–40, pf. RH phrasing as in **A** until end of bar 39 (ending a system, slur carried to barline); **A** then starts a new RH slur from bar 40 note 1; printed sources carry slur without a break to end of bar 40. **A**: bar 40 bass o 8ve higher, tied to preceding o

Bar 40, v. **Es** and **Rc-e** extend < past ♩ 3 (**A** omits it); cf. bar 44

Bars 41–51, pf. **A**:

(then gives the present bar 52 twice, as noted below). Printed sources end bar 42 RH slur above last triplet ♪ (editorially adjusted). Bar 45 ♪ 5 as in **A**; printed sources give it a 6th higher (probably confusion with following beat: cf. bar 41). Bar 48 1st > in **A** and **Es** only (placed in the latter above the ♩ stem), bar 49 − in **A** only. Bars 49–50 accent placing as in **A** at bar 49; **Rc** places 2nd one in bars 49 and 50 ambiguously above dyad, and 1st one of bar 50 above ♩. Cf. end of note to bars 49–52.

Bars 43, v. Main reading as in **Rc-e**, *ossia* as in all other sources

Bars 49–52, pf. *Ritorno al 1° tempo* in **Rc** only, *1° tempo* starting between ♩s 3 and 4 in bar 52 (editorially adjusted). **Rc-e** additionally has *rall.* at the start of bar 49, and places bar 51 ✱ just after ♩ 4. **A** gives bar 52 twice (after the 2/4 bar shown above), with ***p*** midway through the repetition; cf. note to bar 17.

Bars 56–57, pf. Pedal indications in **Es** and **Rc-e** only, but the latter places the second pair under bar 58 not 57

Bar 57–59, v. **Es** and **Rc-e** lead < to the end of bar 58, **Rc-m** ends it before bar 58 ♩ 4; editorially extended (matching pf.), also taking account of **A** which has *cresc.* from bar 58 note 1 (with no subsequent ***mf*** or >). **Rc-e** prints bar 59 ♩ a 3rd lower (with no accidental)

Bars 59–60, pf. Dynamics and accents as in **A** (except that **A** omits to complete < in bar 59 after carrying it past the end of bar 58, ending a system); all printed sources have ***mf*** (not ***sf***) and > matching v., place bar 60 bass ***sf*** left of ♩ 2 (*sic*), omit RH > and give the LH one as > across 2nd half of bar

Bar 62, v. ***p*** in **A** only

Bars 64–65, v. **A**: ♩ ♩. ♪ | o (cf. note to bars 5 etc.)

Bar 71, pf. **A** notates RH as 2 ♩ triads (on lower staff, stemmed upwards), their middle note (*e–e*) tied, 1st ♩ stem touching only the top 2 notes but the note underneath implied as belonging with them (its notehead in alignment and the same size, whereas the bass o is larger and offset to the right). Printed sources omit the tie, slur over the top notes instead, and print lowermost note of 1st RH triad as o (not ♩). As these appear to be corruptions, present edition follows basis of **A**, renotating RH tied middle note as o. Printed sources place ✱ halfway through beat 1 (**A** omits it); editorially adjusted

9. Lydia

Keys: F and G

Hart   First publication: Hartmann [1871], in F (G.H.582). Tempo indication and pedalling absent, dynamics sparse. The subsequent source chain appears to derive from **Hart**.

Es   Choudens [1877], in F (A.C. 3604) and probably *G*; reissued by Hamelle (J. 2697 H. and J. 2697bis H.), the former unamended except for the restoration of a missing ♯ in bar 29. (**Es-e** is traced only in Hamelle exemplars but shows the characteristic layout and typefaces of Choudens *éditions séparées*, and Choudens title pages list it.)

Rc   I/8, in F and G

Priority source: **Rc-e**

Variants

Text. Bars 3, 4, 26: musical sources omit comma. Bar 11: **Rc-m** has *lui* not *luit*. Bars 12, 14: musical sources have comma not semicolon

Bars 3–4, 10, 12–13, 15–17, 19–20, 25, 27–28, 30–31, 35, pf. Sources variously stem dyads/chords together or separately; present edition follows whichever source(s) maintain 4-voice stemming, and editorially adjusts stemming at bar 10 ♩s 2–3 (both hands) and bars 12–13 and 30–31 (LH) where sources have single stems. All sources double-stem bar 35 LH; editorially adjusted in view of the slur, and to match bar 17 and RH bars 16 and 34

Bar 9, pf. **Rc-e** omits <; **Es** starts > mid-bar

Bar 10, v. Slur in **VM** sources only

Bars 10–12, pf. Sources end a page after bar 10 with what look like tie starts from top and lowest notes of ♩ 4 (**Es-e** alone slants the upper one like a slur), omitting to complete the lower one in bar 11 but continuing the upper one as a slur, except that **Rc** and **Es-m** start a new upper slur from bar 11 ♩ 1 (making the prior slur start also readable as an uncompleted tie). Cf. note to bar 29. **Hart** slurs additionally across each RH ♪ pair in bars 11–12

Bars 11–13, v. **Rc-m** omits dynamics, **Es-m** omits ***p***. **Hart** slurs across (just) bar 13

Bar 15, v. **Rc-m**: < not *cresc.*; **Hart** starts *cresc.* at note 3; **Hart** and **Es** omit >

Bar 15, pf. **Rc-m** adds a minor 3rd (*d′*) below RH note 1 (on downstem; cf. bar 33)

Bars 18–19, pf. *A tempo* placed as in **Hart**; **Es** starts it at ♩ 1, **Rc** at barline. Phrase break after bar 19 ♩ 1 as in **Rc-e** (supporting present placing of *A tempo*); other sources break it a ♩ earlier, across the barline (**Hart** and **Es-m** omit bar 18 RH slur)

Bars 19–20, pf. Bar 19 staccato dots in **Rc-e** only. All sources except **Hart** break slurs across bars 19–20, doubtless a makeshift reading of **Hart**, which carries bar 19 slurs to end-of-page barline then starts new slurs from bar 20 ♩ 1. All sources also print bar 19 LH dyads and bar 20 RH dyads with separate stems. Cf. bars 1–2. ***pp*** as in **Rc-m** (clearly a proof amendment, partly overprinting barline); **Es-m** and **VE** sources: ***p*** (absent in **Hart**). **Rc-m** omits ❋

Bar 23, both. <> in **VE** sources only

Bar 25, pf. **Rc** omits LH slur

Bar 27–28, both. **Es-e** continues v. > to bar 28 ♩ 2 and omits pf. RH slurs

Bar 29, pf. RH slur start as in all sources except **Hart** which slurs just across each RH ♪ pair; cf. note to bars 10–12 (**Hart** again starts a new system at bar 29)

Bars 29–33, both. Sources start v. slur a note later (editorially adjusted); ***f*** as in **Rc-e**; **Rc-m** has ***mf***, **Es** no indication. **Hart**: v./pf. < across bar 29, > across bar 30 ♩s 1–3, no dynamics in bars 31–33

Bar 34, both. **Hart** ends last v. slur a note earlier. **Hart** and **Es-e** omit pf. ties across beats 3–4

Bar 37, pf. Dyad 1 stemming as in **Es-m**; **Hart** and **VE** sources omit upstem, **Rc-m** attaches downstem to lower note only. **Rc-e** starts slur at ♩ 2

Bar 40, pf. **Hart**: ***pp*** above LH dyad 2, under present >

10. Hymne

Keys: F and G

Hart First publication: Hartmann [1871], in G (G.H.585). Pedalling absent, dynamics sparse. The subsequent source chain appears to derive from **Hart**.

Es Choudens [1877], in G (A.C. 3850); reissued by Hamelle (J. 2702 H.)

Rc I/16, in F and G. **Rc-e** here exceptionally includes **Rc**→[87] (which gives *Hymne* in G) with **Rc-e**90→; **Rc-m** refers only to the 1890/1908 Hamelle re-editions.

Priority source: **Rc-m**

Variants

Text. Bars 3–4, 55–56: musical sources omit hyphens. Bars 4, 56: musical source add comma after *belle*. Bars 45–46, musical sources: *musc, qui gîs* [*sic*]. Bar 59: musical sources omit comma (**Hart** has *!*). See also note to bars 57–60

Bars 5, 57, v. ***f*** as in **Rc-m**, ***mf*** in other sources (except **Hart** which omits it)

Bars 7–8, 59–60, pf. Pedal releases editorial

Bars 11–12, v. Sources end slur on last note of bar 11 (system break in **Hart**); cf. bars 63–64

Bars 13–17, v. **Hart**: < across bar 13 beat 2, > bar 14 notes 2–6, no *cresc.* in bar 15, < across bar 16, without ***f*** in bar 17

Bars 15–16, pf. Sources break LH slur across the barline; editorially adjusted

Bars 17–18, pf. **Hart**: < (not ***f***) across bar 17, ***p*** > across bar 18

Bars 20, 24, pf. **Es**, **Rc-m**: last LH note a 3rd higher in bar 20, likewise **Rc-m** in bar 24. **Hart** and **Es** continue RH slurs to bar 20, other sources to bar 21, in each case ending a system or page; editorially renotated as *simile*

Bars 21–22, v. **Hart**, **Es**, **Rc-e**→[87]:

Bars 35–37, both. **Rc-e** omits v. > and pf. ***pp*** *sempre* (**Hart** omits all dynamics except pf. ***pp***)

Bars 44–45, pf. Phrasing as in **Rc-e**; **Hart** and **Es** start a new slur from bar 45 (new page), **Rc-m** omits this part of the slur (new page from bar 44)

Bar 51–52, pf. > in **Hart** only (above notes, cf. bars 73–74); **Hart** conversely omits ***f*** (v. and pf.), as well as RH slurs in bars 53–54, but includes all other dynamics across bars 49–54

Bars 54–55, pf. **Hart** prints bar 54 beat 2 to bar 55 beat 1 (spanning a page break) as

Bar 58, pf. **Rc-e**90→ omits 1st RH dyad lower note (cf. bar 6, but also bars 5 and 57)

Bars 59–60, see note to bars 7–8

Bar 61, pf. **Hart**: lower note of 1st RH dyad a tone lower

Bars 65–66, pf. All sources except **Rc-m** start < at note 1, **Rc-m** at 𝄾; editorially adjusted. **Hart** starts LH slur from note 1

Bars 67–68, pf. Bar 67 < in **Hart** only. All sources: < not *cresc.* in bar 68 (starting 3 notes later in **Hart**), ending at middle of bar 69; cf. v. and note to bars 13–16

Bars 70–73, both. **Hart**: *rall.* from bar 70, leaving it ambiguous whether *sempre* at bar 71 refers back to that or to ***f***; other sources omit *rall.* but retain *sempre* (losing explicit justification for pf. *colla voce*); all sources place *Tempo 1°* as in present edition (except **Rc-e**79 which omits it), against pf. only. As *rall.* seems inappropriate to the context, it is editorially reworded and relocated above *colla voce*

Bar 72, v. **Rc-m** omits tie

Bars 73–74, pf. **Hart**: > for just LH, immediately above notes in bar 73, below them in bar 74. Other sources relocate the former midway between staves and add the present RH > in just bar 74. Editorially renotated in bar 73 to match bar 74; cf. also note to bars 51–52

Bar 75, pf. **Rc-e**79 starts 2nd slur 2 notes later; all sources except **Rc-e**[87]→ beam ♪ 6 with ♪ 7–12

11. La Rançon

Keys: c and e

C Manuscript copy, unknown hand, undated: BnF mus., Ms. 419d (ex coll. Malherbe); in b. No dedication is present. The musical calligraphy is remarkably similar to Fauré's (including the opening 𝄢), but details such as system braces, ♪ tails, the opening treble clefs, *Andante* heading and the somewhat formal text calligraphy are distinctly different. A few amendments (such as added or erased accents) are possibly by Fauré. The vocal line has phrasing slurs throughout (absent from printed sources), their logic not always consistent. Pedalling is absent, dynamic markings sparser for v. than for pf. As with *L'Absent*, a few illogicalities in the printed sources relate to calligraphic ambiguities in **C**, suggesting that it formed part of the publication source chain. Whether this manuscript shows the song in its original key or in transposition has to remain an open question.

Es First publication: Choudens [1879], in c (A.C. 4346); reissued by *Hamelle* (J. 2710 H.)

Rc I/19, then I/18 (1908); in c and e

Priority source: **Rc-e**, supplemented by detail from **C**

Variants

Text. Bars 30, 32: printed musical sources place comma after *autre* not *Art* (**C** omits it and in bar 32 has *l'autre est l'Amour*, vocal pitches and rhythm as in present edition). Bar 53: musical sources omit comma

Bars 3, 48, v. **C**: *p*

Bars 7–14, pf. **C** omits RH upper 8ve in bars 9–10 and 13–14 and ties the single note across bars 7–10 and 11–14, > present in bar 11 but erased (still visible) in bar 7. Bar 9 > in **Es** only

Bar 14, v. **Rc-e** omits <

Bars 19–20, both. No dynamics in **C** (which however shows the preceding <). All printed sources: v. > across bar 19 beat 2 in additon to the present dynamics, pf. > in bar 19 (across beats 2–3 after > in **Es**, across the bar after > in **Rc-m**, across beats 2–3 without > in **Rc-e**) then another across bar 20 beat 1. Sources of confusion may have been a system break in the lost *stichvorlage* (as in **C**) or a misreading of pf. >; v. > in bar 19 being in any event illogical, the present edition omits it and merges the 2 pf. hairpins (in which respect cf. note to bars 42–43)

Bar 21, v. **C**: > on last note (without surrounding dynamics)

Bar 25, pf. Beat 3 RH lower 𝄽 in **C** only, which also has a contradictory prolongation dot to the preceding ♩

Bar 27–28, pf. **C** omits to complete tie at bar 28 after a system break; printed sources omit it altogether and print the 4-note slur above the notes. **Rc-m** omits bar 28 accidental

Bars 29–30, pf. LH slur as in **C**; printed sources end it a note earlier. **C** places < > exactly as shown in present edition, omitting mid-system < > and v. dynamics

Bar 42, pf. **C** gives last 2 top-voice notes as ♪s. Printed sources: *sans Pédale*, presumably to cancel the default indication from bar 33 rather than intended literally (editorially rephrased)

Bars 44–47, pf. Dynamics as in **C**, likewise RH lower-voice slur from bar 45; printed sources end slur on last note of bar 45, extend > to ♪3 and omit *dolce*. **C** conversely carries bar 44 LH slur to bar 45 ♩ (omitting bar 44 RH slur; subsequent LH slur as in present edition) and ends bar 46 RH slur a note earlier

Bar 45, v. > in **C** only, at start of a slur to bar 46 (where **C** has *jour!*). Cf. bars 23 and 26

Bar 48, see notes to bars 3, 48

Bar 49, pf. Main reading as in **Rc-e**, *ossia* as in all other sources

Bars 50–51, pf. **C** omits dynamics and slurs last 3 notes of bar 50; bar 51 middle RH slur in **C** only

Bars 55–59, pf. ƒ downstem to penultimate note in **C** only, along with attached slur (the latter in bar 55 only: editorially repeated in following bars); cf. note to bars 60–61

Bars 60–61, pf. RH slur from bar 60 ƒ˙ as in **C**; printed sources lead it to last ♪ of bar 60. **C** ends < midway through bar 60 and adds a ƒ downstem from that bar's penultimate ♪ (probably confusion with preceding bars)

Bars 65–70, pf. Phrasing across bars 65–66 as implied by **C** (which ends lower slur at barline slightly short of bar 66 ♩ 1; printed sources end it at bar 65 ♩ 3), across bars 68–69 as in **C** (printed sources end RH slur at bar 68 beat 3), otherwise as in printed sources (**C** breaks RH slur across bars 67–68 and ends LH slur at bar 70 beat 1). **Rc-m** omits bar 67 ※ and bar 69 ℞. Bass tie across bars 69–70 in **C** only

12. Chant d'automne

Keys: a and c♯

Es   First publication: Choudens [1879], in a (A.C. 4344) and c♯ (A.C. 4345); reissued by Hamelle (*J. 2711 H.* and *J. 2711*[bis] *H.*)

Rc   I/9, in a and c

Priority source: **Rc-m**

Variants

Text. Bar 45: musical sources omit comma. Bars 59–60, **Rc**: *J'aime, de vos longs yeux,*. Bar 66: *!* in **Rc-m** only (other musical sources: no punctuation)

Bars 2, 6, pf. Bass 𝅝 as in **Rc-m**; other sources: ♩˙; cf. also note to bars 4, 6. **Es-m**: additional < > across bar 2 beats 3–4

Bar 3, pf. **Es-e**: *perdendosi* from beat 1

Bars 4, 6, pf. Bar 4 ※ at beat 1 in **Rc**, at end of bar in **Es**. Bar 6 ※ as in **Es-m** (**Es-e** places it under ♪ 8, **Rc-m** under last ♪, **Rc-e** omits it)

Bar 6, pf. **VM** sources print final < as >

Bars 7–8, pf. **Rc-m** carries slur unbroken over bars 7–8. **Rc-e** omits bar 7 LH slur and bar 8 *mf*

Bar 9, pf. Sources single-stem RH beat 1 (top 3 voices all on upper staff through bars 7–9)

Bars 13–15, both. Present pf. *cresc.* editorially replaces < across just bar 13 (which ends a page in **Es**) in all sources except **Rc-e**, which extends it to the middle of bar 14. V. *f* and pf. *mf* as in **Rc-e**; other sources: v. *mf*, no pf. indication

Bar 18, pf. **Rc-e** omits *sempre*

Bar 21, pf. **Rc-m**: *f* not *sf*

Bar 24, pf. **Rc-e** omits < >

Bar 33, v. > as in **Es-m**; **Rc-m** starts it at note 3, **VE** sources omit it

Bar 35, v. **VM** sources start > at beat 3

Bar 35, pf. **Rc-e** omits pedalling; **VM** sources align ※ just before ♪ 5, **Es-e** under ♪ 7 (editorially relocated)

Bars 35–36, pf. **Es** and **Rc-m₇₉** omit *sf* and *p*; **Rc-m**[1871→]: *mf* not *sf*. **Es** starts > at ♪ 1, **Rc-m** at ♪ 6. **Rc-e** omits <

Bars 36–37, v. **Es**, **Rc-e**: ♩˙ 𝄽. | 𝄽 ♪

Bar 39, v. All sources: *sempre* after *cresc.* **Rc-m** omits ♪ (spacing otherwise as in other sources)

Bar 39, pf. Bass 8ᵃ in **Es-e** only, the context implying *coll'8ᵃ* (cf. bar 42)

Bar 41, v. **Rc-e** omits *f* (but prints *f sempre* in bar 43)

Bar 41, pf. **Rc-e** omits bass tie. ※ as in **Es-m**; **Rc-e** places it at last ♪, other sources omit it

Bars 48–49, pf. Fingering in present high-voice edition from **Es-e** (*1 2 3 1 2* etc. for B–B♯–D♯–F𝄪–G♯), no fingering in other sources; present medium-voice edition editorially adapts this for equivalent logic. ※ as in **Es**; **Rc** places it before end of bar 48. **Es-e** gives bar 48 RH ♪ 10 an additional ♩˙ stem; **Es-m** and **Rc-e** show signs of its removal at proof

Bar 49, pf. *Dim.* as in **VM** sources; **VE** sources start it from ♪ 1; **Es-e** follows it with > to end of bar. **Rc-m** ends RH slur at ♪ 9, **Es** and **Rc-e** at ♪ 10; editorially extended

Bars 51, 53, pf. ※ in **VE** sources only, in **Es-e** aligned under penultimate ♪; **Rc-m** also omits ℞. in bar 53

Bar 54, both. V. > in **VE** sources only. Pf. main reading as in **VE** sources, *ossia* as in **VM** sources

Bar 55, pf. **Rc-e**: LH ♪ 1 a 3rd higher (without accidental; *sic*)

Bar 56, pf. − in **Es-e** only

Bar 57, pf. Sources indicate tempo equivalence as *Une double croche pour une croche du Mᵗ. précédent* and pedal as *Pédale à chaque temps* (editorially renotated, leaving pedalling options open at beat 1 in the absence of a preceding ※)

Bar 58, pf. **Rc-m** repeats *pp*

Bar 62, pf. **VE** sources: > from just after ♪ 4 to ♪ 9 (restricted space between staves); **VM** sources place it across beat 1 (above upper staff); editorially extended (cf. bar 65)

Bar 69, v. Main reading as in **Rc-e**, *ossia* as in all other sources

Bar 70, pf. **VE** sources give beat 3 ♩˙ as an 8ve dyad (as present high-voice edition); **VM** sources give just its upper note (as present medium-voice edition), doubtless a pitch-specific variant

Bars 71–72, v. All sources: *cresc. molto* at bar 71, ⟨ across just ♩· in bar 72 (editorially adjusted)

Bars 71–72, pf. **Rc-m** omits beat 3 bass ♩· stem, as does **Es-m** in bar 72; beat 2 bass ♩· stem in bar 72 editorial. **VM** sources omit top voice slur; **Rc-m** omits ⟨ and adds erroneous prolongation dots to bar 72 last RH ♩ dyad

Bar 73, v. *Sempre* in **Rc-m** only

Bar 73, pf. **VM** sources: LH note 6 a 3ʳᵈ lower

Bar 76–77, pf. **VM** sources omit upper cross-bar tie. All sources single-stem last chord (downwards)

13. Les Matelots

Keys: E♭ and F

Es   First publication: Choudens [1876], in E♭. The BnF mus. *dépôt légal* exemplar shows the plate number A.C. 3779, an apparent misprint amended in later exemplars to A.C. 3279 (part of a sequence of Fauré songs). Reissued unamended by Hamelle (retaining the plate number 3279 without the "A.C."), *possibly also a high-voice edition c. 1887 (J. 2696 H.)*

Rc   I/4, in E♭ and F. Hamelle later replaced **Es-m** with an unamended offprint from **Rc-m** (the 1ˢᵗ music page alone numbered J. 2693. bis H. [*sic*]). **Rc-e** appears to have been derived from **Es** rather than **Rc-m**, but shows revisions absent elsewhere.

Secondary sources

C   Manuscript copy reported in *Nectoux* and *Daitz* as by André Messager (c. 1875), unsigned and undated, ex coll. Marc Pincherle; in B. This source was not accessible: any mentions below are as reported in *Nectoux* and *Daitz*.

Af   Signed autograph fragment (bars 3–5, up to "al-lons", v. only, under a lithographed pen-ink portrait by Robert Kastor); undated, probably c. 1890; in F. Beinecke Rare Books and Manuscript Library (Koch Collection), GEN MSS 601, box 324 folder 1763. No tempo indication or dynamics, otherwise concurs with printed sources

Priority source: **Rc-m**, incorporating revisions from **Rc-e**

Variants

Text. Bar 4: musical sources add comma after *profonde*. Bars 29, 48: **Rc** has a comma, **Es** has full stop in bar 29, comma in bar 48. Bar 54: Musical sources have *!*, editorially amended to match bars 16 and 35.

Tempo heading as in **Es** and **Rc-e**. **C**: *Allegretto*; **Rc-m**: *Tempo animato quasi Allegro*

Bar 8, pf. **Es** and **Rc-e** print final LH ♪ a semitone higher (cf. bars 27 and 46)

Bars 11–12, pf. **Es**, **Rc-e**: prolongation dot to each LH ♩

Bar 15, v. ♭ in **C** only

Bars 19, 38, 57, v. **C**: ♩𝄾𝄾 (tied to preceding ♩·)

Bar 22, v. *p* in **Rc-e** only

Bars 41–42, 45–46, v. Main reading as in **Rc-m**₉₀₋; **C**, **Es** and **Rc-m**₍₈₇₎ give rhythm as in bars 22–27. **Es**: *mf* not *f*; **Rc-m** adds *sempre* after *f*

Bars 48–54, both. **Rc** places v. *f sempre / sempre f* at bar 49 (editorially relocated). **Es**: v. *poco a poco crescendo* from bar 49 (following bar 41 *mf*), *f* at bar 54, pf. *cresc.* as in present edition (under the word *crescendo* for v.). **Rc-m** omits pf. *cresc.*

Bar 49, pf. **Rc-e** omits LH >

Bar 52, pf. **Es**, **Rc-e**: LH ♪s 5–6 respectively a third and a second lower (*sic*)

Bars 57–58, pf. **C**, **Es**, **Rc-e**: bar 57 LH notes 5–6 in reverse order, RH an 8ve lower from bar 57 note 5 (8ᵃ sign probably omitted by oversight). **Rc-e** ends slurs at last note of bar 57. **C** omits bar 59

14. Seule !

Keys: e and g

A   Complete autograph: BnF mus., Ms. 419a (showing a 1925 Paris Conservatoire acquisition date-stamp); in e. The music is headed by Fauré "Seule! / poésie de Théophile Gautier", the end signed and dated "1871". The only dynamic indication is pf. *p* at bar 1.

Hart First publication: Hartmann [1871], in e (G.H.641)

Es   Choudens [1877], in *e* (A.C. 3782) and *g* (A.C. 3783); reissued by *Hamelle* (*J. 2703 H. and J. 2703ᵇⁱˢ H.*)

Rc   I/5, in e and g

Priority source: **Rc-e**

Variants

Text. Bars 6, 10, 14, 18: punctuation as in **A** and **T**; **Hart** and **Rc** have *!* in bar 6 and a comma in bars 10 and 14; **Es-e** has no punctuation in bars 6 and 14, comma in bar 10); printed sources have comma not full stop in bar 18. Bar 47: musical sources omit comma. Bar 50: comma as in **T**; musical sources have *!*

Tempo and metre. **Hart**, **Es-e**: *Andante Grave*. ¢ as in **A** and **Hart**; other sources: **C**

Bar 3, v. Main reading as in **Rc-e**, *ossia* rhythm as in other sources

Bars 5–6, 9–10 etc., pf. Placement of ⟨⟩ as in **Hart** and **Es-e** (when present); later sources haphazardly extend or reduce them by a ♩

Bars 11–12, pf. **Es-e** breaks slurs across barline; **Hart** does likewise with RH slur (system break), omitting LH slur

Bars 14, 32, 50, pf. Chord duration ♩ in **A** and **Hart** (**A** follows it with ⁀), 𝅝 in other sources. **Hart** downstems the first LH ♩ (clarifying hand layout at the expense of voice-leading), omitting the slur (as does **A**)

Bars 15, 51, pf. Phrasing slur in **A** only (sources notate all 3 voices on lower staff)

Bar 15–16, both. Dynamics as in **Rc-e**; other sources centre ⟨⟩ a note later, except that **Hart** omits v. ⟩

Bar 17, pf. **A** gives final LH ♩ a 7ᵗʰ higher (bars 35 and 53 as present edition)

Bars 17–18, pf. **Hart**: ⟨⟩ (as in bars 5–6 etc.), to *p* at bar 18 ♩ 4 (doubtless intended for bar 19 as in other printed sources)

Bars 23–24, both. **Rc-e** omits pf. ⟨⟩. V. ⟨⟩ as in **Hart**; **VE** sources place it across just bar 23, centred at mid-bar in **Rc-e**, at ♩ 4 in **Es-e**; **Rc-m** places it across bars 23–24, centred just before end of bar 23

Bars 27–30, v. Main reading of bars 28–30 as in **Rc-e**; *ossia* as in **A**, **Hart** (which omits dynamics), **Es-e** and **Rc-m**₍₈₇₎. **Rc-m**₉₀:

De sa pâ- leur. Ton dô-me blanc, Sain-te So-phi- e,

Bars 31–32, v. ⟨⟩ in **Rc-m** only

Bar 33, pf. **A** omits tie and slur from beat 1, **Hart** and **VE** sources print just a slur across notes 1–3, **Rc-m** prints tie but not slur; editorially adjusted (cf. bars 15, 51)

Bars 33–37, both. Dynamics as in **Rc-m** except for final pf. ⟩ which **Rc-m** extends to ♩ 4. **Hart** and **VE** sources: v. ⟨ across bar 34 to f at bar 35 then $>$ across bar 36; pf. $<>$ across bar 34 (centred at mid-bar in **Rc-e**, at ♩ 4 in **Es-e** and after it (*sic*) in **Hart**, which omits preceding *cresc.*) then $<$ in bar 35 (♪s 2–4 in **Hart** and **Es-e**, ♪s 3–4 in **Rc-e**), bar 36 $>$ as in present edition, bar 37 pp a ♩ later in **VE** sources, absent in **Hart**. In this instance **Rc-m** appears to represent a judicious clarification (and terracing relative to bars 17 and 53) of preceding sources, a revision lost in **Rc-e**. Cf. note to bars 51–55

Bars 41–42, 45–46, v. **Hart** omits $<>$, as do **VE** sources in bars 45–46

Bars 51–55, both. Dynamics as in **Rc-m** (except for pf. [f]); in bars 51–52 other sources repeat their indications of bars 33–34 (cf. note to bars 33–37), then print pf. $<$ across 1st half of bar 53, $>$ as in present edition (except for **Hart** which prints it across 2nd half of bar 53), v. $>$ across bar 54

Bar 55, both. A: v. — (without preceding tie), pf. chord (all 4 notes) ♩ — not 𝅝

15. Chanson du pêcheur (Lamento)

Keys: f and a

Es   **Es-m**: First publication: *Choudens {1877}, in f (A.C. 3288)*; reissued by Hamelle (J. 2701 H.). **Es-g**: Hamelle [c. 1906], in e (J. 5443 H.)

Rc   I/7, in f and a. An offprint from the latter was issued c. 1890 (J. 2701bis H.).

Mz   Metzler [1896], in f (M.7767), as *Lamento*, English and French text (trans. "A.S."). The cover lists the options "N° 1 in F / N° 2 in A" (see under **Source sigla** above); although the covers of all traced exemplars underline "N° 2 in A", their musical text is in f.

Secondary sources

AF   Autograph fragment of the present bars 31–40: BnF mus., Ms. 20293 (ex coll. Clerc); in f. The half-page occurs on the verso of sketches for the A major Violin Sonata op. 13 which also include a fragment of *Au bord de l'eau*; the lower half of the page (including the pf. part for the present bars 38–40) has been removed. Reworking and variant barring is evident over the present bars 31–34; the only nuances are the bar 36 accents. **AF** contributes no readings to the present edition.

O   Transcription by Fauré for voice and orchestra, c. 1891. **OA**: autograph used for engraving **OE** below (showing performance markings): BnF mus., Ms. 20804 (ex Hamelle); in f. Music all in black ink; the stamp "CONCERTS-COLONNE" appears twice; the tempo heading is absent. **OE**: Hamelle [c. 1895], J. 4050.H; in f. Some useful indications from **O** are shown in parentheses, with a few notable harmonic or dynamic variants listed below; otherwise **O** is mentioned only if it impinges on a source problem.

Priority source: **Rc-e**, with remedial input from **Rc-m**

Variants

Text. Bar 6: musical sources omit first comma. Bars 7, 19, 23: musical sources have a comma. Bar 10: **Rc-m** and **Es-g** have a comma; other musical sources omit punctuation. Bar 41: *une* as in **O** (other musical sources: *Une*), matching pattern of bars 35, 37 and 39 (as in all musical sources)

Bar 1, v. p *dolce* as in **Rc-e**; **Es** and **Mz** omit *dolce*, **Rc-m** omits p

Bar 1, pf. RH — in **Es-m** and **Mz** only

Bars 1, 7, 14, 16, 29, 33, pf. **Rc-m** omits ✼, as does **Rc-e** at bars 1, 7 and 33 (**Rc-m** also omits 𝄢. in bar 33)

Bar 6, 7, 22, 23, pf. **O**: harmony across beats 3–4 major 7th not diminished 7th

Bar 8, pf. **Rc-e**: last RH ♪ a 3rd lower (*sic*); beat 4 𝄽 in **Es-m** and **Rc-e** only

Bars 9, 25, pf. $>$ as in **Es-g** (matching v.); other sources end it a beat later (except **O**, which places it across 2nd half of preceding bar, followed by pp, placed as the present [p]). At bar 25 **Rc-e** omits pedalling, **Es** omits 2nd ✼

Bars 14–15, 46–47, pf. Sources break slur over the barline; editorially combined (cf. bar 33)

Bar 18, v. ' in **Rc-e** and **OA** only (in pencil in the latter, non-autograph), probably to indicate non-elision

Bar 25, cf. note to bars 9, 25

Bars 29–34, both. **O** dynamics: v. f unmodified from bar 29, *sempre* f from end of bar 33, orch. $>$ across bar 29 ♪s 3–4, pp from bar 30 until [*subito*] sf / f at bar 33

Bars 31, 38–39, 42–45, pf. All ✼ in **Mz** only

Bar 32–33, v. Rhythm as in **Rc-m**; all other sources: 𝅝 | — 𝄽 𝄾 ♪

Bars 33–35, both. Sources (except **O**: cf. above) end bar 33 pf. $<$ around ♩ 4; editorially extended. **Es**, **Mz** and **Rc-e** then have mf not f (v. and pf., repeated only for v. at end of bar 35); **Rc-m** has f, but placed a note later for v. and 2 notes later for pf. Bar 33 pf. ✼ as in **Es-m** and **Mz**; **Es-g** aligns it 2 notes later, other sources omit it (**Rc-m** also omits 𝄢)

Bar 37, v. $>$ as in **Rc-m**; **Mz** and **Es** start it at note 1, **Rc-e** before note 2. (The difference from bar 35 can be related to textual emphasis)

Bars 38–39, both. Dynamics as in **Rc-e** except that it omits pf. *cresc.* and ends v. $<$ a ♩ early. **Es** and **Mz** omit p and bar 39 dynamics, **Es** also omits pf. *cresc.*; **Rc-m** delays *cresc.* until bar 39 (starting for v. after ♩, notated for pf. as $<$ from ♪ 5)

Bar 45, v. *Sempre* in **Rc-m** only

16. Tristesse

Keys: c and d

Es   First publication: Choudens [1876], in c (A.C. 3278) and d (A.C. 3277); reissued by Hamelle (J. 2694 H. and J. 2694bis H.); then [c. 1912] for low voice (*J. 6461 H.*), key unknown. The original Choudens cover gives title as *TRISTESSE !* (but above the first music system as *TRISTESSE*).

Rc   I/13, in c and d

Priority source: **Rc-m**

Variants

Text. Bars 7, 20, 33: musical sources have a comma. Bars 30, 43, 45, 47: musical sources omit commas, except after *rien* in bar 43

Bar 3, v. **Rc-m** omits p

Bar 6, v. **Rc-m**$_{→[87]}$, beat 2: ♪♪♪ ♪♪

Bars 14, 27, 40, 53, pf. Slur end as in **Es** and **Rc-e** at bar 53; **Rc-m** ends it a ♪ later there, as do all sources in bars 14, 27 and 40 (with RH beat 1 stemmed inversely to present edition, as are bars 7–13, 20–26, 33–39 and 46–52), except that **Rc-e** breaks slur in bar 41 not 40

Bar 29, both. Pf. pp in **Rc-e** only. V. *dolcissimo* as in **Rc-e**; **Es** has *dolce*, **Rc-m** *dolce sempre*

Bar 31, v. **Es**, **Rc-m**$_{79}$: ♩ ♪ ♪♪♪♪♪

Bar 31, pf. Sources: last RH chord as in bar 5; editorially amended to match bar 18 (cf. v.)

Bars 40–54, pf. Accents in **Rc-m** only. Up to bar 53 beat 1 **Es** reprises the RH texture of the previous strophes (without RH 8ves), bar 44 matching bar 5. From bar 46 to bar 53 beat 1 sources start ♪ beam from upper not lower note (with inverse stemming: cf. note to bars 14 etc.)

Bars 49–50, both. **Rc-e** gives last RH ♪ of bar 49 as dyad, adding a 4th below. *Sempre* in **Rc-m** only; **Es** also omits pf. *f*

17. Aubade

Keys: F and G

Es   First publication: Choudens, Paris [1879], in *F (A.C. 4316)* and A (A.C. 4317); reissued by *Hamelle (J. 2708 H. and J. 2709bis H.)*

Rc   I/12, in F and G

Priority source: **Rc-e**

Variants

Text. Bar 10, **Rc-m**: *ent'rouvre* [*sic*]

Bars 1–13, 16–28, 31, pf. Sources print *portato* articulation just for RH, but place LH figurations on upper staff in bars 1–4 and similar; articulation editorially carried over to LH

Bars 3–4, both. Pf. ⟨ ⟩ in **VE** sources only. V. ⟩ editorially adjusted to match; **Rc-m** starts it at note 1, **VE** sources after note 4

Bars 6–7, both. *f* in **Rc-e** only; other sources: *mf* (**Es-e** places it a note later for v.)

Bars 9–10, both. Pf. ⟨ ⟩ in **Rc-e** only; **Rc-m** ends v. ⟨ before ♪

Bar 11–13, v. **Rc-m** ends bar 11 ⟨ a note earlier and omits bar 13 dynamics

Bars 11, 13, 26, 28, pf. ✻ as in **Es-e** at bars 11 and 26 and **Rc-e** at bars 13 and 28; **Es-e** and **Rc-e** otherwise align ✻ under ♪, except that **Rc-e** omits pedalling in bar 11; **Rc-m** sligns each ✻ right of ♪

Bar 22, v. **Rc-e** omits ⟩, **Es-e** places it and preceding *mf* a ♪ later

Bars 25–26, v. **VE** sources omit *mf* and *p*; **Rc-m** places *p* a note later (editorially relocated) and starts bar 26 ⟩ a note later

Bars 32–33, pf. **Rc-e** extends bar 32 } up to include RH chord (cf. bars 16 and 31), adds one across chord 2 (both hands) and another at bar 33 RH. **VM** sources place ✻ at beat 2

18. Barcarolle

Keys: f and g

A   Complete autograph, signed and dated "19 octobre 1873": BnF mus., Ms. 19204 (ex coll. Émilie [Mimi] Risler, née Girette); in g. (Girette was a favoured interpreter and friend of the composer in the early years of the twentieth century, and married the pianist Édouard Risler.) The music shows pencilled autograph revisions, a heading annotation (probably autograph) "en fa mineur" and some pencilled crosses probably flagging renotations to be carried over from the first strophe (presumably for purposes of copying). Fauré's signature and date appear below an original shorter ending (see below) that is deleted, the replacement rewritten underneath the signature at an unknown date. The opening tempo heading and voice rests are absent; dynamics are sparse. Low on the final page Mimi Girette has written (in blue ink), "Donné par Fauré / 12 Juillet 1902 / Mimi".

Es   First publication: Choudens [1877], in g (A.C. 3281); reissued by Hamelle (J. 2700 H.)

Rc   I/17, then II/20 (1908); in f and g. Also printed in *La Musique des Annales* 36 (supplement to *Les Annales politiques et littéraires*, no. 2159), 9 November 1924; musically identical with **Rc-m** except opening pf. dynamic misprinted as *ff*; not mentioned separately below

Priority source: **Rc-m**

Variants

Text. Bars 4, 17, 34: musical sources omit commas. Bar 10: printed musical sources have a comma (**A**: no punctuation)

Tempo heading. **Es** and **Rc-e** omit *con moto*. Metronome indication in **Rc-e**$_{08}$ only

Bar 3 onwards, pf. Sources give many chords (e.g. bar 3 RH, bar 4 LH) on single stems, mixing tied ♩. ♩. notation (rather than ♩) with phrasing slurs; editorially respelt when feasible for legibility (using ♩. as **A** does in bars 3, 5 and similar, and printed sources in bar 7 and similar). In bars 6, 10 and 14 **A** shows some ♪· notation amended to ♪⌣♪· as part of other stemming and voicing revisions that suggest notational indecision at that stage; cf. note to bars 4, 6 etc.

Bars 4, 6, 10, 12, pf. **A** ties bass grace note over to a ♪ (undotted), possibly added later, sometimes incompatible with pedal indications and not carried over to bars 8, 14 or 22 onwards. **A** also shows bar 12 lower staff flagged and repeated in pencil at the bottom of the page minus its bass ♪ and grace note

Bars 4, 8, 22, 26, pf. **A**: ♮ before penultimate RH ♪, deleted in pencil

Bars 5, 9, 23, 27, pf. Top slur and tie as in **A** at bars 5 and 9; printed sources (and **A** at bar 23) have a single ambiguous slur/tie; in bar 27 **A** has no tie or slurs

Bars 6, 10, 14, 24, 28, 32, v. **A**: ♪·

Bars 7–8, 25–26, pf. **Rc-e** ties top voice over barline

Bar 15, v. Main reading as in all sources but **Rc-e**, except that **Es** omits ♭. Cf. note to bar 33

Bar 16–17, 34–35, pf. **A**: , except that bar 35 omits LH upper 8ve and top slur (*p* later pencilled above v. in bar 17, *f* in bar 35)

Bar 18, pf. Sources spell RH as 2 single-stemmed ♩ chords (as also at bar 36), the middle voice tied only in **A** (bar 36 tied in all sources). **A** slurs across just bar 18 (not to bar 19)

Bars 23–27, see notes to bars 5, 9 etc. and to bars 7–8 etc.

Bar 25, pf. **Es** reads as bar 21; see also note to bars 7–8 etc.

Bar 29, both. **A**: *f* (ink) above v., implying also for pf. (no more dynamics until bar 34)

Bar 31, pf. LH slur in **A** only

Bar 33, v. Main reading as in **Rc-m**$_{90\rightarrow}$; **A**, **Es** and **Rc-m**$_{\rightarrow[87]}$ show same musical rhythm but with *Que* across notes 1–2 and *-ni-se* on ♪ ♪. **Es** omits ♭. Cf. note to bar 15

Bars 34–35, both. ⟨ for v. in **Rc-e** only, for pf. in **A** and **Rc-e** only. *Sempre* in **Rc-m** only (which also prints it for pf.; cf. note to bars 37–42). **A** shows *rall.* originally starting above (and just before) penultimate v. ♪, lightly deleted and rewritten just after v. note 1 and repeated in pencil for pf., possibly to match revised ending (see below). See also note to bars 16–17 etc.

Bars 37–42, pf. *f* in **Rc**$_{[87]\rightarrow}$ only, bar 38 RH ♪· (with preceding tie) in **Rc-m** only, its dot in **Rc**$_{[87]}$ only. Original deleted reading in **A**:

19. Ici-bas !

Keys: e and f♯

A Complete autograph, undated but signed at the end: BnF mus., Ms. 20294 (ex coll. Clerc); in f♯. The music is titled by Fauré "Ici-bas tous les lilas meurent!"

Es First publication: Choudens [1877], in f♯ (A.C. 3280); reissued by Hamelle (J. 2699 H.)

Rc I/20, then I/19 (1908); in f♯ and g. An offprint from the latter was later issued [c. 1908], J. 5752 H.

F Feuilleton publication: *La Musique des Annales* (supplement to *Les Annales politiques et littéraires* no. 2019), 5 March 1922; in f♯. Musical text mostly follows **Es**.

Priority source: **Rc-e** (but high-voice key taken from **A**/**Es**/**Rc-m**)

Variants

Text. Bar 21, **A**: *et* not *ou*, the latter then added above

Bars 1, 9, 17, pf. Beat 1 layout as in **A**; printed sources beam ♪s 1–4 together (omitting *m.d.*), with bar 1 RH 𝄾 (not in **Rc-m**) and beat 2 LH 𝄾, bars 9 and 17 RH 𝄾 not 𝄾 and no LH 𝄾

Bars 1–2, 9–10, 17–18, pf. ❋ as in **Es** and **Rc-e**, except that **Rc-e** places it midway through bar 10 as in **Rc-m** (see footnote to bars 1–2). **A** omits pedalling in these bars, as does **F** in bars 17–18

Bars 5–6, 13–14, pf. **A** breaks slur a ♪ earlier

Bar 7, pf. **A**: *pp* (*p* for v., no indication at bar 15)

Bar 12, pf. **Rc-e** prints last dyad a 3rd higher

Bars 13–14, pf. **A**: bass an 8ve higher (matching bars 5–6)

Bar 19 onwards, both. Regarding **A** see Appendix

Bars 22–26, both. Dynamics as in **Rc-e**, except v. > in **Rc-m** only. Other printed sources place *cresc.* at bar 23 (in place of <) and omit pf. *f*; **Es** and **F** also omit v. *f*

Bar 27, pf. Main reading as in **Rc-e**; **Es**, **F**: RH ♩ 1 as in **Rc-m**, otherwise as **Rc-e**

Bar 30, pf. Printed sources stem ♪s 1–2 up but show all the present rests; **Rc-m** beams ♪s 1–4 together

20. Au bord de l'eau

Keys: c and d

Es **Es-e**: First publication: Choudens [1877], in c♯ (A.C. 3754); reissued by Hamelle (J. 2704 H.). **Es-m**: Hamelle [c. 1890], in c (J. 3110 H.). **Es-g**: Hamelle [c. 1909], in b♭ (J. 5820 H.)

Rc I/18, then I/17 (1908); in c and c♯

Secondary sources

AF Autograph fragment matching the present bars 1–28: BnF mus., Ms. 20293 (ex coll. Clerc); in d. 2 pages, among sketches for the A major Violin Sonata op. 13; reproduced in facsimile in Nectoux and Daitz, pp. XVI–XVII. The first voice entry is half a bar later than in other sources, with some 3/8 barring after bar 17. The piano part is blank from the present bar 9 beat 2 to bar 12 beat 1 and bar 13 beat 2 to bar 14 beat 1, and notated just as figured bass from the present bar 14 beat 2 to bar 17 beat 1.

A1 *Complete autograph, listed in Nectoux and Daitz as coll. Gilbert Amat, signed and dated "Sainte-Adresse, août 1875" and dedicated "à Madame Marie Vaudoyer"; in c. This source was not accessible: any mentions below are by reference to Nectoux and Daitz.*

A2 Complete autograph, undated [c. 1875–76]: collection of Thierry Bodin, Paris; in c. Fauré's signature appears at the end, in blue ink and in the handwriting of later years (post-1890), followed by "Quand j'étais petit je n'étais pas grand / Je f'sais des mélodies qu'on chant' maintenant!";[7] this must have been added when he later gave the manuscript to someone now unidentified. Dynamics and articulation are sparse.

A3 Complete autograph, the title page signed and dated "15 aout [*sic*] 1876": BnF mus., Ms. 20291 (ex coll. Clerc); in c. Fold marks, along with a partial postal franking stamp ("HAVRE") at the bottom edge of the last music page, indicate that it was mailed, doubtless to Marie Clerc for her name day. The chronological order of A2–3 is not certain: each shows variant disparities and concurrences with *A1* and printed sources, A3 on balance slightly closer to the published version, suggesting that both were copied somewhat freely around the same time from a common source, possibly *A1*.

To show or list all passing variants of texture across A1–3 (mostly affecting piano chords or bass octave doubling) would necessitate near-complete transcription of each source; only variants of particular musical interest or affecting editorial issues are listed below.

Priority source: **Rc-e**, with parenthesised input from **A**

Variants

Text. Bars 6, 10, 14, 22, 26: musical sources have a comma. Bar 18: full stop as in **Rc-e** and A2; A3 has *!*, other musical sources a comma (T: semicolon). Bar 23: musical sources omit comma

Tempo heading. A1–3 omit *quasi allegretto*

Bar 2, v. *p* in **Rc-e** only

Bars 2, 6, pf. Bar 2 beat 2 RH as in A3; other sources repeat the preceding dyad; A1–2 repeat the dyad at bar 6 beat 2

Bars 2, 6, 14, 30, pf. *A1* and A3 start RH slur a bar later, A2 likewise except starts the 3rd one at bar 16 note 1 and omits the last one

Bars 4, 8, pf. *A1*–3 omit bass tie (present in **AF**)

Bar 6, v. A3, beat 1: ♪ 𝄾 ♪

Bars 10–12, pf. A3: [music example]

A2: chord 1 as A3, otherwise as present edition (*A1* RH mostly as A3, LH as A2). Cf. also notes to bars 4 and 8, 26–28 and 35–36 etc. regarding bass ties

Bars 14–15, pf. Bass slur in A3 only; cf. below regarding v.

Bars 14–15, 30–31, v. Slur in A3 and **VE** sources only, ' in **Rc-e** only (editorially parenthesised; cf. prefatory note on **Tempo, metre and rhythm**). Bar 14 *mf* in **Rc-e** only, bar 30 *f* as in **Es-m/g** and **Rc-e** (*mf* in other sources except A3 which instead has > across beat 2 of bars 14 and 30)

Bar 17, pf. RH tie in A2–3 only, LH tie in A2 only

Bar 18, pf. *Ossia* phrase break as in *A1*–2 (which then give ♪s 4–6 in reverse order; A2–3 then have single-bar slurs until bar 25)

Bar 20, pf. LH beat 2 in *A1*–2 as present LH upper note; A3 gives it a 3rd lower (*A1*–3 all give only the bass upper 8ve from bar 18 beat 2 to bar 26 beat 1)

Bars 21, 25, v. A3: beat 1 ♩ ♪ not ♪ 𝄾 ♪, also *A1*–2 in bar 25

Bar 22, pf. 𝒫𝑒𝑑. in A2 only

Bar 26, v. Printed sources: *cresc.* above < (A2 has just *cresc.*, A3 has just *mf*)

---

[7] Reference to a scatological children's song: *Quand j'étais petit je n'étais pas grand / J'montrais mon derrière* [or *mes fesses*] *à tout les passants* [etc.].

Bars 26–28, pf. A2: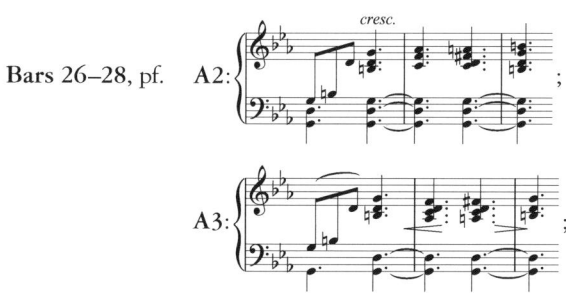

cf. notes to bars 4 and 8, 10–12 and 35–36 etc.

Bar 29, pf. Printed sources extend $>$ across bar, editorially adjusted to match bar 13; **A3** extends it to bar 30 ♪2, omitting subsequent $<$; **A2** marks no dynamics across bars 27–33

Bar 30, pf. 𝄾 in **Es-g** only

Bars 30–31, see note to bars 14–15 etc.

Bars 34–36, pf. RH slur taken from **A2** (which has a slightly variant RH texture)

Bars 35–36, 45–46, pf. **Rc-e** is the only printed source to tie LH over the barline; **A2** (with a variant texture) does likewise, as does **A3** across just bars 45–46; *A1 omits ties across bars 34–36 and 44–46*

Bar 36, v. **A2–3**, beat 2: ♩.

Bars 36–37, pf. Printed sources end $<$ a ♪ earlier, **A3** a note later; **Es-m/g** omit $>$, **A3** places it from bar 37 beat 2 to bar 38 ♪ 2. (**A2** omits $<>$)

Bars 38–39, both. **A3**: v. *cresc.* from just after bar 38 note 1 instead of $<>$, omits pf. $<>$ and subsequent dynamics until bar 46

Bar 40, pf. RH beat 2 stemming as in **A2–3**, RH slur continuation to bar 41 as in **A2** (**A1** and **A3** omit it); printed sources beam RH lower 8ve separately on lower staff with its own slur, both slurs ending at last ♪ (cf. bars 48–50). LH beat 2 a semitone higher in **A3** (D/d♮ not ♭); **A2** originally likewise then amended to present reading (this being the ms. that remained in Fauré's possession)

Bar 42, v. *A1*: ♩. ♩. ; **A2**: ♩. ♪𝄾

Bar 44, v. A: 𝄾 𝄾 ♪♪♪♪, *pp* in **A2**, *p* in **A3**

Bars 45–46, see note to bars 35–36 etc.

Bar 46, v. **A3**: ♫ ♪♩.

Bars 46–48, both. V. *pp* as in **Rc-e**; **A3** places it at the bar 47 entry (above $<>$ for pf., repeating that of bars 36–38), other sources omit it. **A2**: *poco rall.* from bar 47 ♪3, *in A1 starting a ♪ earlier*

Bars 48–51, both.

A2:

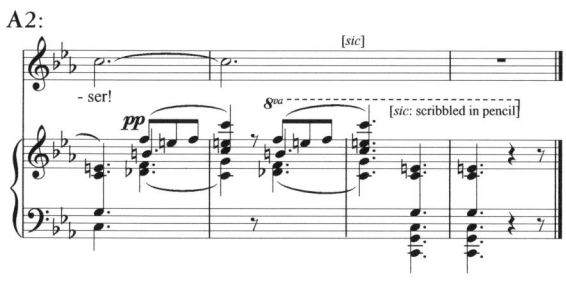

A3:

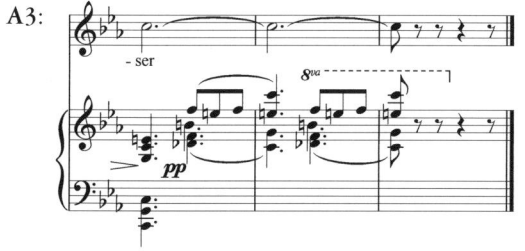

*A1 reportedly as **A2** except omits pf. bar 49 beat 2 and bar 50*

beat 1 (and 8ve indication), and ties final chord over an extra ♪. (The missing v. bar in **A2** might thus imply copying from *A1*.) **Rc** omits pf. upper slur to 1st phrase, **A3** and **Es** omit upper slur to 2nd phrase, **Es-g** and **Rc** omit lower one

21. Après un rêve

Keys: c and d

C   Manuscript copy, unknown hand: BnF mus., Vma ms 1189 (ex coll. Clerc); in c. The musical text shows a few pencil corrections, probably non-autograph; the only dynamics are pf. *p* at bar 1 plus v. dynamics as in printed sources at bars 31, 34 and 43–45.

Es   **Es-m**: First publication: *Choudens* [1877–78], in c; reprinted by Hamelle (J. 2705 H.). A later re-engraving [c. 1923] with English and French texts (J. 7506 H.) is musically identical. **Es-g**: Hamelle [c. 1908], in b (J. 5686 H.)

Rc   I/15, in c and d. An offprint from the latter was issued c. 1890 (J. 2705bis H.)

Priority source: **Rc-e**

Variants

Tempo. C: *Andante*

Bar 4, pf. **Rc-m**$_{79}$: last 2 RH chords same as preceding 4

Bars 15–16, pf. *mf* in **Rc-e** only; **Rc-m** places $<>$ across just bar 16. All sources but **Rc-e** print 𝄾 to last 2 chords of bar 16; faint traces on **Rc-e** attest to their removal at proof

Bar 17, pf. RH beaming as in **C**; other sources beam across chords 1–6

Bars 17–26, both. Dynamics as in **Rc-e**; other sources: bar 17 $<$ for v. only, $>$ at bar 19 for v. only, no other dynamics

Bar 26–28, pf. LH slur in **C** only

Bar 27–29, v. *Cresc.* as in **Rc-e**; other sources: *cresc. poco a poco* from bar 27

Bars 30–31, both. v. $<$ and pf. *f dim.* in **Rc-e** only

Bar 35, both. *mf* in **Rc-e** only

Bar 37, both. Dynamics as in **Rc-e**, pf. *ossia* $>$ as in **Rc-m**. **Es-m** places v. $>$ a bar earlier, no pf. dynamics; **Es-g** omits all dynamics in bars 35–38

Bars 38–39, 43–44, pf. Printed sources break bass slur across bars 38–39 (system change); present edition follows **C**. End of same slur as in printed sources; **C** ends it a note earlier

Bar 40, pf. **Rc-e** omits lowest note of RH chords 3–4

Bars 41–42, pf. *mf* in **Rc-e** only; **Rc-m** also omits $>$

Bar 42–43, v. Sources place *p* at bar 43 beat 1; editorially adjusted. **Es** ends $>$ slightly after ♩

Bar 45, pf. **Rc-m**$_{79}$ prints top note of first two RH chords a 3rd higher

Bars 47–48, pf. Sources give just upper note of bass, **C** with 8va - - - underneath (and the notes of bar 47 tied, doubtless a slip of the pen), printed sources have 8 under each note; editorially renotated assuming intent as *coll'8^{a}*

22. Sérénade toscane

Keys: a and c

Es   First publication: Choudens [1879], in c (A.C. 4320); reissued by Hamelle (J. 2706 H.)

Rc   I/6, in b♭ and c. A musically identical offprint from the former was later issued (J. 2706bis H.)

Secondary source

Es-vc Transcription by Louis van Waefelghem with added cello (or viola d'amore, viola or violin): Hamelle [1901], in a (J. 4691 H.). The separate string parts (derived mostly from the original piano part, which **Es-vc** correspondingly adjusts) show some additional dynamics, perhaps added in consultation with Fauré who knew van Waefelghem well. Some of these, where useful, are shown parenthetically in the present piano part.

Priority source: **Rc-m**

Variants

Text. Bar 3: musical sources liaise *dor-mi* into *e*, with *-po-* across the ♪ pair (editorially adjusted). Bar 12: comma after *toi* editorial. Present edition gives Tuscan as in **T** with underlay editorially adjusted where musical sources mistranscribe it or mismatch syllables to notes, as follows:

In the last of these, *dormire* and *dormir* are editorially transposed here to fit the music's rhythm. Other mistranscriptions of the Tuscan not affecting musical underlay are corrected tacitly

Bar 10, pf. > in **VE** sources only

Bars 11–12, pf. Sources join bass slur over a system break; cf. bars 31–32

Bar 16, pf. 1st ✶ as in **VE** sources; **Rc-m** places it a ♩ earlier

Bar 24, pf. **Rc-m** prints LH ♪ 7 a semitone higher

Bars 26–27. Sources break slur across barline; cf. bars 6–7

Bar 29, pf. End of < as in **VE** sources; **Rc-m** ends it a ♩ earlier

Bar 41, 43, both. **VE** sources: *un pochino* [sic] *più mosso* at bar 41 (pf. only); **Rc-m** removes *un pochino*, leaving *più mosso* in its original location (from ♪ 5), and adds v. *più mosso* at bar 43 (before the v. entry). Bar 43 v. dynamic *mf* in **VE** sources, *f* in **Rc-m**

Bars 41–47, pf. **Es-vc** dynamics (separate violin part only): |*p cresc.* |*f* |*dim.* |*p* |*cresc.* |*f* |*dim.* |

Bars 44, 47, both. Sources place < immediately above bar 47 v., which in **Es** lies below bar 44, probably engraver's misreading of similar placing in the now lost manuscript (i.e. the nuance having been written below and intended for bar 44)

Bars 48–52, both. *Ritorno al 1º tempo* in **Rc-m** only. Sources place pf. *dolce* a ♪ earlier (partly overprinting the barline in **Es**). Pf. 1st bass slur, bar 52 short slurs and v. > in **VE** sources only. **Rc-e** starts bar 49 pf. top slur at beat 2

Bars 54–55, pf. RH tie across barline in **Es-e** only. *Dolcissimo* in **Rc-m** only

23. Sylvie

Keys: F and A♭

Es First publication: Choudens [1879], in F (A.C. 4318) and A♭ (A.C. 4319)

Rc I/14, in F and A♭. Hamelle later replaced **Es** with unamended offprints from **Rc**, retaining the latter's plate numbers

Priority source: **Rc-m**

Variants

Bars 3, 22–23, 44–45, 66–67, pf. **Rc-e** starts bar 3 < at ♪ 3, other sources at ♪ 1. Bars 22–23 < > in **VE** sources only, which start < at ♪ 2. Bar 44 < as in **Es-m**; **Rc-m** omits it, **VE** sources start it at ♪ 2 then start bar 45 > a ♪ earlier. Bars 66–67 < > in **VM** sources only. Placing of < editorially standardised

Bars 3–4, 22–23, pf. Sources break LH slur across barline (system breaks in **Es**); editorially joined (cf. bars 44–45 and 66–67)

Bar 6, v. **Es**, **Rc-e**: *dolce* not *p*

Bars 6, 8, 28, 30, 50, pf. Main reading as in **Rc-m**, footnote *ossia* (flagged at bar 6) as in **Es** and **Rc-e**

Bar 12, pf. **Rc-e** ends LH slur at note 2, other sources at note 3, with new slur in all sources from bar 13 note 1; cf. bars 36–38. (The viable variant phrasing between bars 13–16 and 35–38 is left as in sources)

Bars 14, 34, 36, pf. < > as in **VM** sources; **VE** sources centre them a ♪ earlier in bars 14 and 34, a ♪ earlier in bar 36

Bar 16, pf. < in **Es-m** only

Bar 17, both. Sources place *f* a beat later; cf. bars 39 and 61. **Rc-m** misprints last pf. note as ♪ (followed by present 𝄾)

Bars 19, 41, 63, both. V. > as in **Rc-m**; **Es-m** starts each one a ♪ earlier, **VE** sources start it from note 1 in bars 19 and 63, from (v.) note 2 in bar 41. Pf. > at bars 19 and 41 in **VM** sources only, at bar 63 in **Es-m** only

Bar 20, pf. Sources add *sempre* after *p*

Bars 23, 45, 67, v. > in bars 23 and 67 as in all sources except **Rc-m**, which starts it from ♪ 1. < > centred in bar 45 as in **VM** sources; **VE** sources centre it at barline. Cf. note to bars 3–4 etc.

Bars 28–29, 31, pf. Pedalling for bar 28 in **VM** sources only, for bars 29 and 31 in **VE** sources only. **Rc-m** omits bar 28 1st LH slur

Bars 50–52, pf. Bar 50 pedalling in **VE** sources only, which then place bar 52 ✶ at end of bar. Sources end < at either penultimate or last ♪ of bar 51; editorially extended

Bars 55–56, pf. > in **VE** sources only, *sempre* in **VM** sources only. RH phrasing as in **Rc**; **Es-e** continues slur across the barline; **Es-m** slurs bar 55 as present edition (ending a page) then starts bar 56 with carried-over slur

Bars 59–60, pf. **VM** sources break LH slur across bars 59–60. < in **VM** sources only

Bars 61–63, pf. *mf* in **Rc-m** only. Pedalling as in **VE** sources; **Rc-m** omits it in bars 61–62, **Es-m** places each ✶ at ♩ 3

Bar 64, pf. **Rc-m** omits RH slur

24–26. Poème d'un jour

Keys: B, e, E and D♭, f♯, G♭

A Complete autograph, undated: Harry Ransom Humanities Research Center, The University of Texas at Austin, Carlton Lake Collection (ex Durand archives); in D♭/f♯/G♭. The autograph title page gives the title as *Poème d'un jour. / Trois mélodies* with the present dedication, and ends with the notation "(op. 17)". No. II is titled "Toujours!" No publisher or engraver annotations are visible, but pencil marks throughout the music suggest a pagination cast, doubtless for a transposed scribal copy (now untraced) serving as

D   engraving copy for **D1**. One or two retouches on **A** appear to postdate the copying. Above each song, autograph: "Ténor ou Soprano", along with a key for the edition for mezzo-soprano or baritone (B, e and E respectively). "Adieu" adds an autograph instruction not to employ enharmonic change of spelling for bars 13–22 in the transposed edition ("sans enharmonie dans la modulation en mi mineur"). This central episode of "Adieu" appears twice: the original notation (**A**: see facsimile, p. V) maintains a 6-flat key signature but with sharp spelling across bars 12–22 (amending bar 12 which originally used flat spelling). A laid-in folio on different paper (**AC**) presents bars 11–23 again, recopied mostly in another hand but partly marked up by Fauré. Untransposed, **AC** maintains flat spelling through bar 12 before changing the key signature to 3 sharps across bars 13–22. (Printed sources follow this renotation, though **D1** appears to take some orthographic details from **A**.) **A** shows bar 12 recopied above the system in pencil (see facsimile, p. V) to clarify some untidiness – though this may ironically have introduced a new problem, noted below. The long-delayed high-voice edition (**D2** then **Rc-e**) and all subsequent editions appear to have ignored **A**.

D   **D1**: First publication: Durand, Schœnewerk et Cie, Paris, medium voice only, in B/e/E (D.S. et Cie 2826; engraver: Parent); legal deposit date 26 November 1880. Reprints from 1897 on show a few minor variants and an amended title page that newly lists the work as op. 21 (as in **Rc**), "A. Durand et Fils" as publisher, and different voices (soprano/tenor, mezzo-soprano/baritone); these prints are distinguished as necessary by date (**D1**$_{80}$, **D1**$_{97}$). **D2**: individual offprints for high voice, A. Durand & Fils [September 1894], in D♭/f/F (D.&F. 4843–4845, again engraved by Parent). **D3**: new edition based on **D1**$_{97}$, same keys, Durand (D.&F. 2826, number taken over from **D1**); engraved June 1904 (by Charles Douin), issued February 1905, as of 2014 still the standard Durand edition. **D4**: individual offprints, medium voice (again B/e/E), re-engraving (by Douin) with added English text by F. Bonner, Durand, 1905 (D.&F. 6625–6627). **D5**: re-engraving (by C. G. Röder, Paris) with just German and English texts (*Gedicht eines Tages / One day's poem*) by M. D. Calvocoressi and F. Bonner, 1906, again in B/e/E (D.&F. 6719). **D6**: "Rencontre" and "Adieu" (only), in B/E, Durand [1923], re-engraving by Douin (D.&F. 10 387), as nos. 1–2 of *Gabriel Fauré / Douze Chants / pour Chant et Piano* (medium voice only, followed by extracts from *Le Jardin clos*, *Mirages* and *L'Horizon chimérique*). **D1–2** (and **Rc**) print the title as *Poëme d'un jour*, as do the cover and title pages but not the music headings in **D3–4**.

Rc   II/4–6, in B/e/E and D♭/f/F, as op. 21, with the footer "Publié avec l'autorisation de M.M. A. Durand et fils." **Rc-e** is clearly derived from **D2**, though with numerous variants.

Mz   Metzler and Co. L^{td}, London [1897], in B/e/E (M.7902, 7903, 7903 [sic]), as "Love for a Day / N° 1. Meeting. / N° 2. For Ever. / N° 3. Good-bye" (French titles in parentheses); English and French texts (trans. Paul England)

VE sources: **D2** and **Rc-e**

VM sources: **D1**, **D3–6**, **Mz** and **Rc-m**

Priority sources: **A**, **D3**, **Rc-e**. Text generally as in **Rc-e**, missing punctuation tacitly imported from **Rc-m** and **D3** (no independent text source)

I. Rencontre

Text. Bar 8: **D1–3**, **Rc**: *i-nes-pé-*; **A** shows initially the same amended to *in-es-pé-*. (The initial reading, albeit syllabically incorrect, suggests Fauré's concern for clarity on the initial vowel)

Title, tempo, metre. **D5**: English title *Rencounter* [sic]. **A**, **D1–2**: no metronome indication; **Rc**: ♩ = 72; **Mz**: ♩ = 70 [sic]; **D3–6**: ♩ = 66. **D3–6** render 𝐂 as $\frac{4}{4}$ (Durand house style)

Bar 1, pf. Sources: *Pédale* [or *Pédales* or ℘] *à* [or *sur*] *chaque temps* (in **A** originally written under bar 2 then relocated); editorially renotated

Bars 4, 9, 24, 29, pf. **A** and **D1**$_{80}$ omit beat 4 cancelling accidental, as do **D1**$_{97}$, **D4–5**, **Mz** and **Rc-m** in bars 9 and 29

Bars 7, 27, pf. LH beat 2 downstem ƒ in **A** and **D1**$_{80}$, ƒ· in other sources (editorially adjusted). ⟩ as in **VE** sources in bar 7, as in **D4** and **Rc-e** in bar 27; **A** and **D1**$_{80}$ omit it (and preceding ⟨); in bar 7 **VM** sources start it at ♪ 1 and end it variously at ♪s 4–6, in bar 27 **Rc-m**, **Mz**, **D2–3** and **D5–6** end it at ♪ 8

Bars 13, 33, 34, pf. **A** omits LH beat 3 ƒ stem, as does **D1**$_{80}$ in bar 13 (sources stem this beat inversely, also in bar 14)

Bars 14, 18, 34, 38, v. **A**: ♩. for -mie, -thie and -hie, without the subsequent comma in bars 18 and 38

Bar 19, both. **A** omits pf. ⟨ and shows v. ⟨ deleted, omitting subsequent *f* (v. and pf.); **D1**$_{80}$ also omits *f*

Bar 27, see note to bars 7, 27

Bars 34–35, pf. ⟨⟩ as in **A**; **D1**$_{80}$ omits it, other **VM** sources omit ⟨ and start ⟩ at beat 4, **VE** sources start ⟨ a ♩ later. **D1**,**3–6** and **Rc-m** omit bar 34 1st RH ƒ downstem. Bar 35 penultimate dyad as in **A**; printed sources give its lower note a 3rd higher

Bar 38, both. V. ⟨ as in **VE** sources; **A** omits it, **VM** sources start it a note earlier. Pf. ⟨ in **D2** and **Rc** only

Bar 42, v. **D2**: 𝅝 – [sic]; **Rc-e**: 𝅝

II. Toujours

Tempo and metre. **A**, **D1–2**, **Rc**: 𝐂; **Mz**: ₵; **D3–5**: $\frac{4}{4}$.
A, **D1–2**: no metronome indication; **Mz**: ♩ =76; **Rc**: ♩ =152; **D3–5**: ♩ =144

Bar 10, pf. ⟩ in **A** only

Bar 15, v. **VE** sources omit *cresc.*

Bars 24, 26, both. **A** shows signs of *f* having been amended to *ff* then back again

Bars 30–31, both. **A** leaves v. ⟩ slightly open at the end of bar 30 (end of page) then omits to complete it in bar 31, and conversely starts pf. ⟩ only at the initial accolade for bar 31 (as if carried over from bar 30). Printed sources: v. ⟩ across bar 30, pf. ⟩ across 1st half of bar 31 (starting at ♪ 3 in **VE** sources). Editorially adjusted as doubtless intended in **A** (bar 31 *p* /*pp* as in all sources)

Bars 33–34, pf. **D1–2**, **Rc-m** and **Mz** omit bar 33 final ❋. Pedalling from bar 34 absent in all sources except **A**, which has *pédale sur le 1er et le 3ème temps jusqu'à la fin* [sic, then present indication at bar 43]

Bar 37, pf. Bass accents in **A** only. Sources single-stem LH; editorially restemmed to match bar 36, where the ƒ stems are visibly a later addition in **A**

Bar 38, v. ⟩ as in **A**; printed sources extend it variously to barline or bar 39 note 1, **D3–5** also start it a note earlier

Bar 38, pf. **A**: ♯ not ♮ to last LH ♩, not autograph

Bar 43, pf. 1st LH > in **D3–5** only

Bar 44 onwards, both. **A**:

Bar 47, pf. ✱ (and preceding broken line from bar 43) in **A** only

III. Adieu

Text. Bar 30: colon as in **A**; printed sources have a comma

Tempo and metre. D3–6: 4/4. **A**, **D1–2**, **D4**: no metronome indication; **Rc**: ♩=76; **Mz**: ♩=70 [*sic*]; **D3**, **D5–6**: ♩=72. In **A** *Moderato* overwrites an earlier indication *andante*

Bar 4, pf. Beat 4 RH as in **A**; printed sources stem middle voice down not up

Bar 5, pf. Sources preface *dolce* with *sempre*

Bars 7–8, pf. **A** carries RH slur well past bar 7 (end of system), new slur from bar 8 note 1; printed sources break the slur across the barline, with no slur at bar 7 beat 4 in **VE** sources and **D4**. **D1**$_{80}$ omits bar 8 RH dyad 1 lower note, with ♩ downstem attached instead to upper note

Bar 10, pf. **D2** starts ⟨ at ♩1, other printed sources at ♩2

Bar 11, pf. Printed sources: RH chords 2–4 [music example]; **A** shows the additional notes erased (see facsimile, p. V), **AC** omits them. **A/AC** and **VM** sources follow *dolcissimo* with *sempre*

Bar 12, pf. Rhythm as in **A/AC**; in **A** the version recopied above the system (see p. V facsimile) misaligns RH 𝄾 over LH note 1. Perhaps misled by that, printed sources give LH rhythm for beats 1–2 as 𝄾 then 3 triplet ♪s. Both readings in **A** (see facsimile) show a ♩ downstem from arpeggio note 4 (implying left thumb, practical only in the original ms. key), deleted probably with transposition in mind, absent from **AC**. Present high-voice edition accordingly follows stemming and phrasing of **A** main reading (restoring the ♩ downstem), medium-voice edition **AC** (which shows separate autograph slurs across ♪s 1–3 and 4–9). **D3,5–6** omit ▬, **D1–2,4** place it on upper staff. **Rc** omits pedalling; **D1–6** and **Mz** place 𝄢. under LH note 1 and omit ✱

Bar 13, pf. *Dolce* in all sources except **A** (which has *p*) and **Mz** which alone has *espressivo*. Main reading of beat 4 as in printed sources, *ossia* as in **A/AC** (spelled as e'♯ in **AC**, as f' in **A** within the 6-flat key signature). In **D1** the beam slant and signs of plate disturbance suggest that it was engraved as in **AC** then amended at proof, also removing a cancelling ♮ a bar later. The musical interest of this reading (with its relationship to bar 19 v.) prompts its retention as an *ossia*

Bars 19–20, both. V. ⟩ in **A** only, which starts pf. ⟩ at beat 2. In **A** ⟨ originally extended through bar 19 to *mf* (v. only) at bar 20, with v. *p* at last ♪ of bar 20, *mf* and *p* then erased and ⟨ abbreviated (as in other sources including **AC**); printed sources restore v. *mf* at bar 20 and add it for pf.

Bar 21, pf. LH o as in **A** and **Mz**; other printed sources and **AC** give it as ♩, stemmed with the lower note (**AC** then omits the corresponding o in bar 22). ⟨ as in **AC** (probably autograph); **A** and printed sources start it at or just before RH note 2 (except **D1**$_{80}$, which omits it); **VM** sources end it before final RH ♩

Bar 22, both. *mf* and ⟩ as in **D2**; **A/AC** omit *mf* (as do **D1**$_{80}$, **D4–5** and **Mz**) and start ⟩ at beat 1, remaining sources omit ⟩; cf. also note to bar 21. **A/AC** omit v. *p*, **Rc-e** repeats it in bar 23

Bar 26, v. ⟩ in **A** only

Bar 30, pf. **A**: RH chord 1 minor not major (matching chord 3)

Bars 30–32, pf. **A** leads RH and LH slurs to end of bar 30 (page break, the LH slur curling past ♩4 to the barline), then starts RH slur above initial 𝄾 of bar 31, and new LH slur from bar 31 note 1 to barline ending bar 32; printed sources slur RH as present edition, LH from bar 29 through to bar 32 ♩4. (Some ambiguity is inherent in **A** which, in several bars of this song, starts a RH slur before note 1 and leads what can only be single-bar slurs to the barline. Cf. also note to bars 7–8.) RH staccato dots in bars 31–32 in **Rc** only

Bar 32, v. **A**: ⌒♩▬ (amended thus from ⌒o ⌒♩▬ across bars 32–33)

Bars 33–34, pf. 𝄾 signs as in **A**; printed sources join them across the staves

Bars 34, both. ⌢ in **D3** and **D5–6** only (editorially parenthesised)

27. Nell

Keys: E♭ and G♭

Es First publication: Hamelle [1880], in G♭ (J. 1667.1 H.) and E♭ (J. 1668.1^{bis} H.). A later *édition séparée* (Hamelle, c. 1930), in F (J. 7517 H.), not considered for the present edition, shows orchestral cues from a transcription now untraced, and no viable variants.

Rc II/1, in E♭ and G♭

Mz Metzler & Co. [1896], in E♭ (M.7768), as *Nell*, English and French text (trans. "A.S."). The cover lists the options "N⁰ 1 in E / N⁰ 2 in G [*sic*]" (cf. above under **Source sigla**); under that, between the dedication and the title, is added "Sung by / Madame [Nellie] Melba."

Priority source: **Rc-m**

Variants

Text. Bar 5: musical sources have a comma. Bars 30, 34: musical sources have <u>taira</u> and <u>ne</u>

Throughout. V. phrasing slurs in **Rc** only

Bar 1, pf. **Rc-m** omits *e sempre legato*; other sources slur RH and LH across (just) bar 1 and place *sempre legato* at bar 2, with the linking *e* in **VE** sources only; editorially renotated

Bar 5, v. All sources tie notes 1–2

Bar 7, pf. All sources except **Rc-m**$_{08}$ give RH ♪8 a sixth lower

Bars 8–9, pf. **Es** and **Mz** omit ⟨ and *espressivo*

Bars 14–15, both. **Es**, **Rc-e** and **Mz** add *sempre* after v. *cresc.* (rendered redundant by v. ⟨, present only in **Rc**, ending at ♩4); editorially adjusted. **VM** sources end pf. ⟨ a beat earlier

Bar 16, 27, 35. v. **Es-m**, **Mz**: *mf* not *f* (except **Es-e** omits it in bar 16); **VE** sources omit bar 27 ⟩

Bar 18, pf. **VM** sources end ⟨ at last ♪

Bars 20, 22, pf. *p* in **Rc-m** only; bar 20 beat 3 LH ♩ stem in **Mz** only

Bars 21–22, v. Slur from bar 21 in **Rc-e** only

Bars 25–26, pf. **Mz**: *cresc. sempre* not *poco cresc.* **VE** sources end ⟨ a beat earlier

Bars 30–34, v. **Rc-e** ends slur a note later in bar 30, omitting to start the new slur (end of page), but starts bar 31 with its continuation, then omits to complete subsequent slur in bars 33–34 (after a system break)

Bar 34, pf. ⟨ in **VE** sources only

Bar 36, both. *Subito* for v. in **Rc** only, for pf. in **Rc-m** only

28. Le Voyageur

Keys: f and a

Es   First publication: Hamelle [1880], in f (J. 1669.2bis H) and a (J. 1669.2 H.); also in d [probably post-1908], for bass, in bass clef (J. 1670.2^{ter} H: **Es-g**)

Rc   II/2, in f and g (neither version listed as "ton original", thus implying **Es-e**)

Priority source: **Rc-e**

Variants

Text. Bars 5, 9: musical sources have *dans* and *pour*. Bars 29–30, **Rc-m**: *L'astre*, *vers l'horizon*,. Bar 52: end quotation mark editorial

Bars 1–23, 42–43, 45–53, both. Bar 49 pf. RH tenuto dashes in **Rc-e** only; remaining tenuti, v. bar 3 *deciso* and bars 19–20 *poco rit. / a tempo* in **Rc** only

Bar 10, pf. **Rc-m** omits ⸘

Bars 24–41, pf. Slur as in **Rc-e** and **Es-g**; **Rc-m**$_{\rightarrow[99]}$ omits it, **Es-e/m** omit its completion from bar 34 (new page), **Rc-m**$_{[02]\rightarrow}$ breaks it across bars 27–28, 31–32 and 35–36 (system breaks), ending it finally at bar 39 ♩ 3 (page break), no slur in bars 40–41. **VE** sources omit accidentals to bar 38 ♩ 2

Bars 26–27, 30–31, 33, 35, pf. Sources place $<\!>$ above pf. RH, ending each $<$ at ♩ 3 (restricted space under slurs); editorially adjusted

Bar 33, v. **Es**: *mf* not *f*

Bar 38, pf. **Es-e** omits ♯s to 2nd ♩ dyad

Bar 42, both. **Rc**: *assai deciso* (absent in **Es**); *assai* editorially removed (to avoid confusion between "very" and "rather", via the French *assez*). **Es**: *f* not *ff*

Bar 49, both. **Es**: *poco rall.* not *allargando*, from ♪ 2 in **Es-g**, from ♪ 3 in **Es-e** . V. ' in **Rc-e** only

Bar 50, pf. *al fine* (after 𝒫𝒶𝒹.) in **Es-g** only

Bar 52, pf. $>$ as in **Rc-m** and **Es-g**; **VE** sources start it at note 1

29. Automne

Keys: b and c♯

Es   First publication: Hamelle [1880], in b (J. 1691.3^{bis} H.) and c♯ (J. 1690.3. H.), then [c. 1910] in a (J. 6109 H.: **Es-g**)

Rc   II/3, in b and c♯

Priority source: **Rc-m**

Variants

Text. Bar 21: musical sources omit commas. Bars 22–23, 32: musical sources add commas around *jadis* and after *yeux*

Bar 2 onwards, pf. **Es** omits all LH accents except at bar 33 note 1

Bar 3, pf. **Rc-e**: single RH slur across bars 3–8 (in addition to *sempre legato*)

Bars 3, 7, v. **Es**, **Rc**$_{\rightarrow[99]}$: *mf* not *f*

Bars 8, 11, 18, 21, v. **Es** omits ' in bars 8 and 18, **Es-e** in bar 11; bar 21 ' in **Rc-m** only

Bar 10, pf. **Rc-e**: *mf* not *sf* (cf. bars 11–12)

Bars 11, 16, 32, pf. **Rc-m**$_{\rightarrow[04]}$: lower note of bar 11 RH dyad 5 a tone higher. Parentheses round duplicated notes are editorial; in bar 16 beats 1–3 all sources except **Es-g** give LH upper notes on upper staff, with a shared notehead at that point

Bar 22, pf. LH main reading as in **VM** sources, *ossia* as in **VE** sources and **Es-g**

Bars 24–25, pf. Sources break bass slur across barline (editorially joined)

Bar 28, v. *Meno p* in **Rc-e** only

Bar 29, v. **Es-e/g**, **Rc-m**$_{\rightarrow[04]}$: ' before last ♪

Bar 31, pf. **Es-m**, **Rc-m**$_{\rightarrow[04]}$: RH dyad 3 lower note a tone higher

Bars 31–35, both. Dynamics as in **Rc-e** except that **Rc-e** places *sempre al fine* in bar 33 not 35 (as in **Rc-m**; **Es** omits it). Other sources: v. *poco a poco cresc.* from bar 31 beat 4, then $<$ across bar 33 in **Rc-m** only; pf: $<\!|\!>$ $<$ in bars 30–31 (placed as in bars 1–2), *cresc.* from bar 32 ♪ 5 (bar 34 *f* in all sources)

Bars 36–38, pf. Pedalling in **Rc** only. **Rc-e** omits 2nd $>$ in bar 36. **VM** sources: $>$ on bar 38 note 1

30. Les Berceaux

Keys: b♭ and c

Es   First publication: Hamelle [1881], in b♭ (J. 1882.1 H.) and c (J. 1882.1^{bis} H.), then [1908] in a (J. 5667 H.: **Es-g**); see also below under **Text**. Hamelle later replaced **Es-e** and **Es-m** with offprints from **Rc**$_{08}$

Rc   II/7, in b♭ and c

F   Feuilleton publication: album of the magazine *Musica* 130 (July 1913), pp. 450–452, with copyright acknowledgment to Hamelle; in b♭. Musical text follows **Es-m** (as presently traced, regarding text at bars 5 and 9) except for a few omitted nuances, and is not mentioned separately below.

Af   Autograph fragment (bars 3–4), in c, above the annotation "(Les Berceaux)" and an *envoi* to Lady Campbell Clarke, signed by Fauré and dated "Paris, 15 avril 1899": present location unknown, reproduced in Sotheby's London catalogue for sale of 7 December 2015, lot 157. Musical text as in present edition except for a comma after *quasi*; headed *Andante*, with *p sempre* for pf.

Priority source: **Rc-m**$_{08}$

Variants

Text. Bar 3, musical sources have comma after *quai*. Bars 5, 9: **Rc**$_{\rightarrow[99]}$: *Que la houle berce* and *Que le bras des femmes*; all traced exemplars of **Es-e/m** as **Es-g**, **Rc**$_{[02]\rightarrow}$ and present edition, but with signs of plate disturbance suggesting amendment from an earlier untraced printing that perhaps served as source for **Rc**$_{97}$

Bar 9, v. *Ossia* present in all sources, labelled *ad lib.* except in **Es-g** (which prints both readings on the main staff, the lower pitches in small notes); **Es-e/m** show the 2 readings in inverse positions, the lower pitches labelled *ad lib.*

Bars 12–14, pf. *crescendo poco a poco* in **Rc-m** only

Bar 19, pf. LH accents in **Rc-m** only

Bar 20, pf. LH notes 11–12 as in **Rc**$_{08}$; in other sources they mirror notes 7–8

Bar 21, pf. **Es-g** omits dynamics, **Es-e/m** omit $>$. 1st LH $>$ in **VE** sources only

Bar 25, pf. RH ♮ in **Rc-e** and **Rc-m**$_{08}$ only

Bar 27, v. $<$ in **Rc-m** only

Bars 27–28, pf. Sources omit lower note of last RH dyad in bar 27 and print bar 28 LH ♪ 6 a 3rd lower; editorially amended (cf. remainder of bars 28–29, also note to bar 20)

Bars 28–30, both. **Es**: v. *mf* not *f* (pf. *mf* in all sources). Pf. *p* in bar 29 as in all sources, perhaps an oversight when Fauré revised v. dynamics. Bar 29 v. ' in **Rc-m** only; bar 30 v. $>$ in **Rc-e** only

Bars 36–37, pf. **Rc-e** omits RH tie across the barline

31. Notre amour

Keys: D and E

Es   First publication: Hamelle [1882], in D (J. 1883.2^{bis} H.) and E (J. 1883.2 H.)

Mz   Metzler [1897], in D (M.7886), as *Our Love*, English and French text (trans. "A.S.")

Rc   II/8, in D and E

Priority source: **Rc-m**

Variants

Text. Bars 22, 24, 28–29: punctuation as in **T**; musical sources have *couchants⸲ / penchants⸴ / aile⸲ / cœur⸴*

Bars 3–16, v. Phrase slurs in **Rc-m** only; bars 3 and 9 *e legato* in **Rc** only

Bars 4, 6–7, 16, pf. Sources end bass slur a note earlier in bar 4 (also **VE** sources in bar 16) and break slur across bars 6–7 (page break); cf. bars 18–19, also bars 12–13

Bars 8, 14, 20, pf. ⟨⟩ in **Rc-m** only

Bar 10, pf. **Mz**: last RH ♪ a 3rd lower

Bar 15, v. *Espressivo* in **Rc-m** only

Bars 21–23, v. **Mz** omits each LH ♮ and applies bar 23 ♯ a note later

Bars 21, 26, 37, pf. Triplet numbers editorially carried over from their only source occurrences in bars 1, 25 and 36

Bars 23–24, both. Pf. ⟨⟩ in **Rc** only, ending at ♪ 12 (editorially trimmed). **Es-e** omits v. ⟩

Bar 25, pf. **Rc-e**: LH note 3 a semitone lower [*sic*]

Bars 26–27, both. **Es-e**, **Mz**: *cresc.* at bar 27 not 26, without *sempre and* for v. only

Bars 29–32, pf. LH slurs in **Rc-m** only, which divides them a note earlier across a page break (editorially adjusted)

Bar 35, v. *Ad lib.* option in all sources: **Rc-m** inverts the 2 options (the higher pitch as main reading)

Bar 39, pf. LH beat 1 as in **Mz**, ♪𝄾 in other sources (RH as present edition). **Rc-e**: continuous single 𝄾 across system in beat 2

32. Le Secret

Keys: D♭ and F

Es   Hamelle [1881], in D♭ (J. 1884.3 H.: **Es-m**) and F (J. 1884.3^{bis} H.: **Es-e**); later [between 1897 and 1908] in E♭ (J. 1884.3^{ter} H.: **Es-me**)

Mz   Metzler [1897], in F (M.7819), as *The Secret*, English and French text (trans. "A.S.")

Rc   II/9, in D♭ and F

F   Feuilleton publication: *La Musique des Annales* (supplement to *Les Annales politiques et littéraires* no. 2036), 2 July 1922; in E♭

Secondary sources

Af1   Autograph fragment of vocal line 1 ("Je veux que le matin l'ignore"), in D♭; ironic allusion in a letter to Mme de Chaumont-Quitry, early July 1899, coll. Robert Orledge (reproduced in facsimile in Robert Orledge, *Gabriel Fauré*, London: Eulenburg, 1979, plate XI). Musical text concurs with **VM** sources except omits performing indications and miscopies ♪. ♪ as ♩ ♪

Af2   Autograph fragment, same extract as **Af1** (without the copying error), in D♭; signed and dated "9 aout [*sic*] 1906", Royal Academy of Music, London (McCann Collection). The only performing indication is *Adagio*; otherwise it reads as **VM** sources.

Priority source: **Rc-e**

Variants

Text. Bar 27: Musical sources omit comma

Throughout, v. Slurs in **Rc-e** only, the 2nd and 3rd ones ending a note earlier (editorially extended)

Bars 7–10, pf. Bass slur as in **Rc-e**; other sources start it in bar 9, from before note 1 in **Es-e** (like a carry-over), from chord 1 in all other sources

Bars 8–9, 18–19, 22, 26–27, pf. Sources single-stem each 1st RH chord along with bar 22 RH chord 2, then stem the top note upwards (separately) at bar 26 chord 2 and bar 27 both chords (these last 3 chords thus triple-stemmed), editorially rationalised

Bar 13, v. **Es-me**: note 3 a semitone lower ($c'♭$, as in bar 15)

Bars 13–14, 23–28, pf. Bass slurs (up to bar 28 beat 1) in **VE** sources only, left incomplete in **Es-e** from bar 26 (new system), ending at bar 27 ♩ 2 in **Rc-e** (editorially extended)

Bars 14–17, pf. **Mz**, **Es-me** and **F** omit ⟩ ***p***, **Es-e** and **Mz** omit *cresc.*

Bars 18–20, pf. Middle note of bar 18 RH 2nd ♩ chord in **Es-me** and **F** only. ***f*** in **Rc** only, which then has ⟨ across bar 19 beat 1 (perhaps confusion with bar 18) and ⟩ from start of bar 20 (other sources as present edition)

Bars 23–28, see note to bars 13–14 etc.

Bars 31–33, pf. Layout in all sources:

33. Chanson d'amour

Keys: F and G

Es   First publication: Hamelle [1882], in F (J. 1976 H.) and G (J. 1975 H.)

Rc   II/10, in F and G

Priority source: **Rc-e**

Variants

Tempo. Es: *Andantino* (no metronome indication)

Bars 8–10, 27–29, both. *Senza rigore / a tempo* in **Rc** only. Pf. ⟨⟩ as in **Rc-m**; **Es-m** omits it; **VE** sources omit it at bars 27–28, along with v. ⟩, and start bar 9 ⟩ (v. and pf.) at mid-bar

Bar 15, v. ⟩, ' and penultimate ♭ in **Rc-e** only, the comma placed a note earlier (*sic*; adjusted editorially). **VM** sources start ⟩ a note later

Bar 17, v. **Es** omits ⟨, **Rc-e** omits '

Bars 18–21, v. *Cresc.* as in **Rc-e**; other sources: sources: *poco a poco cresc.* **Es**: ***mf*** not ***f***. ' in **Rc** only

Bars 27–29, see note to bars 8–10 etc.

Bars 28–32, pf. **Rc-m** omits RH slurs, as does **Es-m** at bars 29–32

Bars 36–37, both. Sources add *poco a poco* after *cresc.* (editorially removed)

Bar 40, both. V. slur and pf. ⟩ in **Rc-e** only

Bar 46, pf. ⟨ in **Rc-m** only

Bars 48–50, both. Pf. ⟩ ***p*** in **Rc-m** only. **Es** also omits *poco rit.* and *a tempo*

34. La Fée aux chansons

Keys: D and E

A   Complete autograph: Staatsbibliothek Preußischer Kulturbesitz, Berlin (Mus. ms. autogr. Fauré, G.1); in E. The autograph title page shows a name heavily erased (perforating the paper)[8] above the whimsical annotation "Souvenir affectueux d'un pris de rhum [a pun on *Prix de Rome*]"; after Fauré's signature and the title is the place and date "Villerville 16 [overwriting 15] Septembre 1882". Low on the page appears Hamelle's house stamp. No publisher's or engraver's annotations appear, but some erased pencilling on the title page, plus a pencilled cross after bar 60, suggest pagination marks for a now-untraced scribal copy, possibly transposed for engraving.

Es   First publication: Hamelle [1883], in D (J. 1974 H.) and F (J. 1973 H.)

Rc   II/11, in D and F (the latter labelled *Ton original*)

Priority source: **Rc-m**, with input from **A**

Variants

Text. Bars 7, 11, 28, 81, 99: musical sources omit comma

Dedication as in **Es**; **Rc**: *A Madame Edmond Fuchs*; see above regarding **A**

Bar 1, pf. Nuances and layout as in **A**; printed sources: *p leggiero e legato*, *f* on upper staff

Bar 5, pf. **A**: last RH ♪ a note higher (obvious oversight following a harmonic amendment to lower voice)

Bars 11–18, 30–37, 40–49, pf. < > as in **A**; printed sources start each > from beat 1 (finishing them at end of bars 37, 40 and 49), < from start of bars 11, 16, 31, 35, 42 and 46

Bars 21–22, both. Sources place pf. *cresc.* at bar 22; **Rc** alone adds < in bar 21 for v. and pf. (indications editorially combined here for pf.)

Bars 47–49, pf. **A** omits bass in bars 47–48 (and tie-over from bar 46) at the end of a page, but assumes it by starting bar 49 with a bass tie completion, while omitting to complete the LH upper slur, which printed sources end at bar 48 ♩ 2. Bass tie across bars 47–48 (as in printed sources) might be queried relative to bars 43–44, but cf. the continuous slur above it. See also note to bars 11–18 etc.

Bars 50, 53, 58–59, both. Dynamics in **Rc** only, cf. note to bars 60–61

Bar 53, v. **A**: rhythm ♩ ♪ ♫ ♪ (amended from original reading of ♩ ♪ ♫, then ♫ ♫ | ♪ ♪ ♪ ♪ across bars 54–55)

Bars 60–61, both. **A** omits v. >, pf. > as present edition; **Es** omits both; **Rc** places them across just bar 60, ending a system (editorially adjusted for v.). **A**: pf. RH

Bar 62, both. *Molto* in **Rc** only, placed before barline (doubtless inserted in front of existing *meno mosso* in **Es** from start of bar 62, indication absent in **A**); editorially relocated

Bar 76, both. **A** omits tempo indication; **Es** gives it as *a tempo* (pf. only)

Bar 82, v. **VE** sources start < 2 notes later (**A** omits all dynamics across bars 78–87)

Bars 90–93, pf. *Dim.* in **VE** sources only; **A** has > from bar 90 to bar 92 ♩ 2

Bar 93, v. **A**: rhythm ♪ ♫♫♫

Bar 101, both. Sources: pf. *sempre **p***. **Rc-e**: v. ***mf***, no v. dynamic in other sources. Editorially adjusted in view of surrounding context

Bars 105–106, pf. Phrasing as in **A**; printed sources end slur at bar 106 ♩ 1, then new slur from same note to last ♪

Bars 107–109, both. **A**: pf. *cresc.* from bar 109 not 107 (in place of present ***f***, v. dynamics from bar 105 as present edition), omits *allargando*

Bars 111–125, both. **A** shows multiple erasures and revisions (pencil or darker shade of ink), original reading not fully decipherable but probably

(the final chord and rests in darker ink, possibly added later), bar 117 pf. then amended to [music example] and back again, then the whole passage amended to the final reading:

Bar 113, pf. **VE** sources omit *dim.*

---

[8] Edward Phillips (*Gabriel Fauré: A Research and Information Guide*, pp. 89–90) postulates the erased name to be Henriette Fuchs.

Appendix / Appendice / Anhang

Ici-bas!, **A**, bar 19 onwards